A History of Violence

(1973)

David Cotner

Nine-Banded Books
2022

A History of Violence (1973)

© 2022 by David Cotner

Published by

Nine-Banded Books
P.O. Box 1862
Charleston, WV 25327
United States of America

www.NineBandedBooks.com

ISBN 978-1-7356438-4-7

Frontispiece:

April 17, 1973, photographer unknown
Associated Press image used with permission

Cover art:

4410km/hr Secretor, Adam Chodzko, 1994

Death On The Winds

A skydiver, Steven John Campbell, 24, of Los Angeles, dangled in death from a 12,000-volt power line near Lake Elsinore, Calif., Sunday after a strong wind blew him on to the lines. Officials said he died instantly. (AP Wirephoto)

FOREWORD

I started writing what would become A *History of Violence (1973)* in 2003.

The book started out as a screenplay about an island where the rich and the skilled hunt various murderers culled from three centuries' worth of violent films.

The idea was that these monsters could be cloned endlessly by using cells from the appendix, one of the more poetic organs of the body.

To be thorough – and I am *thorough* – I realized that I needed to research which characters to use. Lunatics in masks and gloves. Staunch cannibals. Home invaders. Orlac and Orloff. Vigilantes. Mad bombers. Spree and serial killers. People dressed as Santa Claus killing people – but also a maniac killing people dressed as Santa Claus.

Anyway.

The violence in the films chronicled in A *History of Violence (1973)* is the kind of violence that builds up inside a person and then explodes outward in mania or vengeance or devouring. Using this metric as a guideline, many genres of film were rejected in favor of a necessarily particular focus.

No Westerns. Westerns are, at their essence – with rare exceptions – concerned with chronology and geography.

No war movies. War movies, at their core, are about various kinds of political systems.

No samurai films or martial arts films. These are also about systems – systems of codes and honor and righteousness.

The crime films included here are mostly Italian *poliziotteschi* – a genre of films in which the main cop is such a crazy creep that he transcends the system by virtue (?) of his own insane inner compass, so much so that eventually he'd explode even if there were no crime to light the fuse.

Jungle cannibals operate with a totally different motivation than cannibals that cannibalize of their own accord and who are as divorced from society as much as jungle cannibals are themselves their own society, embracing cannibalistic behavior because of a more substantial rationale than bottomless hunger and destruction.

I reject most of the futuristic films that are essentially variations on *The Most Dangerous Game* – *The 10th Victim*, *The Purge* or *The Running Man* and so on. These films present a system that bureaucratizes bloodlust to the point that the killing urge is co-opted and exploited by that system. It is the neutering of impulse by way of conformity; actions that previously reduced a man to a pariah are permitted and condoned in these future dystopias.

So much for spontaneity.

The films in *A History of Violence* (1973) are shot through with a very personal kind of violence.

The violence of the individual.

DEDICATION &
ACKNOWLEDGMENTS

TO MOM
Who never in a million years would have read this book but loved me anyway.

DEDICATED TO
Charles Fort, whose curiosity, patience and tenacity remain undying beacons.

Jason Johnson, whose death came too soon but who got to where we said we would go before I did.

Michael Weldon, whose insight and foresight not only showed everyone the way, but suggested that there ought to be a journey in the first place.

Lastly, Dr. Philip Best, whose perception, discernment and eventual abandonment helped guide this book into becoming the epic it always needed to be.

WITHOUT WHOM
Forrest J. Ackerman, Bret Berg, William Connolly, John K. Daniels, Drex Heikes, Greg Luce, Leonard Maltin, Alvin H. Marrill, Adam Parfrey, John Payne, Brian Quinn, Steven H. Scheuer, Tim & Jan Whyte.

Additionally, each and every librarian at the Margaret Herrick Library of The Academy of Motion Picture Arts & Sciences; everyone who dug into their records and memories and rescued information that would have otherwise vanished from the face of the Earth; and the countless legions of people who scan newspapers, fill computer databases and, in the process, safeguard our cultural heritage – for whom this often can seem like a deeply thankless job, let me be the first to thank you, thank you, thank you.

Consulted archives – without which the writing of this book would have been impossible – include those of the Academy of Motion Picture Arts & Sciences, the American Film Institute, Associazione Nazionale Industrie Cinematografiche Audiovisive Multimediali, *BoxOffice*, the British Film Institute, the British Newspaper Archive, Canadian Film Online, *Cartelera*

Cinematográfica, *Cinema Sewer*, the Danish Film Institute, Deutsches Filminstitut, EncycloCiné, *Films & Filming*, the Gay Erotic Video Index, the Google News Archive, the *Hollywood Reporter*, the Hong Kong Movie Database, Horror Digital, the Internet Adult Film Database, the Internet Archive, the Japanese Movie Database, Ministerios de Cultura de España, Newspapers.com, OzMovies, *The Psychotronic Encyclopedia of Film*, *Screen International*, *Sight & Sound*, *La Stampa* {Turin}, the Swedish Film Database, Temple of Schlock, the United States Copyright Office, *La Vanguardia* {Barcelona}, *Variety*, and Video48.

Also, the Internet Movie Database.

The research for this book began primarily through reading the stock lists of the following purveyors of genre cinema: 5 Minutes to Live, All Clues No Solutions, Alpha Blue Archives, Alternative Cinema, American Genre Film Archive, Atlas Visuals, B-Videos 101, Bijouflix, Blood Times Video, Blue Underground, Brutallo, Catalog of the Universal Mind, Cinefear, Cinema de Bizarre, Cinema Wasteland, Classic Movies DVD, Code Red, Cosmic Hex, Crypt Flicks, Cult and Rare, Cult Epics, Diabolik, European Trash Cinema, Excalibur Video, The Fang, Flesh Wound Video, Flikkafilmz, A Ghost House Production, Gravedigger Video, HK Flix, Hollywood Home Theater, Horror Theater Video, Incredibly Strange Video, Just for the Hell of It, Kyonsi Online, Luminous Film & Video, Midnight Video, Milkholes, Movies Unlimited, Mystic Fire, Nightcrew Video, Nightmare Cinema, Nightmare Video, Ninjaforce, Nostalgia Merchant, Odd Obsession, Other Cinema, Pimpadelic Wonderland, Poketti, Putrescine, Rare & Out-of-Print, Rare Television, Rarelust, Revenge Is My Destiny, Rezarected, RHR Home Video, Robert's Hard-to-Find Videos, Ronnie Cramer's Cult Films, Rusted Rare, Sheila B. Devotion, Shocking Videos, Sinerama, Sinister Cinema, Something Weird, SuperHappyFun, Synapse, Tamarelle's International Films, Tapes of Terror, Times Forgotten, Toyboxxx, Trash Palace, Twisted Anger, Vagrant Video, The Video Beat, Video Search of Miami, Videoscreams, Vinegar Syndrome, Visual Pain, Vomit Bag Video, Wildeye, Witching Hour, Xploited Cinema, XTRVID, Yesasia, and ZDD.

In a given landscape, it is some absurdity and not the essential that catches your eye.

- Louis Aragon, *Paysan de Paris* {1926}

One measures a circle beginning anywhere.

- Charles Fort, *Lo!* {1931}

Why do we devote an entire issue to violence and sadism? Because they are there.

- Raymond Durgnat, "Violence in the Cinema" {1963}

Consensus reality seems to have uneven or even jagged edges, and thus we may occasionally and probably all unknowingly pass temporarily from our agreed-upon reality into another.

- Lou Tabakow and George Wagner, 1973

SMUTSIGA FINGRAR
Tuesday, January 2, 1973.

Dirty fingers.

A man tries to hold on to the things he thinks he needs. Even if that means that those things become dirty and repellent.

Harry – played by Heinz Hopf, one of the most wearily urbane scumbags ever etched onto moving pictures – operates a drug ring in Stockholm. One of his clients jumps out a window, she's so high. Her brother and his friend seek revenge. Includes assault by razor-edged glove – a concept explored in last year's *La morte accarezza a mezzanotte* (Death Walks at Midnight), and would also show up six years later in *The Glove* – as well as mass nudity, menace lurking at the edges of every frame, and the unforgiving snows of the Arctic. Hopf graces his villainous roles with an especially annoyed attitude while dealing with his brutal submental lackeys. It's the kind of violence that, once started, becomes difficult to rein in.

The rise and fall.

Today's undercurrents are threats on jets and swift plunges to various miserable deaths. A Roman Catholic cardinal talks down a hijacker in Baltimore. Fraternity brothers – "brothers" – leave one of their own out in the wilderness to "teach him a lesson." Rescuers – "rescuers" – find him at the bottom of a 500-foot cliff. Further up the California coast, shoe-prints are discovered. They may belong to a boy who may have fallen off a 100-foot cliff while hiking. "Futile" is what they call the search for the fallen boy. They simply don't know what happened to him.

And Anthony J. Hussli's body drifts frozen in the Beaver Dam Lake.

Some things can't be learned.

A man plummets from a fishing ship off the coast of California, near the wreck of a luxury liner. Officials search for him for one day. Nearby, onshore, a man fires a pistol in a bar before he has his weapon wrested away from him. He runs. Officials look for him, too. Two vanish. Two fall. Possibly simultaneously.

Meanwhile, in Florida.

A woman's body is found amidst dense saw-grass in the depths of the Everglades. She's the 99th and final victim from one of the worst single-plane disasters in the history of America. Eastern Airlines. The autopilot got disconnected. They fell, too. They think that she's the last one they'll find. They just don't know. It's been five days already. Hey, what's happening here?

Roberto Clemente is still missing.

"Glory."

That's what the Governor of Puerto Rico calls the former Pittsburgh Pirates' 3,000-hit out-fielder during his inauguration. As he speaks, the ocean beckons ceaselessly just beyond the stark white marble of the Capitol steps. A moment of silence for a man who fell. For the man who put baseballs so high into the sky. Clemente died on New Year's Eve, flying to deliver aid to earth-quake victims in Nicaragua.

On a beach nearby, there's a different kind of silence. Clemente's widow Vera scans the ocean as Coast Guard divers continue their search for her husband's body. They never find it.

Going. Gone.

LITTLE MISS INNOCENCE
Wednesday, January 3, 1973.

Full of eerily beautiful images of Hollywood and Los Angeles in the early '70s, this film is the cautionary tale of a dirty old man who thinks he's getting what he wants when he picks up two nubile hitchhikers – scheming Carol and naïve Judy – but eventually his addiction to all that sex becomes too much. His weak and paltry mind snaps. "Poor big superlover!" Carol sneers scornfully, taking Judy with her as she abandons him. In the end, he's become a drooling sex-vegetable. Sandra Dempsey, who plays the incessantly sassy Carol, may or may not have died while boating in or around the Gulf of Mexico on or about May 24, 1975, if the revelation in Candy Samples' column in *Juggs* magazine is any indication. It is unclear.

Sometimes, imagining the violence has just as much impact as experiencing it.

Three people died. 15 injured. A bus carrying a high school swim team overturns on an ice-slickened expressway in the freezing rain near Oswego, New York.

Injured.

That's a word people use all the time. But what does it really mean? A bump on the head is an injury. A cut on the finger is an injury.

And so is gas gangrene.

That Eastern Airlines jet crash into the Florida Everglades also gives the anguished survivors languishing in the wreckage – their wounds cut off from a healing supply of oxygen – an affliction

known as gas gangrene.

Bacteria in. Screams – often and loudly – out. Anthony. Anthony.

Blackened.

TEENAGE JAILBAIT
Wednesday, January 3, 1973.

There's nudity and robbery galore in this film that involves itself with the dangers of giving in to murder and/or lust. Two of the titular teens rope in a couple of angry dopes to invade homes, rob parents and hold hostages. They triple- and quadruple-cross everyone left and right in a de facto morality tale that seems intensely annoyed that it has to deal with morals when it'd rather watch all that illicit sex instead. Violent pleasure and spectacular greed aside, it does not end well. No less an authority than pornography pioneer William Rotsler, writing in his 1973 volume *Contemporary Erotic Cinema*, promised, "This is the kind of film that gives erotic cinema a bad name ... This is an unhappy, anti-erotic film. Avoid it."

In Carlisle, Pennsylvania, Letitia Denise Smallwood sits in a prison cell, accused of arson and murder. She purportedly set a fire last August 29 in the apartments above the defunct Old Strand Theatre. Burned the whole thing to the ground. Killed two – Paula Wagner, 23, and Steven Johnson, 26.

Wagner died from injuries sustained when she jumped out a window. She hit a parking meter on her swift and sudden way down.

"It's my fault, it's my fault, I'm responsible for him being here," a nurse at the Carlisle Hospital hears Smallwood say as she sobs piteously outside the hospital room of Richard "Mike" Baltimore. He was also hurt in the fire. Smallwood herself has also been burned.

Superficially and otherwise.

Assistant District Attorney Edgar B. Bailey Jr. asserts that Smallwood was "considerably" distressed that Baltimore was living with the late

Ms. Wagner when the fire tore through that building. Smallwood's attorney, Herbert C. Goldstein, asserts that Wagner and Smallwood both had many different "dating companions."

One did not necessarily follow the other.

Miner's bodies, found in West Virginia. Anthony J. Hussli's body, frozen in the Beaver Dam Lake in Wisconsin.

They're reopening Southern University in Baton Rouge today. It's been seven weeks – seven; how lucky – since Denver A. Smith and Leonard Douglas Brown were killed by shotgun blasts during a campus protest. "The Southern U Massacre," they call it. Think what it would have been like to be near the protest on that day in 1972. How close could you get to gunfire and still avoid its effects? Just the sound – the imprint of the event, from gunshots to screams to bodies falling to the ground – can you imagine it? Can you hear it, even now?

Shooter or shooters, never identified.

They've now found one of the two knives – two knives – that were used to stab Sandra L. Schooley. Stabbed after she was strangled. Sandra was a nurse. Maybe she'd read about that Everglades crash. She'd know what to do if she were there. She wouldn't have to imagine it. She'd know what to do to comfort the relatives of those four miners whose bodies were finally recovered. They were trapped by explosions and fire in the Blacksville No. 1 coal mine. Last summer. A lifetime ago.

Unimaginable.

SUNDAY - MONDAY - TUESDAY
● 2 FIRST RUN — X RATED HITS! ●

TEEN-AGE JAILBAIT

THEY WENT TO SCHOOL TO LEARN ABOUT LOVE . . .

2 nd Shocker "SCHOOL for LOVE" X RATED

FEATURING 30 OF THE LOVELIEST GIRLS EVER SEEN ON THE SCREEN

"TEENAGE JAILBAIT"

ADULTS ONLY

THE WIFE
Wednesday, January 3, 1973.

Alice (played by Francoise Darc) fools around with her lover Sam while her husband Allan (played by Alain Mayniel) jets off to San Diego for business. Allan comes home from his business trip early. Shit, fan, etc. Sam gets knocked out, Allan dies, and Alice is set upon by two gun-toting hippies named Catwoman (Lyllah Torena) and Catman (Tom Hart). They break into her house and have their distinctly non-hippieish way with her. The ad art for *The Wife* was ripped off countless times over the years to advertise unrelated films like *Playground Sisters* and *Hollywood Starlet*. Directed by Gary Graver, a man who took his porn pseudonym of Robert McCallum so seriously that he denied being Robert McCallum and in the process ironically came off as one of the most embarrassed guys to ever have made an adult film.

The "Death" issue of *National Lampoon* is on newsstands now.

If you were one of the lucky subscribers to *National Lampoon* – something to which boys gravitated and from which they graduated after years of experiencing a distinct lack of bare breasts in *Mad Magazine* – you opened your mail this month and were greeted by one of the most shocking and memorable images ever to grace the cover of a modern humor magazine.

A dog. Unusually expressive. Photographed by the artist Ronald G. Harris. Apprehension and comprehension playing across his furry black-and-white face.

A pistol held to his head.

If You Don't Buy This Magazine, We'll Kill This Dog.

Cheeseface the Dog. Sometimes known as Patches.

Working professionals always have their share of alter egos.

In the early months of 1976, an unidentified person calls the *National Lampoon* offices. Tells copy editor Susan Devins that Cheeseface the Dog is dead.

That he's been tracked down to the farm on which he's lived in his retirement from global superstardom.

Tracked down, and shot dead.

No one knows who did it. No one knows why anyone would.

Or if it was all just a joke.

THE BLUE BALLOON
Thursday, January 4, 1973.

A virginal girl with big expressive eyes sees her lover off to war. She's almost immediately corrupted by a pushy lesbian in chrome-rimmed shades who brutalizes her, whores her out to leering dudes, and gets her hooked on everything she possibly can in this deeply depressing Danish slice-of-(someone's)-life that must have been a real joy to jerk off to in theatres.

They're looking for a woman in Brooklyn who made friends with new mother Nanny Lee Armstrong and, after gaining her trust over time, stole her 5-day old son Jeffrey, beating her insensate with a hammer in front of her 5-year-old son.

$1,000 is the going rate for babies in 1973, purportedly.

That's $6,475.32 in 2022 money. We're told that investing in our children is an important thing to do. Maybe that's why kidnapping babies in New York City in 1973 was a growth industry – another goes missing from a hospital in October, gone as quickly and as quietly as a little balloon floating across a clear blue sky. Both cases are noted in the *New York Times*. Neither is tied together at the time – not by an old grey lady contemplating young black kids, anyway. It is unclear if either of these children were ever found – or, for that matter, if others were kidnapped, their disappearances largely unreported. They may still be out there, not knowing their true lineage; not knowing where they really come from. And yet when, in those rare cases, the link is made and the child is returned to the mother or father – how do you summon forth that parental love after all that time? How do you rebuild that bond? Last month, Steven Stayner was kidnapped in Northern California by Kenneth Eugene Parnell. He's gone until he escapes in 1980.

In a 1984 interview in *Newsweek*, Stayner thinks, "I returned almost a grown man and yet my parents saw me at first as their 7-year-old. After they stopped trying to teach me the fundamentals all over again, it got better. But why doesn't my dad hug me anymore? I guess seven years changed him, too. Everything has changed. Sometimes I blame myself."

"I don't know sometimes if I should have come home. Would I have been better off if I didn't?"

Nanny Lee Armstrong – cowed and berated by neighbors who, in an especially acrid twist of victim-blaming, thought she should have been able to fight back while being clubbed in the head by that hammer – moves to Brooklyn in March to begin her life anew. "That's why I don't ever go back to the neighborhood," she tells the *Times*.

More things are taken away after a kidnapping than just a person. This is the violence of absence.

It's uncertain where Nanny Lee Armstrong went after that.

WE DARE YOU
to keep your eyes open during every terror-saturated scene of "Torso"

Enter...
if you dare
the bizarre
world of the
psychosexual
mind.

Joseph Brenner Associates Inc.
presents a
Carlo Ponti production

TORSO
starring SUZY KENDALL
with Tina Aumont/John Richardson
Carla Brait/Luc Merenda
Directed by Sergio Martino
Produced by Antonio Cervi
Distributed by Joseph Brenner Associates, Inc.

IN TECHNICOLOR

One day she met a man who loved beautiful girls ...but not all in one piece.

To preserve the surprise ending, no one admitted during last 10 minutes.

PINE THEATRE—PINE GROVE
SATURDAY—SUNDAY
Sunday Matinee at 2 P.M.
Matinee all seats $1.00
2 Shows Nightly at 7 and 9
Positively no one under 17 admitted without a parent or adult guardian.

I CORPI PRESENTANO TRACCE DI VIOLENZA CARNALE
Thursday, January 4, 1973.

A woman-hating hacksaw-lover murders and dismembers young girls. A distinctive scarf is one clue. The house in which young girls are stalked and slaughtered is another. The final scene – for which no one will be admitted during the film's last 10 minutes – reveals the killer's occupation. An angry, angry film. Its American title of *Torso*, conjured up for maximum exploitative effect – "parts is parts" – jibes perfectly with the rage that is the lifeblood of this film. Linda Gross – whose reviews of exploitation films in the *Los Angeles Times* really seemed to wear on her over the years – called it "a lazy suspense movie" in the June 20, 1975 edition.

Run from the killer.

A propane torch explodes in a house in the hilly little Pittsburgh suburb of Elliot. An old man catches fire and is consumed. Police have to restrain his wife from running back into the house to try to save him. He's burning. Anthony J. Hussli's body. She can't help herself. She's trying to save him as fast as she can.

Running.

On the opposite side of the country, in the modest Southern California suburb of Cerritos, Carl Eckstrom murders both Cecilia Vasquez, 20, and former Army paramedic Michael Jefferies, 27, in a shopping mall. He then chases down veteran Los Angeles County Sheriff's deputies Carl Wilson and Donald Schneider and murders them, too. With a submachine gun.

Always running.

A shotgun blast from another deputy takes him out. He survives. A shotgun. Neighbors tell the authorities that Eckstrom is "a very quiet fellow." You'd never be able to tell from how he started his day. He tried to pick up Vasquez and another lady in a parking lot by showing them a gun and ordering them to go out with him. Not very quietly. It's the second-worst fatal shooting spree in the region.

Anthony J. Hus li's body.

Eckstrom wanted to be a policeman. Nearsightedness – of one kind or another – cuts those plans short.

He's in a prison in Stockton now.

Nowhere to run.

21

Además, ESTRENO: ¡Un «SUSPENSE» que causa escalofrío!

TECHNICOLOR

ROBERT HOFFMAN
SUSAN SCOTT
SIMON ANDREU
GEORGE MARTIN

PASOS DE DANZA SOBRE EL FILO DE UNA NAVAJA

UNICAMENTE MAYORES DE 18 AÑOS

PASSI DI DANZA SU UNA LAMA DI RASOIO
Friday, January 5, 1973.

A woman casually looks through a telescope one day and inadvertently sees a man in black stabbing a woman in the nude. He then kills various people with a straight razor to ensure that his identity is not disclosed. Further themes of vision: the eyes of the actors are showcased, as are cameras and the persistent importance of light and darkness. Jazz and dramatic pianos abound.

Death carries a cane.

That's the name by which this film is usually known. Death also carries a limp, much like Ted Bundy used to do when he was scoping out his victims. The implied weakness of a cane or a limp puts women at ease; made them easier for Bundy to abduct and destroy. He starts killing in earnest next year. In a few days from today, he stops a purse-snatching at a shopping mall in Seattle, catching the thief.

Giving murderers three names confers upon them a sense of prestige. Notoriety. Legacy. Ability. It's a tradition that stretches back to Lincoln's assassin John Wilkes Booth, strengthened by the press emphasizing the "Harvey" in Lee Harvey Oswald a century later.

In 1973, Robert Christian Hansen is killing women in Alaska. Rodney James Alcala is in jail in California, waiting to get out and kill some more. Randy Steven Kraft is cementing his reputation as The Freeway Killer, murdering young men up and down the Los Angeles freeway system. John Wayne Gacy isn't killing anyone in 1973, but he's out there.

Death does not, however, carry an address book. It's not like these killers all hung out together. It's not like they'd even like each other.

Impressions are important. An image persists. Preconceived notions are pitiless in their underlying sense of tact and understanding.

The speed with which the killer attacks his

victims in *Passi di danza su una lama di rasoio* is astonishing to watch. It is as though the veil of perception is purposefully shredded because of the speed with which he moves. Moving from perception to perception. Quick as a wink. Quick as the opening of a straight razor.

Thalidomide, given to expectant mothers to fight morning sickness, is promoted heavily for years in England by The Distillers Company under the brand name Distaval. It's all about branding, really. The Distillers Company sold a lot of whiskey as well as Distaval. They're handing out millions in settlement money to mothers whose babies were born with birth defects – like flippers for arms, or limps – as a result of taking Distaval.

"Thalidomide babies." That's a phrase that was once perceived as possessing a power almost like a curse. Anthony J. Hussli's body is frozen in Beaver Dam Lake in Wisconsin but no one knows where he is exactly.

Not yet. It's not the right time.

But tell that to Richard L. Fudge, the architect from Chicago who went to Yosemite with his trusty .38 to "see some country." Tell that to the plane trees dying in London of sunstroke because the air pollution to which they had grown accustomed is finally vanishing. Tell that to the workers tearing down the old Rialto Theatre in Rock Island, Illinois. Tell that to the corpses of dead soldiers used as de facto drug mules to smuggle heroin from Asia into America.

Tell that to Ann Leybourne. She's 25. She shot and killed "Friday Night Rapist" Robert Ellis when he tried to abscond with her in Chicago

on New Year's Day. He must have thought she was an easy mark. "Ha, ha," she said, "I'll do anything for you. I'm really scared of guns." She pulled her .38 from her purse when they stopped in a parking lot in Cabrini Green. Slowly. Deliberately. Calmly. She's a cadet at the Chicago Police Academy.

He never saw it coming.

PLAYGROUND SISTERS
Friday, January 5, 1973.

Tchaikovsky's *Waltz of the Flowers* ushers us in to the finer moments of this titillating time capsule, afflicted as it is with the graininess of old home movies but with only a fraction of the wistfulness. A couple of girls have their first sexual experiences and aggressively go after as many guys as they can to get another taste. Pre-AIDS, pre-attitude and pre-alterations of any kind, it's a film that – like many adult films of the '60s and '70s – finds its way into modern life the same way that dirty magazines used to be discovered in the woods. Some kinds of culture find their intended audiences through slightly more arcane and involved methods than most. Imagine a house with many doors – not all of which are immediately visible.

Two children, 9 and 11 years old, play in an empty lot with a few other kids in the Brazilian city of Cascavel. A city dump truck buries them alive with a load of dirt. The driver did not see them. Chances are that the kids saw the driver – looking up at the big truck, watching with the uncomplicated fascination that children have for trucks and construction, not knowing until too late that it wasn't only a game.

It's surprising how many things we don't see coming until it's too late.

A doctor, Ricardo Munoz-Velez, pleads not guilty to killing over 200 patients under his care in Geneva, Illinois. How long do you think it takes to kill over 200 people? Munoz-Velez believes in administering high dosages of sedatives and potatoes (!), taking away anti-convulsive drugs from epileptics and giving treatments for

arthritis to people who don't even have arthritis.

How many things don't we hear about until it's too late?

At Mitchell Field in Milwaukee, passengers boarding jets are frisked and put through a new invention (or inconvenience, or intrusion, depending) known as a metal detector. Exploration of the body: the government's latest way to combat the tiresome phenomenon of hijacking. Starting today, it becomes mandatory at all American airports. A kid with personal problems and a .45 made sure of that.

And yet the hijacking continues throughout 1973.

NOTHING BUT THE NIGHT
Thursday, January 11, 1973.

Peter Cushing was afraid of the dark.

Nyctophobia, they call it. He forced himself out of his crippling fear by taking walks late at night. Into the depths of the dark he strode, surging onward until all fear of it was gone.

Peter Cushing wasn't afraid of death. He welcomed it. It's been almost two years to the day that his wife Helen died. The rest of Cushing's life would be consumed by living it as fully as she wanted him to live it. She urged him, in a parting letter, "Do not pine for me, my beloved Peter, because that will cause unrest. Do not be hasty to leave this world, because you will not go until you have lived the life you have been given. And remember, we will meet again when the time is right. That is my promise."

More than just the night.

Old people are dying, their consciousness seemingly transferred into the bodies of young students so that they can murder or garden or whatever it is that old English people do when they suddenly get another chance at life. Peter Cushing and Christopher Lee try to make sense of all this violent vanity in one of the rare films in which both actors aren't actively trying to murder one another. The film is another of Lee's meditations on themes of paganism, rituals and transference, prefiguring everything from *Like Father, Like Son* to *Get Out*. It also serves as a precursor to *The Wicker Man*, released at the end of 1973 just as *Nothing But the Night* was released at the beginning – an unexpected and providential manifestation of balance, all the way through to the shock

climax. Also starring Diana Dors, the "blonde bombshell" – sex and violence fused together in one enthusiastic metaphor – who claimed she'd hidden away millions in European banks over the years. She gave her husband, actor Alan Lake, the code that unlocked the treasure.

He, however, was so seized by sorrow when she died in 1984 that he burned all her clothes and stuck a shotgun in his mouth an hour after an interview with the *Daily Express* that October.

The key to his treasure died with him.

Successful Separation.

That's what they call the marital separation counseling program at the Mental Health Department of Ventura, California. It's where Robert Frank Reynolds waits in his car in the Depart-

Broncho DRIVE-IN THEATRE
332-6042

OPEN 6:30   STARTS 7:00
ADULTS $1.75   CHILD .50
TONITE   RATED (R)

CHRISTOPHER LEE   PETER CUSHING

"RESURRECTION SYNDICATE"

And

VICTOR BUONO - JOHN CARRADINE IN

MOON CHILD

IN COLOR
Released by
ERICAN FILMS LTD
R

ment's parking lot tonight. Drinking. Smoking. A suicide note scrawled on a brown paper bag. Photographs of the kids spread out on the seat. When his estranged wife Susan and Robert Pate – another man in the program, going through the same thing – come outside, Reynolds says nothing. Shoots Pate in the chest with a .357 Magnum revolver. Shoots Susan in the face. Blows his own brains out. In rapid succession.

A fire truck hoses down the parking lot the following day.

In 1972, Cushing spoke to *The Radio Times*, saying, "To join Helen is my only ambition. You have my permission to publish that ... really, you know, dear boy, it's all just killing time. Please say that."

The way that someone dies serves as a lesson to those who experience the continual rigors of living life.

THE UNTHINKABLE!
THE UNEXPECTED!

Sleep awakens a nightmare of fury that chills until the last terrifying twist!

nothing but the night
...and the terror! PG

CHRISTOPHER LEE / PETER CUSHING / DIANA DORS / GEORGIA BROWN

THE NIGHT STRANGLER
Tuesday, January 16, 1973.

A sinister someone is strangling strippers in Seattle. Intrepid reporter Carl Kolchak figures out what's happening and it's pretty gross. He beats the decrepit old maniac who's using the strippers' blood as an elixir so that he may dance sexier and extend his lifespan every so often (shades of *Nothing But the Night*). Kolchak also gets his own TV series. How many reporters do you know that are out there taking care of things like this? Even if there were – like Carl Kolchak – would you believe them?

Speaking of unbelievable.

A junior high school teacher in Stamford, Connecticut expresses dissatisfaction with his performance review. He takes it upon himself to kill his wife and two sons with a long-handled axe and then hang himself in the garage in front of the family Volkswagen. No note is found. He had been under psychiatric observation.

Shock treatments.

Perceptions of disappointment were clearly – clearly – somewhat different in 1973. Admittedly, massacres set a bar slightly higher than any given storm sewer. Now, at best there's compassion; at worst, no one really cares about what it is you do.

Or, as Thomas Jefferson once put it, "How much pain have cost us the evils which have never happened!"

Occasionally, those evils do in fact really happen. They often go forgotten, the impact of their vi-

140 years ago he began to kill, rising from the caverns beneath the city to claim his victims. Every 20 years he must kill…to live.

The Night Strangler
A real horror story

olence behaving much like the radioactive dust left behind by a depleted uranium round. Kick it back up and watch the cancer spread. The brutality of the crime is eternal. There is no "high bar" for violence like this – the kind of anger, anger, anger that propels a mass murder like this is always going to be astonishing. It's always going to be something hard to explain or understand.

Hard to believe.

In Oxnard, California, a man attempting to reconcile with his wife shoots himself inside her home. He'll live. In Cumberland, Maryland, residents complain about the demolition of the Strand Theatre. Not because the Strand was a beautiful palace devoted to the radiance of cinema – but because they fear the flying debris erupting from its ruination. A little girl in Nashville finds a stray hand grenade. She thinks it's a miniature football.

Another little girl, Anna Christian Waters, vanishes near Half Moon Bay, California while searching in the rain for her pet rooster. Initially, they think she merely fell into Purisma Creek and was washed out to sea. Suspicion is cast on her father, a troubled doctor named George Waters who's been befriended by an enigmatic man named George Brody. The revelations and rumors that emerge in the wake of Anna's disappearance are a murky labyrinth of reincarnation, abduction and dissolution that fascinates researchers for decades. Classified ads brim with hotlines for those who may need to talk to someone before they go on a rampage and commit familicide – thoughts of imminent death jockeying for attention alongside the race results or the lust for a new Pontiac Grand Am. But sometimes you just don't have a telephone handy. Sometimes you want to say what you have to say to someone who knows you. Someone who understands where you're coming from. Even as they claim repeatedly that they don't recognize you anymore.

That they don't know you at all.

One of the very favorite dishes of Vyacheslav Mikhailovich Molotov – he of Molotov cocktail fame – is Aylesbury Duckling à l'Orange. Here follows its recipe.

1 5-pound duckling (preferably from an Aylesbury, imported from England)
½ medium onion, chopped
2 carrots, sliced
1 stick celery, chopped
2 bay leaves
2 tablespoons arrowroot
1 quart veal stock (or beef consommé)
6 oranges
1 lemon
½ cup sugar
½ cup vinegar
½ cup water
2 tablespoons red currant jelly

Heat oven to 375 degrees Fahrenheit. Place duckling in roasting pan with the chopped vegetables and put in oven. When duck becomes brown, pour stock over bird every 15 minutes for about 1 hour. Skin 3 oranges and the lemon, cut skin into strips and cook in vinegar, water and sugar to make a marmalade. When duck is cooked, strain stock into saucepan, adding the juice of the 6 oranges and lemon. Bring to boil, adding currant jelly. Remove excess grease.

Thicken sauce with 2 tablespoons arrowroot, which you blend with a little cold water (or Port wine, if you prefer). Add marmalade to sauce. Pour over duckling and serve, after garnishing with orange slices. Duckling can be flambéed with a glass of Kirsch brandy, or your favorite liqueur. Serves 2 persons.

Or one, if the other person has been set on fire.

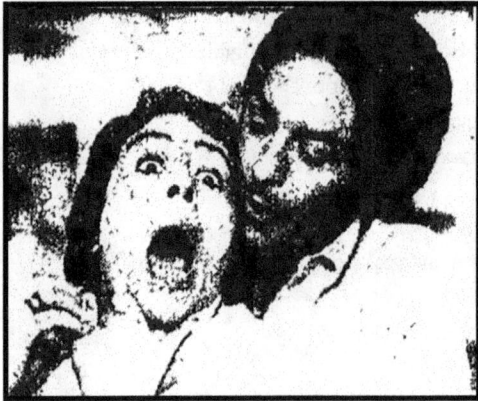

TRAITEMENT DE CHOC
Thursday, January 18, 1973.

Couturier Héléne Masson (Annie Girardot) thinks her life is over at 38 (!), so she goes to a clinic on the coast of Brittany to find herself. Instead, she finds out that the rejuvenation treatments used at the clinic are murderous and addictive. Alain Delon plays the doctor whose woo and wooing both turn out badly for everyone involved. Features therapeutic nudity, frightening calisthenics, and a plot – or at least a statement – that could be updated fairly well in terms of both general overall callousness and the New Age health curatives currently in fashion; generally I tend to exclude references that might make the writing seem dated, but check back in 25 years! It'll be happening all over again by then.

We often think in terms of "finding" the victims of violent acts.

Five children and two adults are shot and drowned in a house that Kareem Abdul-Jabbar gave to a Muslim group in which he put his faith. They're found on the eve of peace talks to end the Vietnam War. One thing does not follow another. One thing eclipses the other. There is nothing else but that in Kareem Abdul-Jabbar's life at this moment in 1973.

Frozen.

Anthony J. Hussli's body is frozen in Beaver Dam Lake in Wisconsin but no one knows where he is exactly until they find him today. He's been missing for several months. Stuck there. 40 feet from shore. In two feet of ice.

The 10-year-old daughter of serial killer Juan Corona is taken to the hospital – suffering from shock – after he's found guilty of killing 25 farm workers and transients over several years. He's found out in 1971. "Guilty of murder in the first degree," says the jury. He's stabbed 32 times in his Vacaville cell in December, then goes on to live a long life at Corcoran State Prison in California, increasingly swallowed up by the great void that is dementia.

They keep him in the Sensitive Needs Yard.

Meanwhile, in the past.

They're looking for the extortionists in the

Ozarks that tied Robert Kitterman, the President of the Bank of Grandin, Missouri, to a tree with his wife and 17-year-old daughter and shot them all. Yesterday, Kitterman had walked into the Bank while it was closed for lunch and taken out $13,000. He told a bookkeeper not to turn on any lights lest a stray charge ignite the dynamite that's strapped to his chest.

Think of what they would have found then.

A guru, a Buddhist monk and a Malay witch doctor attempt to exorcise the evil spirits blamed for the mass hysteria that plagues young women at a General Electric appliance and TV plant in Singapore. Girls collapse left and right and yet neither scientist nor seer can explain why. The assembly line workers can't help screaming when they see the ghosts in the factory.

Apparently, outbreaks of hysteria are normal occurrences here.

The Mounties find an elderly man staggering down a British Columbia highway. In his hands he holds several broken arrows. One is bloodstained, having pierced his neck. They find his son. Arrest him.

A bus driver tries to change a tire in the pouring rain. The bus slips off its jack, crushing the father of six to death while another man tries desperately to save him.

Have you ever found a dead body? I have.

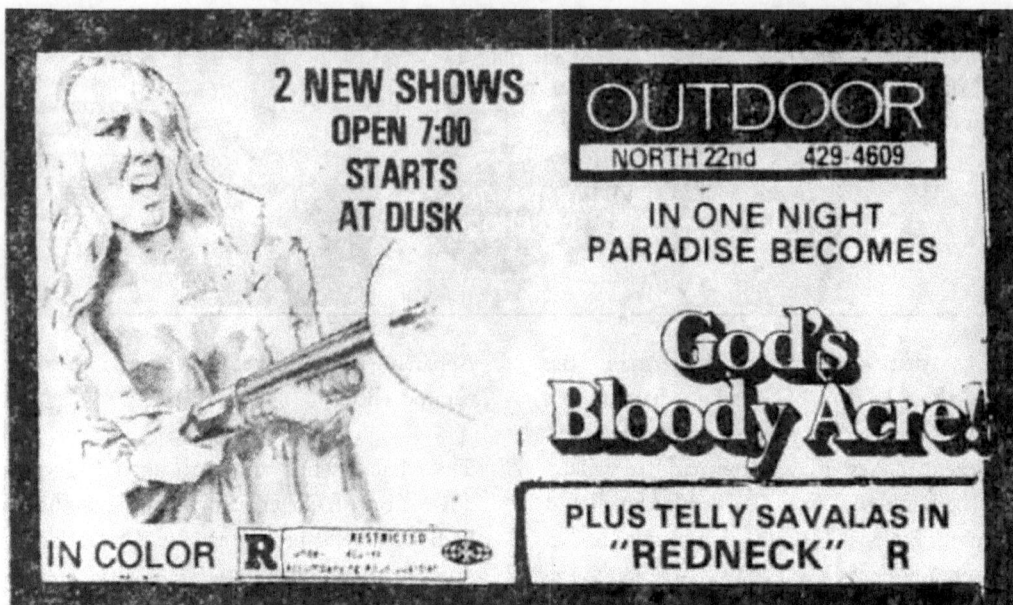

SENZA RAGIONE
Friday, January 26, 1973.

Telly Savalas plays a total psycho and Franco Nero remains deeply stoic as his partner Mosquito in this nuts robbery melodrama. Telly sure does murder a lot of people; after a while, his claims of not being able to stop killing fall just a little flat. In December, Telly starts his five-season television turn as the clever detective Kojak, a role that couldn't be further from the pathology that moves his acting here. At one point, he sings in harmony with the note of a blaring Rolls-Royce horn as he pushes it down a hill and off a cliff. Talk about going in style! He also sends a family to the bottom of a lake in their camping trailer, making him one of the few mass murderers in cinema to use gravity as a weapon. The American version is titled *Redneck*, although who knows how anyone thought that word would have anything to do with all those obviously European landscapes and fashions. Super-bleak ending, too.

The Vietnam War ends tomorrow.

A fourth grade teacher, 20, is raped by a thief at knifepoint in a closet at the front of her class. The students hear everything as it happens.

The Vietnam War ends tomorrow.

Former President Lyndon Baines Johnson died last Monday.

The Vietnam War ends tomorrow.

W. Sherwood Collins, 56, finally dies in hospital from wounds he sustained earlier in the month during a sniper attack in downtown New Orleans. He'd gone to the 11th floor of the Howard Johnson's Motor Lodge to see where all the shooting was coming from.

The Vietnam War will end tomorrow.

Edward G. Robinson – notorious for his rags-to-riches-to-death role in the 1931 gangster film *Little Caesar* – breathes his last at Mount Sinai Hospital in Los Angeles. Bladder cancer. His son, Edward Jr. – actor, alcoholic and tabloid star – will die exactly 13 months later.

The Vietnam War is ending tomorrow.

A Legionnaire, 21, wants to go home to Greece, so he tries to hijack a jet in France. He's shot during the attempt. The live grenade he's holding explodes as he dies.

The Vietnam War. It's ending. Tomorrow.

A man, 24, who becomes rich after becoming the sudden heir to a vast and substantial oleomargarine fortune, kills himself in the home of his father-in-law with a high-powered rifle that blows away a portion of his head.

And yet the Vietnam War will end tomorrow.

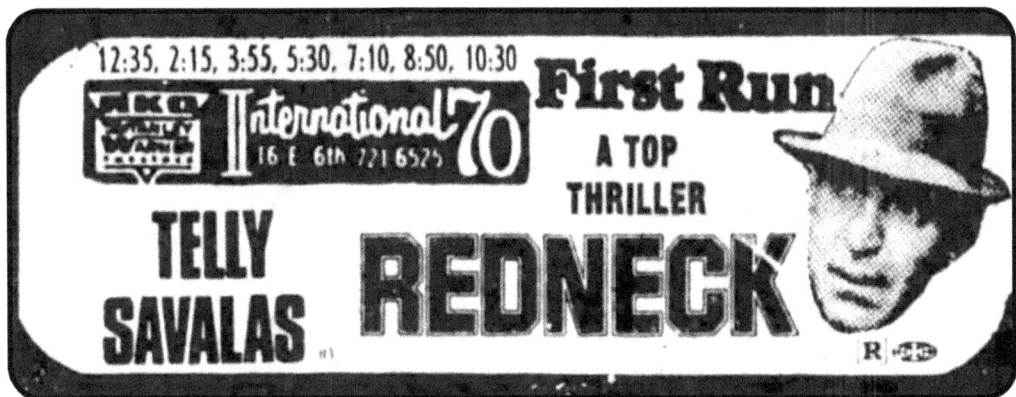

IL BOSS
Thursday, February 1, 1973.

From the opening sequence in which Mafia killer Lanzetta (Henry Silva) totally annihilates a porn theatre full of Mafiosi with four rocket-propelled grenades, you know that *Il boss* is going to be a thrill ride of a crime epic. Everyone double-crosses everyone else except Lanzetta, a natural killer – and orphan! – who kills every-one he can on orders from head capo Richard Conti. Lanzetta rescues the daughter of the Mafioso who raised him and taught him every-thing he knows – including the fact that Rich-ard Conti's character is God and the person with whom one does not trifle – who theoretically would be his sister but then he ends up having sex with her for a week and falls for her. Kind of? You can never really tell with Henry Silva – he's like a wall, impossible to read! Almost everyone who dies ends up in a blast furnace operated by a helpful giant mute guy. When one of Lanzetta's fellow killers sets him up in a remote shack loaded with dynamite and sneaks up and blows the whole damned thing to hell – will Lanzetta escape? The Luis Bacalov soundtrack cues are incredibly obvious and manipulative but when the drums and fuzz-guitar kick in, you know you're in for some freakishly violent action. "To be continued," says the card at the end of the film. Promises, promises!

A man lights his pipe at a Burbank, California lunch counter. The man sitting next to him pulls out a pistol and shoots him. The victim dies a cou-ple of hours later. The killer walks into a police station a few blocks away and hands over his .38.

"I've had enough," he tells the cops.

In Houston, Joseph Lyles, 17, is taken by serial killer Dean Arnold Corll. Lyles' body is eventually found buried at Jefferson County Beach in 1983, but won't be identified until 2009.

The fullness of time.

Corll's killers will have enough of him in August, when he's shot multiple times trying to murder some of them.

Dr. Peter Steincrohn's syndicated column runs

with the headline "'Normal' People Commit Slow Suicide." In it, he asks his readers a question uncharacteristically progressive for a syndicated newspaper columnist in 1973: "What's your definition of unbalanced? Normal?" He proceeds to assert that the people who speed, smoke multiple packs of cigarettes each day, and fly into rages are in fact unbalanced, abnormal, and seeking death a bit too leisurely.

Because how much is enough? When is it enough?

Prison guards at Western Penitentiary in Pennsylvania work a 16-hour day. Not enough guards. The violence of need.

A judge in Pittsburgh calls for handguns to be outlawed because "People are being attacked in their homes and shot in broad daylight," further stating, "Handguns, used in 90 per cent of robberies and murders, should be outlawed. There is no reason why anyone should possess a handgun except peace officers and the military." The violence of plenty.

Nathan Heard serves six years for armed robbery in the late '60s. He becomes a professor of creative writing at Rutgers University – and, this year, an actor, beginning with *Gordon's War*, which comes out in August. He – along with Chester Himes (who, like Heard, ultimately dies of Parkinson's disease) and Donald Goines – becomes a pioneer of the genre of prison literature, chiefly with his million-seller *Howard Street*.

The potential of violence.

THEMROC
Wednesday, February 7, 1973.

Themroc gets fired from his job and decides to annihilate his role in modern French bourgeois society by demolishing his apartment until it's like a cave and he becomes like a caveman. His neighbors witness his example and do the same. With zero intelligible dialogue throughout, this film is either a quaint and irrelevant time capsule or a direct and impassioned mission statement, depending on where you currently stand in the life you've been living. Not that the filmmakers want you to capture and cook a cop to the point that he becomes an actual pig – but you get the general idea.

A Navy fighter jet slams into an apartment block in the night in Alameda, California. 50 dead. Possibly more. Everyone home from work. Getting ready for the morning. Going to work. Always more work. Thank Heaven for those rescue workers.

The ones in the asbestos suits.

The fire chief marvels, "I can't see how anyone could survive that. It just cremated them."

In Adamsville, Alabama, three people die in an explosion at a grocery store. A leak in the natural gas line. Those who die are found in living quarters behind the store.

Attached to it.

Fire does not choose favorites. It kills a grocer as easily as it does an empire.

It's not all about work.

A dog is found playing with a skull in Miami.

This leads police to the skeletal remains of a hospital volunteer who vanished from an area bus stop in June of 1971.

Debbie Rehfuss, found at last.

14 years old. Always 14. Effortlessly 14. Doing something she loved, and kind until the end.

It's the end for Georges Simenon, the author whose detective Inspector Maigret could have been called in to solve the mystery of the missing girl were he aware enough to know that he could become something more than a mere fictional character. Simenon retires from his mountain château above Lausanne to an apartment in Lausanne below. He needs to stop writing. For his health.

His daughter Marie-Jo will kill herself in Paris five years later. A gunshot in a locked room.

In Frankfurt, another skull takes the spotlight. The State Prosecutor announces that a skull found in Berlin last December 7 – a day positively bristling with infamy – was in fact that of the elusive Martin Bormann, personal secretary to Adolf Hitler. It will take until 1998, using rigorous DNA testing, to conclusively prove that this skull was Bormann's.

A detective's work is never done.

ONE DAY, THEMROC, JUST BLEW UP—

HE CHUCKED HIS JOB, DESTROYED HIS FLAT, MADE IT WITH HIS SISTER, DINED ON A COP, AND TURNED ON THE WHOLE NEIGHBORHOOD.

THEMROC

PORTRAYED BY MICHEL PICCOLI, IN A NEW FILM BY CLAUDE FARALDO. Distributed BY THE OTHER CINEMA

ONE DAY, THEMROC JUST BLEW UP— HE CHUCKED HIS JOB, DESTROYED HIS FLAT, MADE IT WITH HIS SISTER, DINED ON A COP, AND TURNED ON THE WHOLE NEIGHBORHOOD.

THEMROC

PORTRAYED BY MICHEL PICCOLI, IN A NEW FILM BY CLAUDE FARALDO. Distributed BY THE OTHER CINEMA

THEMROC
THE URBAN CAVEMAN

THEMROC
THE URBAN CAVEMAN

PORTRAYED BY MICHEL PICCOLI IN A NEW FILM BY CLAUDE FARALDO. Distributed BY THE OTHER CINEMA.

'A MUST' WHAT'S ON   'NOT TO BE MISSED' THE LISTENER

'... A COMEDY AND A VERY GOOD LOOKING AND ENJOYABLE ONE AT THAT! TIME OUT

THEMROC

DISTRIBUTED BY THE OTHER CINEMA

"THE URBAN CAVEMAN"

PORTRAYED BY MICHEL PICCOLI IN A NEW FILM BY CLAUDE FARALDO.

He was taught to kill.

Rape was his own idea!

forced entry X

STARRING:
LAURA CANNON PLAYBOYS PORNO QUEEN

NO ONE UNDER 18 ADMITTED!

Exclusive Area Showing
• **STARTS TOMORROW** •

FORCED ENTRY
Thursday, February 15, 1973.

Horrors of The War in Vietnam haunt gas station attendant and ex-soldier Harry Reems in this uncompromising, genuinely shocking adult film. He targets various female customers and does all manner of unspeakable violence to them because of what he endured over there. Endless footage of war and atrocities plague the nameless veteran as he stumbles through his violent life in a haze of rapes, murder and brutality. At the end, he's shown affection by a couple of hippie girls. The prospect of tenderness – after everything he's done – makes him blow his brains out. Most people had absolutely no idea what they were in for when they sat down in theatres for this one. *Deep Throat* was still gaining in popularity as a cultural touchstone, released as it was about eight months before *Forced Entry*. In this strange, brief period of openness, audiences of every race, color and creed found themselves sitting next to one another, watching pornography like it was just another film. A film that also just happened to have explicit sex in it. For once, though, it didn't seem like you could keep telling yourself "It's only a movie" when it came to *Forced Entry*.

How many Vietnam veterans does it take to change a lightbulb? YOU DON'T KNOW BECAUSE YOU WEREN'T THERE, MAN – YOU WEREN'T THERE!

"We're so shocked and horrified we can't say anything." – Martin William Mullin, father of mass murderer Herbert William Mullin.

The NEW Plainfield 6-5477
LIBERTY
Today: 7:00-8:25-9:30
• X No one under 21 •
• • •
**He was taught to kill
... his other acts
were his own idea!**

forced entry

STARRING:
**LAURA CANNON
PLAYBOYS PORNO QUEEN** COLOR X

• Also X & Fun •
**101 ACTS
OF LOVE**

He says this after his son's arraignment yesterday in Santa Cruz, California. Six murders. Ten bodies alone since January 1 have been discovered littered throughout this placid seaside hamlet.

"If our son is found guilty, God help him," Mullin's father continues. It's a distinct rarity to hear from the parents of serial killers, partly because mass murderers occasionally kill the mothers and fathers who would ordinarily have relevant insights on the topic.

Mullin purportedly changed drastically as a person while at Cabrillo College in Aptos, California. He became "freaked" on psychedelics during his time there.

Some people have adverse reactions when they take such drugs. Mullin's reactions included stabbing Father Henri Tomei, 46, to death in his own confessional in order to stave off the next big earthquake that would have otherwise ripped apart the state of California.

Martin William Mullin – an Army captain in World War II, now a postal clerk – was accused by his son of sending telepathic messages that urged him to kill. In Mullin's testimony to a court later this year, he says that, "In 1972, I was on the verge of becoming matured. Instead, my father drove me kill crazy."

This is also the father that attends every court meeting and embraces his son. After everything he's done.

By September, Mullin's father and mother will sit quietly in the front row of the courtroom. Waiting for the verdict to come.

Two first-degree murder convictions. Nine second-degree murder convictions. Served consecutively.

They leave in silence.

FURYÔ ANEGO DEN: INOSHIKA OCHÔ

Saturday, February 17, 1973.

In this highly entertaining and inventive period piece, Inoshika Ochô keeps her promise to a dying gambler and searches for his sister, sold into slavery and iniquity lo, those many moons ago. As she kills lots of people and becomes nude suddenly and often, she discovers that she's getting closer to finding the people who killed her own father and made her into the vengeful unblinking maniac she's become. She believes that she'll triumph – *and so she does!* One particularly clever scene involves Ochô coating her body with poison, seducing a killer and watching as he dies between her thighs. Nudity connoisseur – and no slouch at revenge herself – Christina Lindberg shows up, is hassled and does hassling. Ochô – expressions perfectly captured like ancient engravings carved in real time – swiftly and surely hurtles headlong into an epic finale involving death, death and still more death. Also: snow.

They found four more of Herb Mullin's victims today.

They don't know it at the time, but in a town as small as Felton, California, it doesn't take long to put four and four together. "It's foul play. There's blood all over the place," said Santa Cruz County Undersheriff Lee Davis. Four boys goofing off in the wilderness were warned by Mullin, posing as an authority figure, about "polluting" nature and that they should leave.

They didn't. He came back. They died.

The same day as Mullin's arrest, they found two

headless victims of Edmund Kemper, 60 miles away.

Ray Gallagher runs a hardware store in nearby Aptos. "If they looked hard," he argues, "I'll bet they'd find a lot more bodies. I think those hills are full of bodies."

Parts of another coed washed up in Monterey Bay in January.

Something in the water.

Herb Mullin believes that by killing people, he's able to prevent earthquakes from destroying California. His birthday falls on the anniversary of The Great San Francisco Earthquake of 1906.

Great.

During his trial, he points out that there haven't been any earthquakes on his watch.

He's planning her memorial service today. The murder remains unsolved.

In April, the musical drama *In the Eyes of the Beholder* is undertaken by a group from Gustine High School at the First Presbyterian Church.

With original music by Sarah Louise Gammons.

He goes to prison for life anyway, for all his troubles.

In Noya, Spain, the dust is still settling after director Claudio Guerin's 10-story plunge to his death yesterday. He fell from the bell tower on the set of his film *La campana del infierno* (A Bell From Hell). Doubt persists for decades about whether he jumped, or simply fell. Doubt clings tightly to the imagination like the tolling of an incessant bell, sounding a clarion call that summons forth even more doubt.

What do you want to believe?

Police announce that Sarah Louise Gammons, a Presbyterian minister's wife in Gustine, California, was murdered last night in a youth building at her husband's church. A week before her 32nd birthday. Stabbed multiple times. In both eyes. Blood-drenched Bibles surrounding her where she fell. She's found by her husband.

WALKING TALL
Tuesday, February 20, 1973.

Former professional wrestler Buford Pusser moves back to McNairy County, Tennessee and is positively agog at all the crappy corruption and gambling happening around him. Tired of all this mediocre sinning, he fashions a club out of a branch off a tree down at the mill and goes to work clobbering anyone who would try to stop him from cleaning up the county. People eventually get with the program and band together to expel the crooks from their community. He cries. The film was so successful that it spawned two sequels, three remakes, a TV version and a 1981 NBC series starring former Philadelphia Eagles guard Walter Barnes as Pusser. The real Buford Pusser was supposed to be in the sequel but he wrecks his Corvette on August 21, 1974 – the same day that he signs a deal with Bing Crosby Productions – and is thrown to his death. His daughter finds his body mere moments after it happens. Elizabeth Hartman, who plays Pusser's wife Pauline, jumps out a fifth-story window in 1987. Depression. Lifelong. You may remember her as the voice of Mrs. Brisby, the heroic mouse in the 1982 Disney film *The Secret of NIMH*.

With a death like that, how could you forget her?

Authorities announce that they're looking for the mother who gave birth to a newborn girl last night on a United Airlines flight from Washington, D.C. to Youngstown, Ohio. A worker finds the baby, umbilical cord still attached, jammed into the lavatory toilet bowl.

With a birth like that, how could you forget her?

The measure of a man is how tall he walks.

He was going to give them law and order or die trying.

The story of a real man who became a living legend

"WALKING TALL"

CINERAMA RELEASING presents "WALKING TALL"
Starring
JOE DON BAKER   ELIZABETH HARTMAN
ROSEMARY MURPHY   Written by MORT BRISKIN   Executive Producer CHARLES A. PRATT
Produced by MORT BRISKIN   Directed by PHIL KARLSON   A BCP Production   A service of Cine Broadcasting Corp
In Color   FROM CINERAMA RELEASING   Title song sung by Johnny Mathis   On Columbia Records
EXCLUSIVE ENGAGEMENT STARTS FRIDAY   R
PACIFIC'S PANTAGES THEATRE HOLLYWOOD

A week later, Betty Jean Anderson, 22, asks for custody of the child. Claims she did not know she was pregnant at the time. The FBI charges her with violating a federal law that states that it's a crime to attempt murder on board an aircraft. She gets two years for attempted manslaughter. Her daughter, later adopted, grows up to be Zuri Lazaro. "Plane Jane Doe," they named her. Lazaro even opens up to *People* magazine about it. She's still looking for Betty Jean Anderson, even in her 40s. Tells them about her search. She finds Anderson's sister – her aunt, who calls her on the telephone.

She tells her, "We have been looking for you your whole life."

Poor Betty Jean. She didn't make it.

Searching for reasons for suicide and searching for reasons for abandonment are opposite sides of the same question. It's the violence of emptiness. The violence of banishment and vanishment. Silence can be just as brutal and punishing as any blow struck or curse screamed.

Silence. Still hits as hard as a fist.

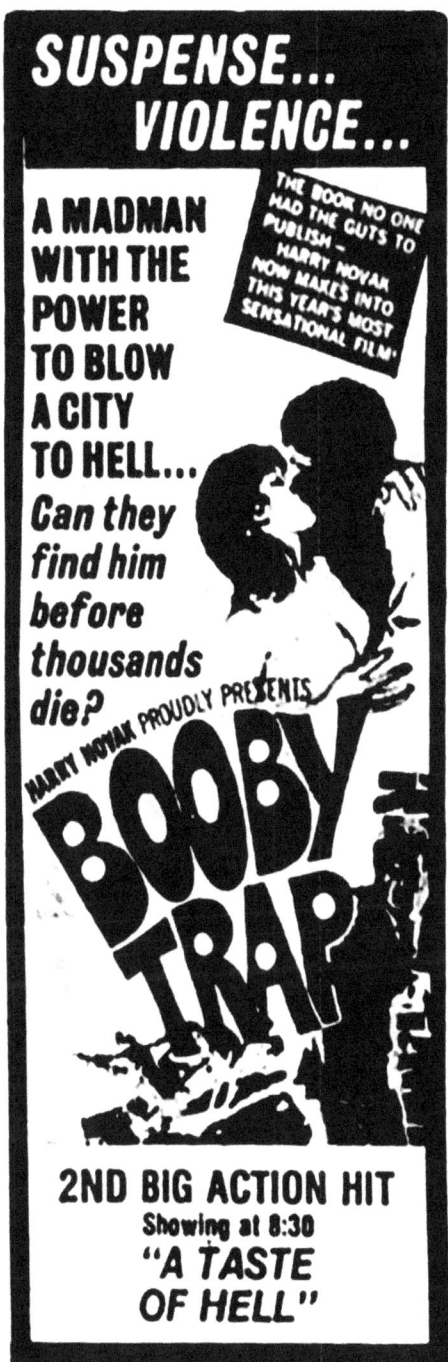

SUSPENSE...
VIOLENCE...

A MADMAN
WITH THE
POWER
TO BLOW
A CITY
TO HELL...
Can they
find him
before
thousands
die?

THE BOOK NO ONE HAD THE GUTS TO PUBLISH - HARRY NOVAK NOW MAKES INTO THIS YEAR'S MOST SENSATIONAL FILM'

HARRY NOVAK PROUDLY PRESENTS

BOOBY TRAP

2ND BIG ACTION HIT
Showing at 8:30
"A TASTE
OF HELL"

BOOBY TRAP
Thursday, February 22, 1973.

More energetic insanity presented by veteran huckster Harry H. Novak that promises that "Even a madman can enjoy having sex!" A crazed Marine gets his hands on a bunch of Claymore mines and travels the nation in his recreational vehicle, blowing up hippies and wiping out people with his shotgun, laughing and laughing. "A dragnet for a psychopathic killer zeroes in on the Sunset Strip" hollers one headline. He sure does get around. Plenty of vintage location shots of Los Angeles make this a real gem in the nostalgia department. Also: bazonks.

White protestors outnumber black supporters of the Kawaida Towers housing project in Newark, New Jersey. Scuffles turn into fights turn into riots and police wade in and waylay the melee. Cops are punched in the face; one gets his leg broken in the heat of the violence. In a few years, the foundations of the ill-fated housing project will be filled in with dirt.

Dead and buried. Again.

Few will notice. More will mourn yet another lost opportunity to construct housing for low- and middle-income people in the then-majority white North Ward area of Newark.

On the desolate French prison island of Île d'Yeu, on the Atlantic coast, they're burying Marshal Philippe Pétain.

Again.

His coffin had been exhumed by nationalist

agitators who demanded that the man who had been a beloved hero in World War I be buried with honors at the Douaumont Fort he'd defended against German aggression – despite his collaboration with the Nazis during the War's sequel. Four of those who made off with Pétain will be charged tomorrow with violation of a sepulcher. A Pétain sympathizer at the re-interment who tries to speak is stopped by Pétain's grandnephew. "I forbid you," says the man, dropping this philosophical bombshell: "This is a time for silence. The Marshal was a silent man and you, who never knew him, should learn that."

Silence. Like a fist.

In Las Vegas, Elvis Presley announces that he's not pressing charges against the four guys from Lima, Peru who stormed the stage during his set last Monday evening at The Hilton. He and a guitarist from the TCB Band karate-chopped two of the men and sent the rest packing.

Elvis got a standing ovation.

Again.

ARLECCHINO

Un nuovo divertente spassosissimo film
Un comico d'eccezione

EURO INTERNATIONAL FILMS
JACQUES-ERIC STRAUSS
JEAN-LOUIS TRINTIGNANT

**UNA GIORNATA
SPESA BENE**

UNE JOURNÉE BIEN REMPLIE OU
NEUF MEURTRES INSOLITES DANS
UNE MÊME JOURNÉE PAR UN SEUL
HOMME DONT CE N'EST PAS LE
MÉTIER

Wednesday, February 28, 1973.

Jean-Louis Trintignant directs this story of a
baker who vows to kill all nine of the jurors who
condemned his son to death. People are burned,
shot, stabbed and crushed to death in cars. Its full
title, translated, is *A Busy Day (Or, Nine Unusual Murders in the Same Day by One Man and It
Wasn't Even His Job)*. The killer drives around in
his motorcycle with his mother riding in the side-
car, dispensing justice dressed entirely in black
and not saying a whole hell of a lot as he kills.
Usually when actors try their hand at directing

it's a real mess but not Trintignant, who has a
real flair for black humor and the potency of his
imagery.

With violence comes resolution. Sometimes.

A man gets a new kidney today at UCLA
Medical Center. It comes from a mother of four,
crushed to death by a boulder as the family drove
back home to Santa Cruz up the Pacific Coast
Highway. The boulder – millennia in the making
and, in a more cosmological vein, existing to be
shaped and placed at this spot in particular – falls
somewhere south of Point Mugu in Southern
California. You can see that stretch of highway
– and the Big Rock emblematic of that drive –
gracing the background of many films.

Just in there. With her family. Riding along.

Speaking of chasing boulders long after they've
fallen, four members of the Manson Family
are judged sane enough to be sentenced for the
recent robberies of a Covina beer distributor
and a Hawthorne surplus store. Theoretically,
they did it to raise funds to help break Charles
Manson out of jail.

Theoretically.

I wonder what Charlie (the Viet Cong) thought
of Charlie (Manson) thought of Charlie (boss of
Angels) thought of Charlie (the perfume) thought
of Charlie (the Company that fought the Cong).
And vice-versa.

Underworld figure Meyer Lansky is in court today. Coincidentally, his crimes have helped send
many people over the years to a different kind of
underworld. They find him guilty of contempt

of court because he didn't answer a federal subpoena. One can only guess at how someone like Meyer Lansky perceived people like the Manson Family, stuck at opposite poles of history and larceny and violence as they were. It is as though the passing of one era has overlapped with the fading of another, differently brutal time. Fifty years is a vast gulf that brims with lost traditions and translations beyond measure.

Meanwhile, in another courtroom, a mother of eight children is acquitted of voluntary manslaughter in the shooting death of her husband. He came home one night, drunk and looking for money and savagery. Beating her. Reaching for the gun. Telling her he was going to shoot her. A long struggle suddenly becomes a brief one.

A mother of eight children.

Self-sacrifice is much more violent than you might think.

IL PRATO MACCHIATO DI ROSSO
Friday, March 2, 1973.

Known by its more ominous English title of *The Bloodstained Lawn*, this film concerns itself with the adventures of a rich brother with terrible taste in bow ties, his haughty aristocratic sister, and the hitchhikers, hookers and hippies they lure in to drain their blood with a robot (!) after acting like they really cared. What could be seen as an incisive satire about how bloodless and amoral rich people can be might also be seen as a more cynical take on humanity in general. Or, how riches simply amplify the kind of person that you really were on the inside all along. Then again, some people are just flat-out fucking assholes. Additionally, if you're out in the middle of nowhere and see a big field of pretty red poppies, this is called foreshadowing. Get the hell out of there!

14 people will ultimately die in today's collapse of the 26-story Skyline Towers apartment complex in Bailey's Crossroads, Virginia. At this moment, they only know about six of them. The workers had only finished 23 stories; it was the 24th that collapsed and took the entire thing down in a matter of a few agonizing dust-soaked moments. They'll find out that it happened because the job was rushed. Structural supports were pulled out too early from beneath freshly poured concrete sections that hadn't set as completely as they needed to in order to support the weight. The project won't be finished until 1977. Regardless.

The bloodstained lawn.

In the little town of Sebastopol, California, two men frying on LSD get pulled over, freak out and shoot two sheriff's deputies before running away. They then invade a home and hold hostage a mother of five and a reporter that got sucked into his own story. They surrender after their high finally fades.

The manicured lawns.

Throughout the Mississippi River Delta, some of the worst flooding of the 20th century inundates the surrounding states through June. Millions in damage to property. 33 dead. That we know of. The same water that falls into the ruins of the fire-gutted Sand Theatre in Gulfport, Mississippi after it burns to the building's bare brick and steel tomorrow morning. Pitiful ponds collect in the mud of the abandoned lot where the 2,300-seat Warner Theatre in Memphis used to stand. Its demolition throughout 1973 was a long and torturous process. The building held on. Didn't want to go. Didn't want to die.

The drowning lawns.

In Khartoum, the Palestinian terror faction Black September holds a group of diplomats hostage. Kills both the American ambassador and chargé d'affaires to Sudan after 26 hours. 26 hours of waiting, fearing, anticipating. It's an event that marks the crest of a wave of Black September terror attacks around the world that will end – appropriately enough – this September. Its campaign ended because its adherents came to believe that no good would ultimately come of attacks outside of the Occupied Territories of the West Bank and the Gaza Strip.

Some people don't think that blood makes the grass grow.

SEXY CAT
Friday, March 2, 1973.

Boozy, twitchy cartoonist Grahame hires louche private dick Mike Cash to prove that Paul Karpis, creator of popular pulp comic strip "Sexy Cat," stole the idea from him. Someone who looks suspiciously like Sexy Cat is running around killing as many people as possible. Using everything from a knife to a snake to a metal shearer, victims meet their respective gory fates at the paws of this karate-chopping, razor-clawed maniac. One guy steps out of the shower and gets relentlessly and impressively mauled when he opens up his closet to pick out his outfit for the day. Is nothing sacred? Sexy Cat just laughs and laughs. The filmmakers even made up copies of Sexy Cat comics for the characters to read during downtime on the set. Then, when you think it's over and the credits start rolling, there's even more murdering!

A three-ton concrete slab comes down fast in downtown San Francisco. It's a surprisingly swift 40-story drop from the top of the Tishman Building. Flying debris from that shattering monolith injures five luckless people during the morning rush hour.

"I thought it was an earthquake," says one of the injured, rightly traumatized.

Still.

In Springfield, Massachusetts, an eight-year-old boy is arraigned for stabbing to death his classmate, a seven-year-old girl, at Tapley Elementary School. "Delinquency by reason of murder."

A non-criminal charge, according to authorities.

What happens to the boy? After a week of reports from the wire services published in many American newspapers, he is heard of no more.

Unsurprisingly.

City Hall in Phoenix, Arizona is the scene of a mystery involving fumes that seep into a room of telephone operators, incapacitating them for the third time in four months. The fumes could be from remodeling taking place elsewhere in City Hall. They find their way into the room through the outside hallway every time the door opens.

"Positive pressure," they call it.

Director of Maintenance Services Ronald W. Jensen says that the telephone operators are currently working in the room that used to be his. "The new space is where my old office was, and we never had any such problems in there." And yet.

Criminal charges are still pending in the cold case of the rape-murder of Ann Woodward, the owner of Woody's Bar in Moab, Utah. Her husband, finding his bed empty upon awakening, looks for her at the bar this morning.

Cash register empty. Body between the pool tables. Strangled with her own slacks.

The case is still open. DNA technology advances. Continually. Year-by-year.

Former Moab Police Chief Melvin Dalton tells the *Deseret Morning News* that evidence from the case may have gone missing. "People were going in and out like they were going to church," he says. "There wasn't a sign up, no tape up, nothing that said 'Police Line, Do Not Cross'."

Dalton keeps the case file on his desk for years and years.

"I always felt if we had a really good trained detective, we'd have been in a lot better shape," Dalton says.

If only.

WENDY'S NAUGHTY NIGHT
Friday, March 2, 1973.

Wonderful scenes of the San Francisco Bay Area in the early '70s grace this tale of suicidal Wendy and the stories she lays on her psychiatrist after she has a lot of sex and indulges in all manner of perversions. The term "roughie" often conjures images of a certain type of violent sex film, but every so often a film is a roughie because it's really rough getting turned-on watching someone go through various levels of everyday anguish. Someone who then kind of forgets about the whole thing until an ending which comes out of nowhere in a moment that's more perceptive about death than anyone had any right to expect with a film like this. Another film from busy director Nick Millard's Irmi Films conglomerate – an outfit with longtime connections to everything from '60s European erotica to '80s shot-on-video works like *The Cemetery Sisters* and *Death Nurse*.

In Pensacola, four women become the first women to undergo flight training in the U.S. Navy. Lieutenant Junior Grade Barbara Allen Rainey of Chula Vista. Ensign Kathleen L. McNary of Plainfield, Illinois. Lieutenant Junior Grade Judith A. Neuffer of Wooster, Ohio. Ensign Jane M. Skiles of Des Moines.

By summer, McNary had been disqualified. Fear of flying. That's as far as she goes.

It would be somewhat illuminating to study the effects of fear on the history of the American military.

Another time.

Skiles ultimately retires at the rank of Captain

in 1997. She's the most senior female aviator in the Navy at that time. She could only go so far. Congress mandated that women couldn't serve in combat. "It's very discouraging to know the best you can play on is the junior varsity team no matter how good you are," Skiles says.

By 1977, LTJG Neuffer is set to become the first woman astronaut. She'd already become the first P-3 fighter pilot in the Navy. She got as far as Director of the Safety and Mission Assurance Directorate at Goddard Space Flight Center.

She could only go so far.

Allen dies at 33 in 1982 with a trainee ensign during a touch-and-go landing exercise at Middleton Field near Evergreen, Alabama. The aircraft crashes after banking and dropping like a stone. It's so thoroughly destroyed that a suit against manufacturer Beech Aircraft Corp. fails in part because the cause of the crash could not be conclusively determined.

Some people are defined by their lives. Others, by their deaths.

Which do you think yours will be?

PORUNO NO JOÔ: NIPPON SEX RYOKÔ
Saturday, March 3, 1973.

Perpetually nude Christine Lindberg goes to Japan, gets into the wrong taxicab and is waylaid by a tragically anxious cabbie who takes her to his apartment and proceeds to rape her again and again (to the strains of Beethoven's *Symphony No. 6 in F Major*, no less). He keeps her gagged and chained up while he rants and pontificates. She escapes to an after-hours psychedelic bar, only to be gang-raped by a bunch of other maniacs. Freaking out over having "lost" her, the cabbie finds her wandering in a daze. She winds up falling for him. As one does! He quickly gets sick of her but the die is cast and she's his forever. She also sings "Nobody Knows the Trouble I've Seen" in English. Eventually the cops close in and bring about a more dynamic and philosophical conclusion that likely none of them expected when they got up to go to work that morning.

They're baring their hearts at Wounded Knee.

200 Oglala Lakota Indians and supporters from the American Indian Movement (AIM) have, over the course of five days, taken over the South Dakota town on the Pine Ridge Indian Reservation. They're protesting current tribal leadership, as well as the countless broken promises and dashed hopes visited upon Native Americans by the American government. The occupation lasts until May 5.

When the dust settles, there are dead and wounded on both sides. Dust, however, is not something that disappears when it settles. Dust is cosmic. Dust kills. Dust is us. The microscopic dust that erupts from the skin around the wounds

caused by the bullets of the government snipers during the occupation is probably still out there, borne on winds carrying it to every corner of the state of South Dakota.

It gets kicked up whenever someone visits the past.

May 5, 1973. At the time, it seems like it takes forever to get from here to there.

Ray Robinson is on his way to the siege.

On his way to forever.

In Moscow, at the Sheremetyevo Airport, 25 die when their iced-over Balkan Bulgarian jet crashes.

Final approach.

No survivors. It's the third fatal crash at that airport in five months.

You'd think you'd get out while the getting's good.

Some people just can't get out.

A highway patrolman in Los Angeles has his right foot severed when his patrol car is struck by a drunk driver. He's pinned between his car and the unforgiving concrete of the center divider of the Harbor Freeway. This happens while he's investigating another accident. Lightning, twice, etc. A sudden shock. No one ever goes to work even vaguely daydreaming that they might come home lacking a limb.

Something that anyone would rightly expect would always be there.

Survivor Shōichi Yokoi waits in an airport lounge in Guam. His bride Mihoko waits beside him.

He was found last January. He's going to show her the jungle hole in which he lived for 28 years, despite knowing that World War II was over.

Two more Japanese holdouts will surrender in 1974. At his homecoming, he says, "It is with much embarrassment that I return." On returning, he is fêted and celebrated. He tours Japan, experiencing much curiosity and fascination; ironically beloved by a curious post-war public for living so simply – and simply because he is who he is, which is to say: himself.

Yokoi was terrified to come out of hiding. Japanese military training dictated that being captured alive was a fate worse than death. He lived his life in accordance with that training.

If you can't maintain a state of war, you maintain a state of fear.

SI PUÒ ESSERE PIÙ BASTARDI
DELL'ISPETTORE CLIFF?
Monday, March 5, 1973.

Inspector Cliff – played by stalwart saint of the square-jawed himself, the reliable Ivan Rassimov – busts up Mama the Turk's drug ring with a lethal combination of smarts and savagery, scored by a jazzy Riz Ortolani soundtrack throughout. With a gang of young crooks that perform musical accompaniment to crimes, a nutjob with a thing for rabbits, and more car chases than you can shake a nightstick at. One of the best chases involves a black Citroën's long fall down a hill, mesmerizing in its seemingly endless ballet of destruction. The personalities of the characters rise above the usual constraints of the *poliziotteschi* genre, and they're about as demented as they come. Even the gunshots sound more violent than usual. Character and charisma – if only actual crime and violence were quite so colorful. Leon Vitali – who plays a Mod licking a Popsicle – wound up being Stanley Kubrick's right-hand man and confidant for decades. Go figure!

What's the most violent thing that's ever happened to you – and how did that change you?

Leon Vitali (speaking in summer 2017): "Me? I wouldn't know where to start! (laughs) I had a pretty volatile childhood. I would say that that did have an effect on me, because over the time that that was happening, those were my most formative years. When that period was over, I'd already kind of ... I don't know how to say it ... "mastered" the art of knowing when to step back. To stay out of a thing you knew you couldn't possibly win – and have much more of an idea of self-preservation. And dealing with

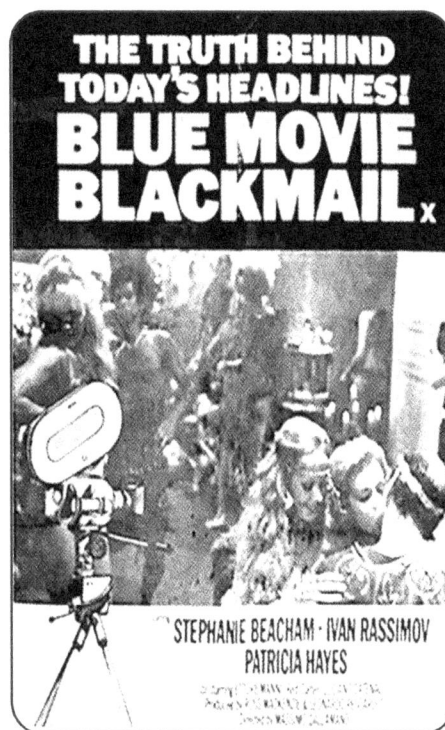

people who were volatile, you know? You could take a step back and let them vent – because often it's just venting, and that's what sometimes can spill into far more dangerous territory."

A man accidentally touches a high-power wire in Hermosa Beach, California with a chainsaw. In an instant, the 16,000 volts carried by the power line course through his body, burning off his clothes and all of his hair.

Elsewhere in California, a judge rules that a Hells Angel on trial for murdering two men during an initiation ritual will have testimony brought against him by the prosecution. The Feds got it from another biker.

That biker, William "Whispering Bill" Pifer, died in San Francisco. Throat cancer. Hence the whisper. He testified on his deathbed – through a lip reader! – that the two victims died after having their drinks spiked with LSD. One of them freaked out on acid, became violent and was killed.

The other guy died because he was in the wrong place at the wrong time.

Not 16,000 volts' worth of wrong timing, but still.

An avalanche crushes a ski hut in Schliersee, Germany. One of four injured people frees himself from this icy sarcophagus and finds his way down the mountain.

To get some help.

The ice and snow falls in just the right way that allows him to struggle free and find an escape route in the cold. The way that it falls seems carved out of nature explicitly and specifically for him. As though he were destined to survive.

A two-year-old dies, along with three others.

A hut collapses one way. An air pocket opens up another way. A storm passes. Lightning strikes. A man breaks free and another man stays buried.

It's all a matter of timing. Random and capricious timing.

As much as people talk about timing, it must also be understood that spacing is always as important as timing.

POWs returning from the war tell stories today of watching massive fireballs erupting near Ha-

noi and cheering.

Later, they learn that these were American B-52 bombers. Shot down, falling to earth and exploding on impact.

One POW remarks, "(It was) the greatest show on Earth." So great was this show on Earth that watching those burning clouds of annihilation made imprisonment somehow bearable. "I didn't want to go home a loser," the man said.

A school principal gets out of prison today.

He shot his wife yesterday in a suburb of Milwaukee. He did it because his wife was going to file for divorce and didn't want to reason with him. Reason. His sons, 6 and 8, watched him pull the trigger. Then they watched as he pointed that .25 revolver at them.

It did not discharge.

Timing.

SI PUO' ESSERE PIU' BASTARDI DELL' ISPETTORE CLIFF?

COUSIN PAULINE
Wednesday, March 7, 1973.

Pauline visits Paris from America. Reminiscent of the plot of *The Blue Balloon*, she's drugged by her cousin Jenny, who rapes her and then passes her over to two scumbags so they can rape her some more. This is what's known in some quarters as "The Devil's Threesome." They also take a lot of blackmail photographs while she's being raped. Film inside a film: kaleidoscopic; voyeuristic. The final shot of the Eiffel Tower drives the point home in an instant. It's a chance to see France as it was – briefly – in 1973. A France in transition. The France of the dying Picasso. An evolving France, besotted as it is with Nixon-blessed clandestine nuclear weapons program. The anxious France that in January saw the publication by Éditions Robert Laffont of *The Camp of the Saints*, Jean Raspail's fear-soaked screed about immigration. Not that you'd be able to step back and extract enough perspective to see all of this amidst everything that befalls Cousin Pauline.

Just because you're on your back doesn't always mean you're looking up.

Czech astronomer Luboš Kohoutek first sees the comet Kohoutek today.

A Great Comet – so-called – it unveils itself nicely each evening throughout 1973. It is, however, nowhere near the cosmic object of death that inspires so many charlatans to have such an astronomical effect on their followers.

David Berg – founder of the Children of God cult – promises his followers doom, death and destruction by this time next year. Dave Berg – writer of "The Lighter Side Of" cartoons in *Mad Magazine* – promises his readers chortles, chuckles and cognitive dissonance in his book *My Friend God*, available at B. Dalton, Waldenbooks, Borders, and finer newsstands and drugstores everywhere.

The confusion is palpable.

The faithful and fearful flock and cluster amongst themselves accordingly. The enlightenment of the '70s carries with it an undercurrent leading to many fantasies of extinction – popular Cold War anxieties notwithstanding – that saw everyone from the Worldwide Church of God to the Jehovah's Witnesses to the Brahma Kumaris in India get in on the booming business in apocalypses.

Cult figure Sun Ra undertakes the "Concert for the Comet Kohoutek" in December. Cult band Yahowah 13 titles their first album *Kohoutek*. The slightly more grounded Kraftwerk name their first single *Kohoutek-Kometenmelodie* after it in 1973. All of these recordings are beautiful. Evanescent. Effervescent. Transcendent.

You take your opportunities for ascension where you can get them.

They're ready to die at Wounded Knee.

Women and children are leaving today. Something in the wind. Ralph Erickson, Special Assistant the U.S. Attorney General, alleges that the Indians spearheading the siege are demanding nothing less than "Total capitulation by the U.S. government to their illegal demands or violence."

Is today a good day to die? For whom?

In Macon, Georgia, eight-year-old Debbie Brown walks along the side of the road. No shoes. Torn clothing. She tells the police, "My daddy threw me away." When stopped by the police, Daddy – 22-year-old George E. Southerland – throws his three-year-old son David over a cop's head. The child sinks into a watery ditch. His father attacks anyone who tries to rescue the boy. "God told me to kill them," he shouts.

1973. Something in the air. Or the water.

In Manhattan, Luis Ortiz is stabbed 38 times. His penis is mutilated. Ortiz is one of the victims of never-caught serial killer Charlie Chop-Off, so named because of his habit of disfiguring the genitals of young boys.

In Bakersfield, Texas, they're still picking through the remains of a Greyhound bus that collided with a truck and exploded tonight. Authorities reveal that most of the 15 who died were burned "beyond recognition."

The flames were so hot that the bottom of the bus disintegrated. Bodies fell through. It's a small town, Bakersfield. Everyone knows everyone in a small Texas town in 1973.

The front of the frame of the annihilated bus shows where a person, burning, tried to escape through the front door.

"He didn't make it," one reporter observed at the scene.

Newsflash.

Clyde Tuttle, 41, falls three stories from the top of the soon-to-be-destroyed State Theatre in East

Liverpool, Ohio. Contusions of the head. Contusions of the body. He's lucky to be alive. It happens minutes after he shows up at the demolition site and asks for a job. He gets it.

Moments later, the real work begins.

The Carnival in Rio de Janeiro ends today. A legendary celebration. After four days, 150 people fill the city morgue. Shot. Stabbed. Drowned.

Fallen from heights.

THE MARCUS-NELSON MURDERS
Thursday, March 8, 1973.

"My name is Theo Kojak. It's interesting how matter-of-fact death can become." So begins the television dramatization of the true story of the 1963 Career Girls Murders. The career girls in question – *Newsweek* researcher Janice Wylie, 21, and schoolteacher Emily Hoffert, 23 – were stabbed over 60 times with their own knives in their New York City apartment. It was also a case of collateral damage that presently involved innocent George Whitmore Jr., wrongfully imprisoned for close to four years for those murders. He was abused, beaten and gaslighted by authorities to get a confession – so much so that his case was one of the many miscarriages of justice that led to the Supreme Court issuing rules that protect suspects under arrest: Miranda Rights. In Whitmore's case, it was the right to remain silent. Turns out that he was in New Jersey watching Dr. Martin Luther King Jr. give his "I Have a Dream" speech on television the whole time. Irony of ironies. The Supremes, duly aghast at his treatment, cited Whitmore's case as "the most conspicuous example" of police coercion in the country when it issued its landmark June 13, 1966 ruling. In the film, Kojak – in this, his first appearance – is the only good cop around, drowning in a sea of corruption and suspecting that his fellow cops are railroading a young black triple-homicide suspect just to get a conviction. Kojak's anguish and disgust is truly compelling. The luckless artistic kid paints Kojak's portrait and gives it to him at the end. "Well, you gave me a lot of hair ... and I'm good-lookin'!" The cops still say that the kid did it. They just can't get off of it. The violence of self-delusion. "It was as if we were all sleepwalkers, watching a terrible pageant that nobody cared about anymore."

James Richard Finch and John Andrew Stuart spend their night plotting a different kind of excitement.

They light two six-gallon drums of diesel fuel at the Whiskey Au Go Go nightclub in Fortitude Valley, Brisbane, Australia. Grease the fire doors to make them impossible to open. Grease the steel stairs in case the impossible happens. 15 patrons and workers die. Choked to death on carbon monoxide fumes.

It all comes down to plots of terror and extortion that the pair meant to level against Brisbane nightlife. Stuart dies in 1979 after a hunger strike. "Australia's most violent criminal," they call him.

Finch eats wire and part of his little finger in the days preceding the trial.

In case anyone wondered how competent he was.

TV Film Based on Murders Here

Next January 16, Barbara McCulkin and her two daughters, Leanne, 11, and Vicki, 13, will be abducted from their home in the Highgate Hill area of Brisbane. They're taken into the bush. Barbara, strangled. The girls, killed in some other way. Bodies, never found. In 2017, Brisbane crime figure Vincent O'Dempsey will be found guilty of the family's murders. Garry "Shorty" Dubois, his partner in the murders, will be convicted for his role in the crimes in 2016. The elder McCulkin was killed allegedly because they thought she knew too much about a fire set by Dubois and Brisbane's notorious Clockwork Orange Gang that annihilated Torino's Nightclub in Brisbane this past February 23. The children, however, knew nothing. The criminals thought the Whiskey Au Go Go fire would be pinned on them if it was connected to the fire at Torino's. In fact, there never was any connection in the first place.

Collateral damage.

Above El Centro, California, three F4 Phantom fighter jet pilots parachute to earth. The Blue Angels, they call them.

Their $9 million fighters, worth about $58.5 million in 2022 dollars, were following each other too closely when they collided.

Competence.

At a National Press Club luncheon in Washington, D.C., violently competent actor Rex Harrison bemoans – and decries – the entertainment quotient of modern cinema. "I don't enjoy endless brutality," he says, adding, "But the only things that seem to make money are sex and brutality." In case you thought he undercut his argument later by appearing in a film that was either sexual or brutal – nope! Ever the bearer of courageous convictions, Rex Harrison was genuinely distressed about the current state of affairs of his chosen profession.

Umbrage. Have you taken yours today?

In Corte Madera, California, organist Ron "Pigpen" McKernan – whom bandmate Mickey Hart described as "the *musician* in The Grateful Dead" – is found dead by his landlady. A gastrointestinal hemorrhage. He's 27. At his funeral, Jerry Garcia calls this momentous occasion "the end of the original Grateful Dead."

Burying a friend is a terrible pageant of an entirely different color.

VAULT OF HORROR
Monday, March 12, 1973.

Five men take an elevator down to a gentlemen's club. The elevator won't go back up. They pass the time by telling stories about some of the shitty things they've done in their lives. A brother (Daniel Massey) kills his sister (Daniel's real-life sister Anna) for inheritance money. A neat freak (Terry-Thomas) marries a young babe (Glynis Johns) who drives him to fits until he screams at her, "Can't you do *anything* neatly?" Another fellow (Curt Jürgens) and his wife (Dawn Addams) go to India looking for new magic tricks to learn. One character climbs up a rope and vanishes in the ceiling. The patch of blood that appears is a nicely surreal touch. Two back-stabbing insurance scammers (Michael Craig and Edward Judd) find out too late about the real nature of their deal. An artist (Tom Baker!) learns voodoo techniques to create more vivid paintings and then mutilates the portraits of his tormentors, after which his own self-portrait undergoes a drastic and sudden revision. The anthology is based on the American horror comics of the '50s published by EC that, due to the restrictions and nausea that greeted them from lawmen and psychiatrists alike, were shuttered or neutered by the end of the decade. No one likes a ghost story told by a scold. In April, the film premieres at The Wiltern in Los Angeles. You got in to the theatre if you screamed real loud for KDAY DJ Wolfman Jack, a man who knew screams better than most anyone.

A girl dies at a temple fair in Chachoengsao Province, east of Bangkok, when a soldier dislikes the choice of music being played. He decides to throw a grenade into a crowd to make his point slightly more emphatically.

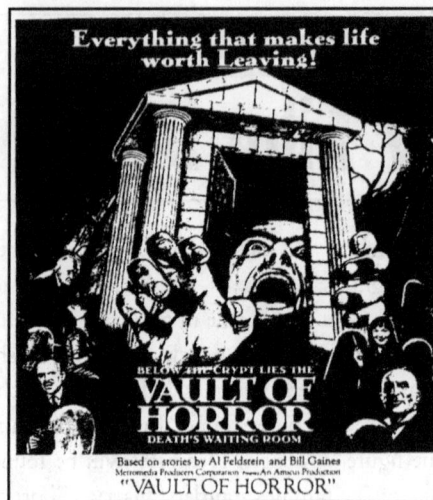

Everything that makes life worth Leaving!

BELOW THE CRYPT LIES THE
VAULT OF HORROR
DEATH'S WAITING ROOM

Based on stories by Al Feldstein and Bill Gaines
Metromedia Producers Corporation presents An Amicus Production
"VAULT OF HORROR"

In Brisbane, Finch and Stuart are subdued by six cops. They tried to break out of the courtroom as they appeared before a judge. They will continue to appear in the news over the years, constantly denying that they set the Whisky Au Go Go fire. False confessions. Coercion. If only they'd had Miranda Rights to guide them.

In Rio de Janeiro, the parents of a seven-year-old mourn him after he's devoured by giant ants. He was sick in bed. He didn't have a chance. Four of his siblings are also attacked by the marauding beasts but neighbors come to their rescue.

Kenneth B. Davenport is 18. He slaughters both his parents and both his younger brothers as they slept early in the morning in their home in Abington, a suburb of Philadelphia. He's arrested the same day – caught while driving around in the family car. Running red lights. That was fast. He bludgeons them to death with a shotgun barrel. Apparently their wounds were so grievously intense that initially police suspected that he had shot everyone. Kenneth excels at chess. People

taunt him. Call him "Martian Head." He brings copies of The Watchtower with him even while he's out camping. That doesn't stop his Jehovah's Witness father from arguing with him over the length of his hair and the quality of his grades at school. The level of violence visited upon men with long hair in the '60s is often forgotten, even though it became almost a civil rights issue unto itself. As will be revealed during the trial, Davenport is a certified paranoid schizophrenic. Gets hospitalized for four years. Then gets four consecutive life sentences.

Three young men are arrested in Washington, D.C. after robbing and shooting Senator John C. Stennis twice outside his home in Cleveland Park. Wire reports reveal that the three men are "all from the predominantly black and lower-class northeast section of the city." The notoriously hard-of-hearing Stennis had been a big supporter of segregation, opposing Voter Acts and Civil Rights Acts with equal fervor. It must have made his predicament doubly galling.

Justice for whom? When? In what regard, exactly?

THE BAIT
Tuesday, March 13, 1973.

Donna Mills plays policewoman Tracy Fleming, who's out to stop a murderous serial rapist targeting young working women in and around the Hollywood Hills. The psycho has a habit of covering his victims' faces with their own long hair. She's also a widow and her mom is helping raise her son. The super-competent policewoman busts three different crooks on one bus ride alone! That was Los Angeles in 1973, I guess – if nothing else, it's a highly entertaining look at the city through a certain lens at a very particular point in time. She also reads the criminals their rights using an early version of the Miranda Rights, before the police got the litany standardized. She lays it all on the line as she gives herself up as bait to catch the wily bastard – as far as you can lay anything on any line in any ABC Movie of the Week, anyway. She gets cornered and tries to reason with him. "I really like you," she says soothingly. "Now you like me ... but in time it will be different! All women are alike!" he scoffs, grinning maniacally. She dispatches him forthwith. As if there were ever any doubt!

White House Counsel Howard Dean tells Richard Milhous Nixon in the Oval Office that CIA officer and Watergate conspirator E. Howard Hunt Jr. wants a cool million in hush money. "There is a certain domino situation here," Dean counsels Nixon. "If some things start going, a lot of other things are going to start going." In 18 months, Nixon will himself be gone. You can see Army One – the helicopter on which he departed the White House after resigning the Presidency – at the Nixon Library in Yorba Linda, California.

It is not for nothing that horror films are littered with cursed objects.

Nixon's Army One may be the most cursed-at object in the history of the Presidency, flipped off and spat at by people below who watch it fly him home to San Clemente, California after he leaves office.

More cursing and aircraft.

At Portland Airport in Maine, George D. West, 27, and Arthur Smith, 56, both pilots for the International Paper Company, fly a Beechcraft King Air turboprop to meet with FAA Inspector George Phinney, 48, to get a rating on West's pilot's license. The "emergency maneuver" that West executes on approach makes the aircraft crash and burn. West and Phinney both die.

If you go back and review cockpit voice recordings and flight transcripts from aircraft accidents, the most popular last words are "Oh, shit!"

Popular. Well, shit.

A principal from Los Angeles' Crenshaw High tells a bunch of members of the Assembly Education Committee in Sacramento that he's had to confiscate 15 guns so far this year. Half of those weapons are purportedly being carried for protection.

Youth gangs, you see.

These gangs invade the schools and cause panic. The theme of terrible and temperamental teens is one that will swell and intensify throughout the '70s in the media. America becomes like an alien world to the clutchers of pearls and passers of laws. America as seen through a particular lens, that is.

After a President resigns, all bets are off.

Keep going.

Wind and rain erode Chimney Rock in northwestern Oklahoma. It's a well-loved and well-worn landmark that for decades guides wagon trains westward. It is unknown if it's the rain or the wind that topples the Rock first. Credit or blame – it's all the same to entropy.

Milestones and gravestones.

Louis Williams steps off a curb and walks onto the Santa Ana Freeway in Los Angeles. He's struck by a car. Gets up. He's hit by a second car. Then a third. Knocked down by a fourth, he's then run over by a fifth, which kills him. All but one driver takes off. They never find out why Williams did it. He's buried over in Woodlawn Memorial Park in Compton if you want to ask him yourself.

Slightly more than 12 miles north of Salta, Argentina, an engineering student sees a white 5'2" diving-suited being with an opaque helmet gliding alongside a newly landed UFO. It vanishes. Suddenly sick, the student is taken to a clinic. After eight days, he's released, never knowing the diagnosis of his ailments.

In this month's edition of the planetary science journal *Icarus*, there's a paper by MIT radio astronomer John A. Ball. Titled "The Zoo Hypothesis," it maintains that extraterrestrials deliberately avoid this slice of space because we Earthlings are too backward and violent for

The Bait
8:30 pm

A sex maniac has already killed four girls. Will his next victim be the lady cop set to trap him? A suspense drama starring Donna Mills, Michael Constantine, June Lockhart.

Tuesday Movie of the Week

words. As such, they conceal themselves from view so that they may study Earth civilizations like scientists studying animals in a zoo.

Some things are going to start going. Some are already gone. Others just got here.

HUNGRY HYPNOTIST
Wednesday, March 14, 1973.

"A modern-day hypnotist who preys upon the dreams and aspirations of the easily-led!" intones the narrator. Thank God he's not just another fucking pervert. The hypnotist in question mesmerizes various lovers by making them susceptible via a drug he slips into their drinks. Apparently his previous subjects have become corrupted, ruined sex maniacs in the wake of his influence on their lives. The classical music crescendo that mirrors the climax of one performer is a nice touch. Psychopaths get a lot of attention, whereas sociopaths like the Hungry Hypnotist are much more plentiful in a society. At times the unsynchronized, dubbed dialogue could be from another film entirely, achieving consciousness and forming a narrative of its own, ultimately escaping from the film itself to enjoy unheralded pleasures of its own, elsewhere.

Country musician Carl Phillips is 42 when he dies outside his home in Goodlettsville, Tennessee. He's pulling an old car up a steep hill with a tractor. The tractor rears up because of the hill's incline. Throws him back between the car and the tractor. Crushing him.

In Santa Cruz, earthquake repeller and conscientious objector Herb Mullin is indicted for the murders of 10 people. Families, campers, prizefighters – it didn't matter. He killed them all. His friends claim that he's "strongly against killing."

Conscientious. Not consistent.

A woman in Milwaukee is found by her daughter after she electrocutes herself while installing insulation.

In a closet.

A short in a broken electrical cord got her when she touched a water pipe.

It is the everyday and the banal that is infinitely more hypnotic in our lives than a man with a pendant or a drugged-up drink. The days pass, painless as the slow drip-drip of blood lost from an unknown wound. Ordinary things glisten and gleam in their own way, implanting concepts of comfort and calm more powerfully than any mentalist.

Nanny Lee Armstrong still prays for her baby's safe return.

Vera Clemente still wishes like mad that she could

touch Roberto again, even if only for a moment.

Thomas Pynchon's novel *Gravity's Rainbow* still exists.

Betty Jean Anderson of Garyville, Louisiana is indicted in Cleveland. A federal grand jury charges her with attempted murder for leaving her newborn daughter inside a toilet on that fateful flight to Youngstown. She gets two years in prison next year.

What did she think would happen?

Expectations are some of the most powerful illusions under which a person can labor.

You think you know what you're doing. And yet how present are you? How aware are you in this moment? Of this moment?

THE MIDNIGHT HUSTLER
Wednesday, March 14, 1973.

Fresh-off-the-bus Gail – here played by Sandy Carey – gets picked up by Angie The Leech (played by durable and reliable Norman Fields, a journeyman in life who worked as everything from an electrician to a folksinger) from a bus bench. He takes her back to his flophouse apartment. Shows her kindness. Feeds her. Offers her a pickle. She's annoyed when he tries to put the moves on her. He tells her how things really are in the big city of downtown Los Angeles. They have sex. A lot of sex. They then venture into the depths of Hollywood, accompanied by one of the most intense drum-and-bongo breaks ever heard in a film of this nature. He takes her to a den of debauchery: the pad owned by whoremonger Vince, who wears a horrible fringed leather jacket and asks her, "So, you want to meet some groovy people, huh?" It's all a set-up to get her gang-raped by the guys hanging out at Vince's. Still more bongo music plays. She turns up back at Angie's place. He realizes the spot he's put her in and acts cold to her. They wander somewhere in the Los Angeles Harbor and discuss their possible futures, finally having found one another – regardless of what it cost to find themselves.

Faded people, fading lives.

Water seeks its own level.

In Gila Bend, Arizona, Burt Reynolds takes the stand to testify in support of actress Sarah Miles, whose business manager David Whiting was found dead here on February 11 during location shooting for the film *The Man Who Loved Cat Dancing.* "He started beating her and throwing

CENTER 17th & Market   LO 4 4942
        Cont fr 8 45 Open All Nite
  2 (XXX) MIDNIGHT HUSTLER (X)
Rated Hits SLIPPERY WHEN WET (X)
    $2 00 till 11 AM Mon - Fri

her around the room," Reynolds says. Why?

Because she'd declined to tell Whiting where she was that night.

The next morning, they find Whiting on the floor of a hotel room. Dead where he fell. Contorted in a rictus of agony. A bottle of pills clutched in the hand behind his back.

"He's dead, he's dead," Miles kept repeating, sobbing as Reynolds picked up the telephone and called the police. Methaqualone. Benadryl. Something librium-adjacent.

The unexplained presence of blood around the room.

Sometimes you don't realize what you've done even while you're doing what you're doing.

Ken Baldwin, a survivor of a suicide leap off the Golden Gate Bridge in 1985, thought that too – even as he saw the railing from which he'd jumped receding rapidly into the distance above. "I instantly realized that everything in my life that I'd thought was unfixable was totally fixable – except for having just jumped."

John McCain returns from the war, released today by the North Vietnamese with over 100 American POWs. He's a Navy pilot. He's been in captivity for five long years. A Russian missile shot down his Skyhawk divebomber. By the time his parachute and ejector seat had delivered him to the drowning embrace of a lake near Hanoi, he'd broken his right leg, his right arm in three places, and his left arm. He suffers phenomenal, agonizing tortures over the breadth of those years. The stocks. Solitary confinement. The Vietnamese rope trick. Now he can't even lift his own arms over his head.

He has no earthly idea what he's going to do next.

First Exclusive Detroit Showing

"THE MIDNIGHT HUSTLER" and "ROMP AROUND"

Both Color

X-Rated For Adults 18 and Over

SISTERS
Wednesday, March 14, 1973.

Margot Kidder stars as a woman with a very specific kind of personality disorder. People die trying to find out what her problem is. A reporter tries to help but is scorned and otherwise dismissed because she writes articles critical of the police and/or has been hypnotized. The murders are shocking and deeply personal, while everything having to do with the medical profession is depicted as either surreal or downright inhumane. With Charles Durning as a tenacious telephone pole-sitting detective and the thematically pristine narrative device of the split screen. An unusually claustrophobic film.

As if the last three months' worth of a formerly extinct volcano erupting in Iceland wasn't enough – now Iceland's Westman Islands have a new problem: poison gas.

It seeps in and chokes people, knocking them to the ground. It's not like you can simply hop in a car and speed away. The gas stops engines cold, too. Since last January 23, an entirely unexpected fissure has opened near the church on the island of Heimaey. Lava everywhere. Eldfell is the name of the new volcanic cone that forms in the wake of the eruption from the depths of the chasm. Immediately south of Eldfell is Helgafell, an inactive volcano that last erupted 5,000 years ago.

You never know what might blow up next.

In Raleigh, North Carolina, politicians bring the death penalty back to life.

It's squarely in line with President Richard Milhous Nixon's current pressure on senators

to restore the death penalty nationwide. One representative says, "All you have to do to do away with capital punishment is not to murder, rape or burn down homes." Rep. Herbert L. Hyde counters by saying, "If we continue to kill our fellow man, whether you call it legalized or not, crime will continue to increase. Violence begets violence."

Inextricably linked.

In Lumberton, North Carolina, four children – aged 3, 4, 5 and 7 – walk into an empty house and take a radio. They give the radio to a mentally handicapped person. An attempt to communicate. Local police charge them with breaking and entering, and larceny. No credit for kindness served.

A moment like that is a bond that lasts a lifetime.

72

HUNTED
Thursday, March 15, 1973.

Edward Woodward plays a guy who does his Charles Whitman thing and holds a real estate agent (played by June Ritchie) hostage. He threatens to waste various innocents in the streets with his sniper rifle in this British film that unspools methodically, bristling with tension and riveting character studies throughout its brief 41 minutes. It would be reworked only slightly as an episode of *Alfred Hitchcock Presents* in 1988, with Woodward reprising his role. When he asks Ritchie's character to talk him out of killing all those people, it does seem as though he doesn't really want to do it; like Texas Tower Sniper Whitman and his brain tumor, however, it also seems like he can't really help it. Ultimately, it led to Woodward being cast in the CBS series *The Equalizer*, which ran from 1985–1989. Oaks, acorns, et cetera.

20 people die in a Buddhist pagoda in Saigon. Communist terror is blamed. It has something to do with anticipating an upcoming Canadian mission to examine the effectiveness of the current Vietnam War ceasefire.

A dozen grenades. That's no way to die.

"That's no way to die." You'll hear people say that a lot in old movies. Did the saying come before it was used in the movies – or did movies make people think that that's what you should say when a dozen grenades kill and injure a house full of worshipers? Or when the scoop of an industrial steam shovel collides with a passing German train, tearing open the side of a car and killing someone?

STUNNING TERRIFYING SUSPENSE

COLUMBIA PICTURES PRESENTS

EDWARD WOODWARD
and
JUNE RITCHIE
in

HUNTED ⓜ

written by
MICHAEL SLOAN
directed by
PETER CRANE

produced by
THE PEMINI ORGANISATION

At the Eastern side of the Berlin Wall, Horst Einsiedel, 33, wants to return to the West. He misses his mother and sister. A mechanical

73

engineer, he knows the perils of the Berlin Wall better than most. Using ladders to scale two fences at the Wall that divides East from West at the Pankow Cemetery – where his father lies in rest – he gets over one of them. Moments away from freedom.

At the Wall, border snipers immediately open fire. The Stasi cover up his death. Monitor his wife's telephone calls and mail in East Berlin. Find out that she has doubts. The secret policemen come back later. They tell her about the condition of Einsiedel's corpse. In detail.

They recommend that she doesn't come and see.

George Douglas McFly is shot to death today in Hill Valley, California.

That's no way to die.

Mostly because he's a fictional character.

ABC 2. BRISTOL ROAD, BIRMINGHAM
440 1904

PORTNOY'S COMPLAINT (X)
Richard Benjamin, Karen Black.
3.15. 6.00. 8.50.
HUNTED (X)
Edward Woodward.
2.20. 5.00. 7.50.

74

SEIZURE
Thursday, March 15, 1973.

A writer of horrific fantasies (played by Jonathan Frid) finds that his dreams may be coming true to menace and murder his friends and family. They manifest in the archetypes of the seductress (Martine Beswick), the colossus (Henry Judd Baker) and the imp (Hervé Villechaize), preying on the fears and desires of the people gathered at the writer's stately country manor. Mary Woronov is especially sighworthy in all her Woronovness. I wonder if Andy Warhol ever saw this. A dynamic, energetic film with off-kilter camera angles and a real sense that nothing any of these people could do would ever prevent their deaths. As Beswick's character tells them after Villechaize and Baker kick all their asses and pit them against one another, "Don't ask us who we are, or where we come from. We are without beginning, or end. And our purpose – our only purpose – is death. Some of you will seek an answer in what follows – and some of you will find it. For the others – there will be darkness, damnation and a meaningless death." Meaningless! Inspired by a nightmare that writer/director Oliver Stone had last August, it likely spawned countless variants on Stone's original nightmare well after it had come to a theatre near you.

"This is the way Susan died."

That's what 15-year-old Kim Bradley looks up and says to his mother Mary as he dies today in Tallahassee. His sister Susan died of the same thing – primary pulmonary hypertension – that he has.

Had.

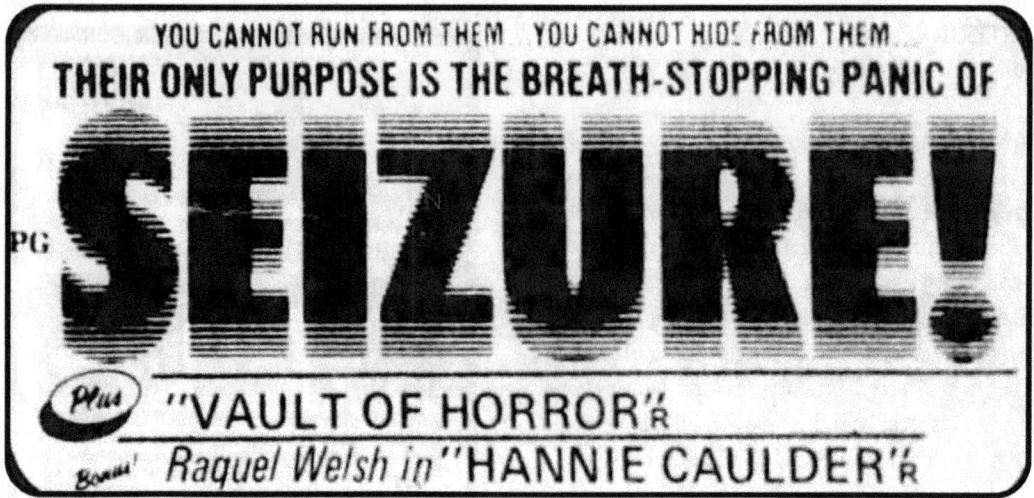

Rare. Incurable. Imagine living through multiple random heart attacks and you'll understand. Imagine having children that you know will die as children.

They have another daughter. Mary Faith is 11. She had two other siblings.

They didn't make it.

Their father John says, "The doctors said the odds against one member of a family getting it are 1,000-to-1 ... but we've had three. The odds on that must be ... well, I just don't know. We'll keep praying it won't be four."

Prayers, hopes, dreams and nightmares.

At the Smithsonian Institution's National Museum of History and Technology, Arthur C. Clarke suggests that sounds from the distant past might be recaptured from ancient objects.

He discusses the work of Richard Woodbridge, a New Jersey electrical engineer working to extract sounds from the surface of antique clay pots on which were etched the ambient sounds heard around the potter's wheel. Spoken words unwittingly projected onto an unlikely canvas; sounds of the natural world, extracted from the brushstrokes on a work of art.

Dreams, prayers, hopes and nightmares.

In Miami, thousands of fish are seen "dancing and twirling in the water" of Biscayne Bay. They end their terminal terpsichore by dying. Scientists are perplexed. It's their natural state. The scientists, I mean – not the fish. 100 square miles of the Bay are closed so that they may more completely understand why death came swimming.

Hopes, dreams, prayers and nightmares.

NIGHT OF FEAR
Friday, March 16, 1973.

A crazed loner catches and torments a woman after she wrecks her car and stumbles across his rat-choked backwoods shanty in Australia – which, being Australia, is already fairly horrifying because of all the myriad venomous animals trotting around the continent. Banned by Australian censors for its perceived obscenity, it's a film for which the path to public consciousness was itself deeply tormented – because, you know, without censors, we'd really be drowning in violence as a society. Little-seen, with little intelligible dialogue – it'd make a great double-bill-for-the-deaf with *Themroc* – and a constitutionally vivid awareness of the harrowing terror that flows through its panicked cinematic veins.

Ernest Holmes, defensive tackle for the Pittsburgh Steelers and one of the most-feared members in the lineup, has a mental breakdown driving down the Ohio Turnpike at 90 miles per. He shoots at some trucks. Gets off some shots at a police helicopter. Hits the pilot in the ankle. One of Holmes' tires blows off. He streaks down the road, spitting sparks and bullets everywhere. The cops surround Holmes as his annihilated car comes to rest in a lonely field. He throws down his gun.

No one over at Steelers headquarters can believe it.

"The Holmes I know wouldn't do this," the home office scoffs, adding, "He's just not that type of guy."

He gets five years' probation. In Holmes' own estimation, he was "stone crazy." Acute paranoid psychosis. Troubles with the wife. Troubles at home. He plays for the Steelers until 1978 and later become an ordained minister, with his own church.

35 years later, he dies in a car wreck. No seat belt.

A family of three in Mill Valley, California is shotgunned to death late tonight, execution-style, outside their home. Their house is then set on fire. Melvin Schallock, the father, is the brother of former Yankees pitcher Art Schallock. Their son Daniel is found in the nude. It turns out that a grocery store bag boy, Brent William Bedayan, 22, did it. Police describe the scene as something done by "an insane person" – which, considering the relative peacefulness of Mill Valley in 1973, is a pretty good lead for once. The suspect's mother calls the cops. Says she heard about the murders. Thought her son might have had a hand in it. The Schallocks' son was in a rock band called Sound Hole. His bandmates are his pallbearers. Eventually it will transpire that the killer had schizophrenia. He thought that Daniel could induce pain in his genitals merely by driving past his house, or that he could use ESP to reach out and grab them. That his father Melvin was evil, and everyone in that family had to die.

Bad blood.

Both were musicians. "It seemed as if his mind were somewhere else," the killer's former boss recalled.

Sometimes you just don't know. You think you know, but you don't know.

LA PADRINA
Friday, March 23, 1973.

A wife (played by Lydia Alfonsi; a.k.a. Costanza, a.k.a. The Godmother, a.k.a. Lady Dynamite) is married to the Mob in her betrothal to Brooklyn capo Genco Cavallo. At their 10-year wedding anniversary (when you're supposed to give your spouse aluminum, for some strange reason), he's assassinated. His last words are "Giarrattana from Palermo." She goes to Palermo to visit her well-deserved revenge upon powerful politician Don Giarrattana. The crooks cut her brakes and put all manner of obstacles in her way but she keeps on coming. The opening credits, with all those shots of New York City in the '70s, make you realize that the world romanticizes that city far more than America does. *La padrina* is occasionally known as *Lady Dynamite*, something that was confusing for audiences throughout the '70s because of the Lady Dynamite that's Kathy Shang and the Lady Dynamite that's Colleen Brennan. The film moves at a slightly slower pace than do most of these Italian *poliziotteschi* films – but what better way to be respectful of a widow getting violent revenge than by giving her a little more time to process her grief and deal with it in her own way? During filming, a motorboat accident off the Sicilian town of Syracus lands Alfonsi in the hospital. Director Giuseppe Vari suspends production so she can recuperate. It'd be a shame if anything happened to her.

As of today, John Lennon has 60 days to leave America.

His wife Yoko Ono gets to stay, though. Some blame Nixon for his expulsion. Others blame drugs. They'd both wanted to stay in America to look for Kyoko, Yoko's daughter by impresario Anthony Cox. Currently, both are missing.

The violence of estrangement.

They'll write the song "New York City" about their travels and travails for The Plastic Ono Band's *Some Time in New York City* album.

Elsewhere, in New York City.

A wife and husband die together in The Bronx. It's been three days since their daughter got a telephone call telling her, "Keep cool if you want to see your mother alive again."

The apartment of Carmen and Fernando Ortiz had been ransacked. Television set stolen. Carmen strangled. Fernando beaten and stabbed.

Dead for days by the time their daughter – who's also their neighbor in the apartment building – gets to them.

The violence of separation.

In Lorain, Ohio, they find nine-year-old Roxie Ann Keathley's body. She and her sister were out collecting soda bottles to get the deposit. She tells her sister, who's going home, that she'll be back soon. During this week's intensive search for the missing girl, her third grade teacher tells her classmates, "God knows where Roxie Ann is."

God knows.

They find her, buried in leaves, less than a mile from her home.

It might be "fitting" or "just" to tell you that there's someone waiting for her killer when he gets out of prison. That there might be a Lady Dynamite or a god or a mother out there to pull a trigger or cast a spell or mete out the revenge that is desired. But those are movies. Those are wishes. Those are some of the basest desires available.

Sometimes, there's only a killer behind bars, and a little girl who was killed.

So where do you go from there?

What kind of life do you save for yourself and everyone around you?

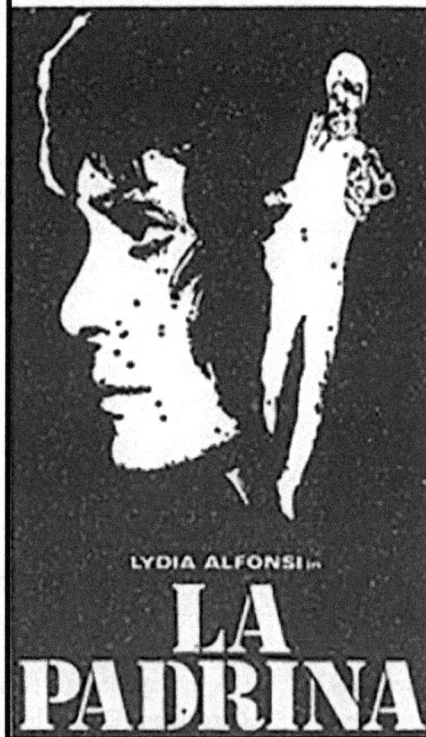

al Regina

Le imprese alla
F. Coppola   L. Liggio
V. Genovese   L. Luciano
rivivono in una
GRANDE
PRIMA VISIONE
che potrete ammirare a
META' PREZZO
d'ingresso sulle altre
« prime » della città

LYDIA ALFONSI in
LA PADRINA

THE SINGLE GIRLS
Friday, March 23, 1973.

On a Caribbean island, a doctor believes that sexual indulgence for men and women will increase their capacity for empathy. In counterpoint to his premise, someone's running around slaughtering a bunch of those selfsame sexually indulgent men and women. The maniac slashes out the crotches of various panties, which the free-loving girls think is cute. The killer, somewhat less-than-loving, also scrawls the word "cunt" on a bathroom mirror, a word that's somewhat shocking to see in a film from 1973. For some of the stars of *The Single Girls*, the future wouldn't turn out to be quite so utopian; lead Girl and *Playboy* Playmate Claudia Jennings will die in a horrifying head-on collision in 1979 north of Topanga Canyon Boulevard on Pacific Coast Highway in Malibu. She drifts into the path of an oncoming truck. No one knows why. It happens as she's driving over to pick up her things from an ex-lover's house. Another Girl, Chéri Howell, starred in a couple of other films – including the underrated *Sisters of Death* – and then simply disappeared.

Just drifting.

A 17-year-old kid gets four years in prison. All he wanted was to get out of the Navy. Winning big points for initiative, he kidnaps a rear admiral's daughter. When he'd captured her last October, he told her all about how crummy the Navy was for him. Her father, fuming at the relatively light sentence, tells anyone who'll listen, "This could very easily have ended in murder."

Sometimes it's what doesn't happen that's more violent than what actually does.

Augusta Road
Tri Custom Theatre

TONIGHT   open. . .6:30
starts 7 p.m.

FIRST AREA SHOWING

Searching for a man was a way of life

R. rated

THE SINGLE GIRLS

no. 2   HALF CLAD - ALL BAD!
"THE SINS OF ADAM & EVE"

The human mind is one of the deepest and largest torture chambers ever dreamt up.

It must be stressed.

A policeman, Raymond Peterson, 38, is arrested today in Detroit. He's charged in the shooting death of Robert Hoyt on March 9. Claims Hoyt tried to slash him with a knife.

The knife turns out to be Peterson's own.

He's part of the city's STRESS unit of crime-busters. STRESS stands for Stop The Robberies, Enjoy Safe Streets.

Safe for somebody.

He's been involved in nine different shooting incidents since joining STRESS three years ago. Ultimately, he kills nine of 13 people he shoots on those streets. Self-defense. Every time. Later, recalling the response he got down at the station after each one of these altercations, he said, "They were happy with me. Whenever I shot someone, I would have to go to headquarters to fill out a report and the guys would cheer me when I walked in. I was the fair-haired boy – as long as everything worked their way. Who doesn't like to be the fair-haired boy? Who doesn't like applause?"

In Ireland, political struggle takes on a more erotic dimension when two women proposition four British soldiers.

"A good time," the single girls say.

The promise of sex is met with the reality of death. Armed men ambush and kill three of the soldiers and grievously injure the fourth. His jaw is shot away. There's a bullet in his spine.

Alive. Survived.

It is not for nothing that the alternate title for *The Single Girls* is *Bloody Friday*.

Raymond Peterson dies in 2016, aged 81. A long life. "You're no better than a rotten murderer," he'd think to himself, his mind consumed with the deaths he'd caused. Where once there had been a boy "with a lot of love for everybody," now there was a man who said he was "out on the street killing people, and it not really bothering me."

"I'll tell you," he said, supernally aware of what he'd become, "If that ain't sick, boy, I don't know. I don't know."

GENERAL MASSACRE
Sunday, March 25, 1973.

Stark and brutal Belgian-American morality story by director Burr Jerger that finds the titular General still waging war using his experiences from World War II and the Vietnam War. Belgian audiences got to see the film first, in those first weeks after the end of the Vietnam War. At one point, the General believes his daughter is his wife and rapes her. In order to return to the purity of his particularly psychotic current, he sits and repeatedly watches footage of Vietnam War atrocities. The sequence during which the General declares a cow to be an enemy combatant is depressing and gory and revealing all at once. The Belgians know a thing or two about war and annihilation, which gives the film an especially incisive point of view. In a 1975 interview, American filmmaker Jerger alleges that the CIA had a hand in the censoring and banning of *General Massacre*, which may also explain why it remains obscure. A "protest against war," Jerger calls it. Possibly the authorities didn't cleave to General Massacre's musings on war and life, which include chestnuts such as "Politics are the extension of war" and "Civilians are as much the enemy as men in uniform."

They've finally traced the license plate of serial killer Gerard Schaefer in Fort Lauderdale.

It only took them six months.

In the interim, two teen girls vanish. Schaefer eventually kills nine young girls throughout Florida and Iowa. Schaefer claimed the body count went a little higher. The violently misogynistic killer blamed the women for making him kill them. Evidence in his trial included Schae-

fer's lurid short stories overflowing with rape, violence and general overall mayhem. The bodies of some of the girls were accidentally discovered by men looking for soda pop cans to cash in. Schaefer, a onetime deputy sheriff, dies in 1995, murdered by his own cellmate.

Stabbed in both eyes.

In Oklahoma City, the *Oklahoman* newspaper claims that the 1968 massacre at My Lai was in fact an orchestrated bit of theater. One source indicates that the idea was approved and sanctioned up the Central Intelligence Agency chain of command – an agency that is itself merely one tool in a vast arsenal of weapons and tactics. That it was a coördinated effort by the Agency to destabilize and demoralize the population.

That it meant to teach them a lesson.

To make them see the futility of war.

HOUSE OF TERROR
Sunday, March 25, 1973.

A man hires a nurse to care for his demented wife, the suggestion being that he himself no longer cares for her. Presently, the wife (played by perfectly-named Jacquelyn Hyde) dies. Suicide. Her sister – also played by Hyde – shows up. So does the nurse's boyfriend. They all want the family money. More plots, more double-crossing. More murders. And ... scene. Remember: just because you may not have felt terror when you watched this film doesn't mean that the characters in the film didn't. On some level, for some amount of time.

Even the music charts are dripping with violence in 1973.

The top song today? "Killing Me Softly With His Song," by Roberta Flack.

It jockeys for position with "Last Song" by Edward Bear, the doomed disco jazz of Eumir Deodato's "Also Sprach Zarathustra" – and, because people love a good backwoods banjo number, "Dueling Banjos" off the *Deliverance* soundtrack. That song holds on to public consciousness for a long, long time. *Dueling Banjos* is also the number one album in the country. Number two?

Don't Shoot Me I'm Only the Piano Player, by Elton John.

Maybe these songs are playing on the radio the day that Special Agent Pilot George F. White of the Bureau of Narcotics and Dangerous Drugs hits a utility pole with his twin-engine Cessna on takeoff near Tucson. 30 feet up. Cleared High-

way 93. Came to rest in an open field, fresh from plowing. Probably saved some lives, even at the very end.

Eight years in Vietnam. Teacher of fighter pilots. Fought the Dominguez cartel in Sonora.

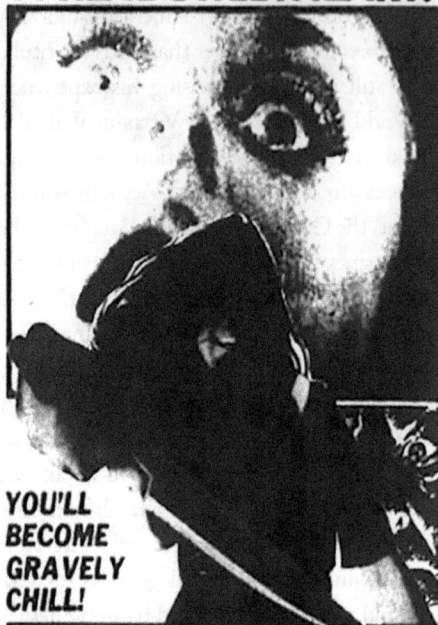

THE NEXT WORLD IS GETTING A REAL SWEETHEART!

YOU'LL BECOME GRAVELY CHILL!

the FIVE at the FUNERAL

Jenifer BISHOP · Arell BLANTON · Mitchell GREGG guest star Jacquelyn HYDE
Screenplay by Tony CRECHALES and E. A. CHARLES · Executive Producer George A. EADE
Produced and Directed by Sergei GONCHAROFF EASTMANCOLOR · · · SANKATSA ASSOCIATES, '72

NOW SHOWING!
CINEMA II
379-9331

R

2:30-4:05-5:35-7:20
9:15

In the seas off Virginia, they're pulling a lone sailor – Stein Gabrielsen, 23 – from a forlorn, tempest-tossed raft that's about ready to fall apart. He's the only survivor from the wreck of the Norse Variant, which went down three days ago and left no trace of either the ship or its 30-man crew. They abandoned ship within moments of the flooding of its holds. Laden with coal. 40-foot seas. 60-mile-per-hour winds. Its sister ship, the Anita, sank in the same massive storm. All hands lost. Vanished. Nothing left.

In newspapers later this year, reporter John Wallace Spencer blames UFOs and The Bermuda Triangle for making the ships vanish.

Tell that to Stein Gabrielsen.

In Oakland, Maryland, a man takes his wife for a drive. Later, he tells the cops that she's been kidnapped. Presently, beneath the weight of questioning and evidence, he admits that it's all been a hoax. His wife, however, remains missing. Paradoxically, she's sighted in the area from time to time. In July, her remains will be found in the countryside by ginseng hunters. The husband will be indicted for murder in February of 2017, spending time in prison ever since.

For now, he's free. Free to listen to Roberta Flack. Free to build a new house for himself. Free to build new realities.

Free to crash and burn, too.

BECAUSE OF THE CATS
Thursday, March 29, 1973.

"To know all is to want all! To know all is to dare all!" chants the cult of young rich psychopathic dudes who pull home invasions dressed in formal suits. They wear black stockings for masks and rape the women they find when they break in, forcing their husbands to watch it all unfold. An early look at affluenza – a sickness that consumes kids who think they're untouchable because they're rich – informs this grimy, unflinching look at sociopathology as a communicable disease. Also, "betrayal is death," they vow – in case you wonder how insular and hardcore a mindset can become when shared amongst like-minded maniacs. Sebastian Graham-Jones is a revelation as Jansen, the leader of the psychotic cult – genteel one moment and ruthlessly cold-blooded the next, he twists these young men so that they're convinced that they're pursuing the sanest and most justifiable course of action. The title of the film makes more sense when you hear Jansen's last words. Mixing psychodrama with the tone of a police procedural slows down the timing of the film slightly – and yet, much like life, violence doesn't often unveil itself rationally or in a timely fashion. What seems like an eternity may be really only a minute. What seems like ten minutes may only be one. Adrenalin, stress, fear and anger do different things to one's sense of time passing during acts of violence.

The last U.S. soldier leaves Vietnam today.

Today is not the Fall of Saigon, with its dramatic images of people clinging to helicopter pontoons lest they fall into the hot lava of advancing Communism. That's not until 1975.

The last U.S. soldier that leaves Vietnam today has a name.

Master Sgt. Max Beilke.

You get to be so much a part of the Armed Forces, if you serve in it long enough, that it becomes part of your identity. Part of your being. You respond to "Master" or "Lieutenant" with as much iron-clad sureness as you did when you were very young and you first realized that you

doing, or who you knew. The violence of the moment pins you to your memories like a butterfly pinned to a box of shadows.

Like the moment you shake off your shock and realize that your wife of four months has been swallowed by a hole that opens up beneath her in Cairo, Egypt and pulls her down so deeply into the earth that she's never found.

It traps you there, be it ever-so-momentarily. Sometimes you wonder what kind of person you'd be if it never happened. You wonder who you were and how you felt, way back then, way back when.

Sometimes you wonder how you ever got out in time.

had a name to which you should answer in the first place. A name so inextricably linked with your person that it becomes part of you. There are many Master Sergeants like you, but this name is yours. You even come to cherish the dot in the abbreviation for the word Sergeant.

It's you. It's always you. For as long as you live.

Master Sgt. Max Beilke will die on September 11, 2001. At The Pentagon. Helping war veterans.

The calendar is one of life's great unheralded control mechanisms.

When you suddenly realize what day it is, you transport yourself back to a time you can't forget – which is not necessarily the same thing as a day that you remember. You recall what you were

Plus
"YOUNG
SECRETARIES"
9:20
11:55
(X)

CINDY
WEST

LACKLAND
OUTDOOR THEATRE
7170 Somerset   924-4591

DEVIL'S
DUE

Who said the Devil
was a man?

7:40
10:35
(X)

DEVIL'S DUE
Thursday, March 29, 1973.

Scheming and intrigue are the two axes straddled by the plot of *Devil's Due*, in which a promising young student gets drugged and inseminated by her scuzzy dean. After she finds out that he'd done the same thing to other girls, she plots her revenge. In the big city, however, she gets waylaid by the cult of Kampala. Everyone has *a lot of sex* while organ music plays incessantly. She conspires with the lesbian acolytes of said cult to overthrow Kampala by smothering him with her poison-soaked breasts! Of course, scheming and intrigue are always much more entertaining and exciting than the day-to-day business of running a cult. Can you buy phallic red candles wholesale? Is a satanic altar a tax write-off if no Satan appears? And when *is* The Devil due, anyway? Everyone look busy when he gets here! Mark Suben, who plays Kampala, graduated Fordham Law and also acted as District Attorney for Cortland County in upstate New York.

He was ousted as DA after a 2012 scandal during which the brother of one of his opponents in his re-election campaign exposed his earlier career appearing in movies like these. Suben denied it at first but finally had to admit the truth. Intrigue indeed!

Activist H. Rap Brown gets convicted today of possessing illegal weapons and robbery during a 1971 hold-up. Attempted murder charges against him and three co-defendants don't stick, though. Mistrial.

Brown previously led the Student Nonviolent Co-ordinating Committee.

Ever the leader in technology and progress, prison guards in America try out their first plastic bullets.

They'll be used for the first time in Ireland later in the year by the Royal Ulster Constabulatory. A new tool in the arsenal of The Queen's official riot-putter-downers.

Almost three years ago, the Constabulatory first started using rubber bullets. How time flies.

Time. Occasionally less-than-lethal rounds. Whichever.

The 75 rioting inmates in the Maryland Penitentiary in Baltimore hold seven prison guards hostage all night. They demand to see newsmen. They want to tell their various truths.

It's always nice to be wanted.

100 cops storm the prison. Two of the captured guards are found hanged.

They are, surprisingly enough, not quite dead.

They'll carry the scars of their ordeal around their throats for months. If not years. If not life. Mutilated and returning to that hot Thursday

night in prison every time they look in the mirror to shave or wipe the mist off after a shower. Or a bender.

There are still wounds on the flesh of those who are hit by those non-lethal rounds. There's blindness. Disability. Bruises that never fade. New birthmarks which can't be disguised. Can't be forgotten.

In Detroit, five men – including the Reverend Lonnie Demour and two volunteers for the city's poverty outreach program – are found dead in a derelict house. They may have been dead for as many as six days. No motive. No clues. Only the telltale signs of an execution. Bludgeoned. Strangled. Slashed. One after another. Sgt. Roy Awe from the Detroit Police Homicide Bureau casually suggests causality in these casualties. "Other than a history of homosexuality on the part of these people – and that's neither here nor there – we have nothing to go on at this time. That's what really has us puzzled right now - why?"

How soon we forget.

THE HOUSE IN NIGHTMARE PARK
Thursday, March 29, 1973.

This modern take on the hoary old dark house genre – which involves various people being invited to a house to get good stuff and die miserably over the course of one night – finds Ray Milland as the crusty, crotchety patriarch of a family at a remote country mansion. British comedian Frankie Howerd shows up, playing an actor invited to give a performance. He cracks wise and makes smutty jokes while a meatcleaver-bearing baldie lurks in the attic. The part where some of the actors dress up like dummies and dance is especially bizarre. You can almost hear the hulls of the ships that are two very distinct time periods – 1870s vaudeville and 1970s comedy – scraping with a particularly slow and agonized clank as they pass in the night, generating a very specific kind of atmosphere in their wake. Toward the end, it feels like you're watching a movie from a bygone era, before kids as young as 7 learned how to roll their eyes.

"Goodnight, my darlings, I'll see you tomorrow."

They buried Noël Coward today.

Friend to actor and Queen Mother alike, the writer and professional wit was buried in a private service amidst the simple beauty of Firefly, his estate in Jamaica, where he was neighbors with Ian Fleming and Richard Burton. Halfway across the world, his packed memorial service in St. Martin-in-the-Fields in London stands bedecked in culture and filigree. John Betjeman, the Poet Laureate of the United Kingdom in 1973, reads a poem especially composed for the dearly departed. Laurence Olivier reads Psalm 100. Coward's understudy John Gielgud recites

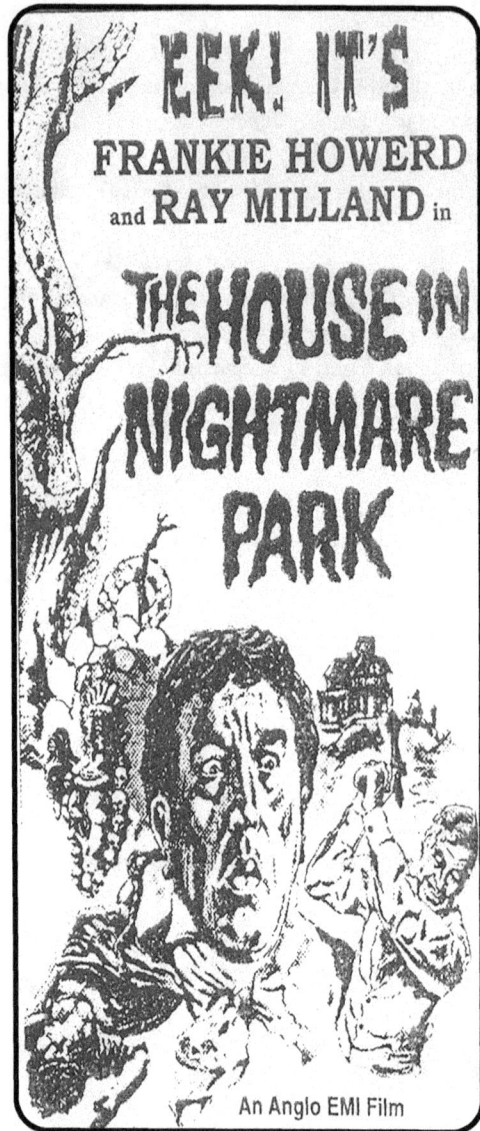

EEK! IT'S FRANKIE HOWERD and RAY MILLAND in THE HOUSE IN NIGHTMARE PARK

An Anglo EMI Film

Shakespeare's "Sonnet XXX" ("But if the while I think on thee, dear friend, All losses are restor'd and sorrows end."). Violinist Yehudi Menuhin plays a sonata by Bach.

Shout for joy to the Lord, all the Earth.

CAMPBELLTON Drive-In
Morshead Road
Narellan
2 2498
730: Bruce Lee in "FIST OF FURY" (M). PLUS: Frankie Howerd In "THE HOUSE IN NIGHTMARE PARK" (NRC).

Three employees of the 202 Drive-In Theatre on Concord Pike in West Chester, Pennsylvania nurse their wounds after last night's battle with two men they'd asked to stop trashing the men's room and leave. Cuts, bruises, et cetera.

The film that was showing that night at the drive-in?

Cabaret. Starring Liza Minnelli.

In Washington, they're recalling 2,000 bottles of Pure Silver Plate-Polishing Solution distributed last year in shops up and down the East Coast.

No, they're not fondly remembering those 2,000 bottles.

It's that there's cyanide inside them.

Were someone so graceless as to accidentally sip some of that silver polish – as apparently enough people have done up until this point that a Food and Drug Administration recall becomes necessary – an instant death is promised.

Guaranteed.

Think of the children.

In the Ottawa River, the body of eight-year-old William J. Haas is found after he goes missing on February 19. Fell through the ice. Taking a short-cut to save some time. Found 300 yards from where firemen dragged the river initially.

Searching.

In the shadow of a Chevrolet plant in Flint, Michigan, two boys run away when their play-mate, six-year-old Gene A. Barlow, falls into the Flint River and drowns. He isn't found until April 20. He'll float away, almost a mile from where he fell in. He stays there. For now.

Stays there until he's found by two different boys.

Sorrow ended.

'RACE' 3:20, 6:40, 10:00
'PARK' 1:30, 4:50, 8:10
DAVID CARRADINE. DEATH RACE 2000

IN THE YEAR 2000 HIT AND RUN DRIVING IS NO LONGER A FELONY. IT'S THE NATIONAL SPORT!

A CROSS COUNTRY ROAD WRECK!

3rd WK!
RIDEAU

ADDED HIT: "HOUSE IN NIGHTMARE PARK"

LES GANTS BLANCS DU DIABLE
Friday, March 30, 1973.

A killer named Cartoni – played by the wonderfully moody and expressive Yves Afonso – enters The Whisky Bar and shoots the bartender. Deputy Caron, a heroin trafficker and former owner of the Bar, gets the cops to investigate and head off any trouble that might taint his election campaign. Turns out that Cartoni got out of prison in exchange for giving one of his eyes to Caron, who's now going blind and needs another operation. Apparently there's no one else in France that's a match! In between all the murders, Cartoni drinks, carouses, learns to kill by sound alone and doesn't look nearly as haunted as these roles generally tend to require. The Karl Heinz Schäfer score ranges from freaked-out fuzz guitar to murderfunk jams to easy listening soundtracks for rants and screeds in this madcap nihilistic adventure.

Flights of fancy.

In Detroit, Evel Knievel revs his motorcycle and rockets over 13 cars. It's a feat that he repeats all weekend at the State Fairgrounds Coliseum, ultimately jumping five times. Last Tuesday, he creates a new kind of spectacle on his way to his Fairgrounds engagement by leading police in Jackson County, Michigan on a merry little chase, with his Ferrari hurtling down the I-94 doing 100 in a 70 m.p.h. zone. It costs $25 for Knievel to post bond and continue on his way.

Spare no expense when it comes to showmanship.

In October, he crashes his Harley-Davidson in Kaukauna, Wisconsin while trying to jump 10 cars and three trucks in a ramp-to-ramp leap.

FILMS

NFTA screening: Les Gants Blancs du Diable plus Un Neveu Silencieux, Paddington Town Hall, Sunday 7.30 pm.
Government Information Service screenings: London's Burning, Noise Annoys, Elie Wiesel's Jerusalem and others, Monday to Friday, 12.15 pm — 2.15 pm.

Bruised kidneys. Fractured bone in his hand. Those fractures in his lower back that the X-ray finds? All fractures from years of prior accidents.

He's still recovering from a wipeout that happened during a practice jump nine months ago which compressed his vertebrae at the Lakewood Speedway in Atlanta. 1972 was a brutal year for the stunt motorcyclist who jumps everything from cars to trucks to rattlesnakes. He suffers a broken back and concussion, as well as a broken collarbone caused by crashing into a wall during a year filled with at least a dozen jumps.

By the time he retires in 1980 after 15 years of grueling stunt work, his wounds have become the stuff of legend.

"There are a lot of myths about my injuries," Knievel once revealed. "They say I have broken every bone in my body. Not true. But I have broken 35 bones. I had surgery 14 times to pin and plate. I shattered my pelvis. I forget all of the things that have broke."

Evel Knievel. A larger-than-life figure whose fans come to see if he'll die.

CANNIBAL GIRLS
Thursday, April 5, 1973.

Clifford (SCTV's Eugene Levy) and Gloria (SCTV's Andrea Martin) play a couple stranded in a backwater hamlet near Ontario in Canada. An old lady at a motel tells them the legend of the Cannibal Girls – who, as a matter of tradition, seduce, stalk and/or slaughter their victims. The Reverend Alex St. John shows up and seems to hold a mysterious influence on the entire town. Gory murders continue apace. Clifford freaks out and betrays Gloria in order to survive but she double-crosses him. The whole movie turns out to be a story that the old lady is telling to yet another stranded couple. And so on, and so on, and so on, and on and on and on.

In Chile, the Mt. Hudson volcano erupts after two years' silence. It rains lava throughout the surrounding 30 miles and annihilates five shepherds as they camp in its shadow. Over 1,500 sheep, cows and horses also perish in a conflagration the likes of which they'd probably had no concept in their ovine, bovine or equine minds.

Death from above.

Gravediggers go on strike in Buffalo today after contract negotiations fail. 75 of them hit the picket lines near the Cemetery Division of the Buffalo & Western New York Hospital and Nursing Home Council. Burials are expected to be impaired and curtailed for the duration of the strike.

Death from below.

In Rochester, New York, police announce leads in the kidnap and murder of Wanda Walkowicz,

NORTHSIDE DRIVE-IN THEATER
NOW! 3 BIG SHOCKERS
EXCLUSIVE FIRST LANSING SHOWING
CANNIBAL GiRLS
THE PICTURE WITH THE WARNING BELL!
When it rings — close your eyes if you're squeamish!
at 9.50 only
R
"CANNIBAL GIRLS"
EUGENE LEVY · ANDREA MARTIN · RONALD ULRICH

11. She vanished on Monday. She's found the next day at a rest area off State Route 104 in Webster, seven miles from Rochester. Violated. Strangled with a belt. A girl matching her description was seen being forced at knifepoint into a Dodge Dart on Monday near where she lived. News reports draw a line between her death and the 1971 death of Carmen Colon, found near Churchville in New York, murdered under similar circumstances.

In time, they'll be considered casualties of the enigmatic '70s serial killer known as The Alphabet Killer, whose victims all had names with double initials and whose bodies were found in places the names of which matched their initials.

Death.

Pioneer 11 lifts off from Cape Kennedy in Florida tonight.

The spaceship, following in the footsteps of the

Pioneer 10 probe which is already 13 months ahead of it on its voyage into the depths of the cosmos, is scheduled to rendezvous with Jupiter, and then Saturn beyond it.

They're looking for life, there beneath the Jovian clouds.

Stowed aboard Pioneer 11 is a plaque displaying the nude forms of male and female humans. In case an advanced form of alien life somewhere finds the spacecraft.

Designed by astronomer Carl Sagan, his wife Linda and astrophysicist Frank Drake, the 9"x6" gold-anodized aluminum plaque carries with it images of where the Sun sits in relation to the universe; a map of the Solar System; and a silhouette of Pioneer 11 in relation to humans.

So everyone can see how small we can be.

Pioneer 11 has to slingshot onward using Jupiter's gravitational field to reach Saturn, depending on how strong that field might be.

It's always something.

It gets there. Almost collides with tiny Saturnian moon Epimetheus. Determines the moon of Titan is too cold to sustain life.

Life as we know it.

It's out of the solar system now. NASA hasn't heard from it since 2002. Its signal ultimately moved out of alignment with Earth.

In four million years, it's projected to pass close to a star in the constellation Aquila. The heat that

unevenly emits from Pioneer 11 as it sails through space has slowly pushed it off course over time.

Symbols of the human race.

Just drifting.

THEATRE OF BLOOD
Friday, April 6, 1973.

Vincent Price plays a touchy, narcissistic Shakespearean actor who fakes his own death, teams up with a bunch of hobos and comes back a couple of years later on March 15 (the day that Julius Caesar was murdered – what an egomaniac!) to get revenge on all his critics. His stylized murders are patterned after various death scenes from Shakespeare's plays. One critic has his head cut off while he sleeps (as in the play *Cymbeline*); another is force-fed his annoying poodles until he chokes to death (*Titus Andronicus*); still another gets wasted by the hobos à la *Julius Caesar*. Every murder is a tour-de-force by endlessly hammy Price; even while dying, he performs King Lear's final screed. Price got one good thing from starring in this insightful satire, for all his troubles as an actor – he met his future wife Coral Browne on the set of the film. Browne was reportedly a woman whose love of foul language was such that future "Dame Edna" Barry Humphries recited this verse at her 1991 memorial service: "She left behind an emptiness / A gap, a void, a trough / The world is quite a good deal less / Since Coral Browne fucked off."

Today marks the final Freedom Flight from Cuba to Miami.

In the slow space of nine years, the entire demographic of Miami changes because of those flights. Nearly 300,000 refugees finally find a home in Miami's Little Havana. Fidel Castro is not happy. Freedom and opportunity clash with harassment and pressure. Castro knows that some of his best and brightest are trying to get out any way they can.

Caridad Caballero, 69, the last Freedom Flyer out, says, "I am not able to believe it will be the end."

It is, however, the end for Basil Raoud al-Kubaissi.

Al-Kubaissi, a law professor at the American University of Beirut in Paris, is assassinated by Israeli agents. Operation Wrath of God. Revenge for Palestinian militant group Black September's assassination of 11 Israeli athletes during last year's Summer Olympics in Munich.

Eight shots. Point-blank. With silencers.

Like *that*.

It's the third killing this year in Paris that authorities begin to suspect might be related. That Palestinian and Israeli operatives are waging an underground war.

In plain sight, no less.

Activist and future actor Russell Means meets with White House representatives.

A peace treaty.

It's a treaty that doesn't necessarily guarantee an end to conflict, says Means, the American Indian Movement figure, discussing the ongoing strife at Wounded Knee. A deal to lay down their arms – even knowing that this might simply make it easier to put on handcuffs – is made in exchange for federal oversight and investigation into corruption among the politicians at the Pine Ridge Reservation in South Dakota.

They can't believe it's the end, either.

A 15-year-old girl plays records at home in Milwaukee when a man walks in. Puts a gun under her chin. Tells her, "I'm going to shoot you."

She pushes it away. Gets shot in both breasts when the gun goes off.

While she's in the hospital, across town, a mother is charged with neglecting her child. She'd been drinking for an hour yesterday at the Club House Tavern when the suitcase next to her seat started to cry.

Some people in the bar open it up. Her 13-month-old son is inside.

She tells the cops that she took her son with her to the bar because she didn't want her husband to take him away.

Why she chose a suitcase to do that, she didn't say.

"There is only one valuable thing in art," the painter Georges Braque once said. "The thing you cannot explain."

LIDO ADULT THEATRE
1112 Bethel Street   Tel. 537-6872
Continuous Shows—9 A.M. to 2 A.M.
"WANDERING INTRUDER"
"HOOKERS HOLIDAY"
New Show Every Friday • Sound & Color
Validated Parking at Cinerama Parking
Admission $3.50   Visit Our Sex Boutique Shop

WANDERING INTRUDER
Monday, April 9, 1973.

Occasionally a film exists in the continuum of cinema that is so arcane that it only emerges to wider attention through the weirdest quirks of fortune. This is one such film. It originally emerged under the title *Wondering Intruder* in Tampa – a typo that stands as an example of regional accents or bad telephone connections becoming the modern-day flyspecks that transform the Bibles of history – and was screened in passion pits throughout the South until its "world premiere" in Los Angeles on May 4. At this point, the film itself is seized by the Los Angeles police. The presence of a new print is trumpeted by overheated newspaper ads as your only chance to catch the film before Vice twists the vise. In February 1974, Royce Adams Enterprises Inc. of Miami will be fined $2,200 for screening the film and bringing the seamy scourge of obscenity to the fair city of Syracuse, New York. The arrests, seizures and shamings of the '70s relating to adult films hinge on the Supreme Court's 1972 decision that "community standards" are the metric by which a movie can be judged as obscene. In other words: you know it when you see it. Later in 1974, Joseph Royce Adams, 42, will appear in Syracuse to answer for even more obscenity charges. He vanishes into the mists of history after this. As for the film itself, taglines like "See what could happen when an unexpected visitor knocks on your door." and "The fear of attack was not on her mind until..." are tantalizing enough to include it here. I know it when I see it. Are police department evidence lockers one of the final frontiers in film preservation? Do police now think that pursuing obscenity cases back then ultimately made a difference?

Picasso died last night.

His lungs filled with fluid. Pulmonary edema. Aged 91. He dies in Mougins, a village in the middle of a forest near the French Riviera. He and his wife Jacqueline Roque were entertaining friends at dinner when Death, ever the uninvited guest, came for Pablo Picasso.

Imagine the kind of life that flashed in front of his eyes.

The final inspiration. Are future lives as well as a past life seen at the moment of death? If not, why not? Why not demand more from your death than a clutch at the heart or a fumbled last word or a finger of accusal pointed at an intruder?

Picasso's grandson Pablito, 24, kills himself by drinking potassium chloride bleach on April 12 after Jacqueline forbids him from attending the funeral.

In 1986, she dies when she puts a gun to her head after years of grieving and isolation.

His lover Marie-Thérése Walter hangs herself in France in 1977. "Women are machines for suffering," Picasso once tells his mistress, the artist Françoise Gilot. She ultimately leaves him, marries polio vaccine pioneer Jonas Salk and, as of 2022, enjoys a pleasantly forward-thinking life as a painter in her dotage at age 100.

At Camp Pendleton in California, Sgt. Ronald Ridgeway tells a news conference how a fellow POW showed him a magazine during his time in captivity.

In it were images of his burial and his family. Weeping.

In 1968, he was the only survivor of an ambush that killed 43 members of his patrol. He appeared on the casualty list at the time.

He wants to visit his grave, now that he's free.

The wondering intruder.

IL PLENILUNIO DELLE VERGINI
Tuesday, April 10, 1973.

La Contessa Dolingen de Vries uses Count Dracula's big shiny red ring to hypnotize virgins and bleed them dry so she can have a nice hot bath with their blood on The Night of the Virgin Moon. La Contessa (played by Rosalba Neri) is plenty alluring, so it's unclear why she needs Count Dracula's anything in order to zap these already-dopey virgins. Mark Damon finally gets his ass in gear for the bloody climax in which he hassles the evil cultists with an axe and a pike, pitting his snazzy Egyptian amulet against Dracula's ring. Your eyes will roll out of your skull when you see how it all ends. This Italian production is long on nudity, atmosphere and alliteration (in its American, Paul Frees-narrated trailer); American audiences experienced the joy of seeing it over the next few years as *The Devil's Wedding Night*, sometimes triple-billed with *In the Devil's Garden* and *The Devil's Nightmare*. In South Carolina, duly scandalized newspaper editors titled the film *The Devil's Crypt* because God forbid that The Devil would get married and have a happy honeymoon! La Contessa is based on Countess Elizabeth Báthory de Ecsed, a Hungarian noblewoman who put a big greasy hair in the otherwise-pristine cupcake of the Renaissance with her sadistic shenanigans that purportedly involved killing tortured virgins and bathing in their blood to stay young.

More than 100 people die when an Invicta International Airways Vickers Vanguard turboprop returning to England after a day of shopping in Basel, Switzerland crashes into a hilltop in a blizzard in the Swiss hamlet of Herrenmatt.

A survivor says it happened when a wing hit the trees. The airplane spins in mid-air. It takes two hours for rescuers to make it through the blizzard. Pilot error gets the blame. So does bad soldering and ineffectual navigation devices.

The victims are English housewives. Cheddar Mums' Night Out members. Axbridge Ladies Guild members. Skittles players. Out doing some shopping. 55 children – motherless in an instant. One woman loses 11 members of her family.

Survivor Joan Young later recalls, "You go on, you live your life – but of course you never forget. I will never forget the kindness – it's marvelous how people pull together."

Outside of Pittsburgh, something unforgettable happens.

A single-engine airplane flown by retired Air Force colonel Charles G. Anderson hits some trees on approach. Wings shear off. Passenger John Thompson, his leg broken, crawls to a home they'd nearly hit on their way to their crash landing.

He knocks on the door and presents his calling card to the lady of the house.

At the Ben Gross Restaurant in Pittsburgh, they're looking for vestal virgins. To have dinner, watch a roaring fire – and enjoy Don Brockett's riotous production of *Amen, Amen, Etc.*

Someone had to say it.

WHITE HORSE
DRIVE-IN THEATRE ★

HWY. 123 & U.S. 25 BY-PASS
PH. 269-3641 OPENS 7:00 P.M.
STARTS AT DUSK!

ADULT HORROR TRIPLE!

TONIGHT
A NIGHTMARE OF HORROR!

SATAN IS COMING!

DARK DESIRES
UNLEASH THE LEGIONS
OF LUCIFER!

The DEVIL'S CRYPT R COLOR

DON'T COME OUT ALONE!

PLUS! ——————— ALSO!

BEAST OF THE YELLOW NIGHT

R

CREATURE WITH THE BLUE HAND

THE NIGHT GOD SCREAMED
Wednesday, April 11, 1973.

Incessantly mortified Jeanne Crain helplessly watches her husband get literally crucified by a cult of religious maniacs led by Billy Joe Harlan (Michael Sugich, going out in a blaze of acting glory). The judge sentences Harlan to be executed. He gets up and screams, "You dumb sonofabitch – you're making me immortal!" I guess! Hooded crazies come after Crain while she's babysitting the asshole kids of the aforementioned judge and things get really nuts from there. With James B. Sikking from *Hill Street Blues* as a deacon whose sly smile belies his awareness of the kind of film he's gotten himself into. What generally gets ignored about this film is Crain's portrayal as a widow, with maniacs acting as metaphors for the various challenges through which people must suffer in the process of becoming a new person after their old life is instantly, decisively swept away. There had already been at least 14 adaptations of the 1969 Charles Manson saga by the time *The Night God Screamed* came along. Originally released, fittingly enough, on a double-bill with 1971 Manson ripoff *I Drink Your Blood*.

Today in California, federal anti-smog regulations decree that new cars have to use lead-free gasoline. The general idea is that this will cut levels of smog that have led to days of air quality that are so bad it's like living in a fog.

A fog that can kill you.

The final Stage-3 alert will come next year. Until then, when those alerts come, factories close, kids are pulled indoors and non-essential driving is forbidden.

The state sets stricter emissions standards than the rest of the country. The new catalytic converters in California cars use chemistry to turn exhaust riddled with carbon monoxide and other harmful gases into slightly-less-toxic carbon dioxide and water. It takes a couple of years before the other states in America fall in line and do the same.

There is a school of thought that links lead absorbed into the body – from gasoline, from paint, from pipes – to rates of violent crime. The effects of lead on the mind are many.

Hyperactivity. Learning disabilities.

Lack of impulse control.

Impulses that race through the mind like the fire that rips through an elevator shaft today in the almost-completed Sears Tower in Chicago, killing four mechanics between the 33rd and 42nd floors in a sudden storm of flames.

Maybe God screamed because, in 1973, He just couldn't help Himself.

In Washington, the National Transportation Safety Board lets it be known that it was shitty piloting that led to the deaths of 22 people when a Sabre Mk. 5 jet piloted by Richard L. Bingham crashed into a Farrell's Ice Cream Parlor in Sacramento last September 24.

It's the third-deadliest accidental air crash involving bystanders in America's history. So far.

Little League football players. Sitting down together to celebrate with some ice cream. One child lost nine family members in the crash.

The Sabre was owned by businessman William Penn Patrick, who will himself die on June 9 when his P-51D Mustang enters an inescapable spin and crashes in Lakeport, California. You can tell where the ultraconservative Patrick was coming from when he announced to the world, "Those who condemn wealth are those who have none and see no chance of getting it."

If only his Leadership Dynamics Institute – with its group awareness training techniques of sleep deprivation, sexual torture, and crucifixion – could have taught him the techniques he needed to pull his life out of that tailspin.

Sometimes, God tries to tell you things. Don't make Him have to scream at you.

EL JOROBADO DE LA MORGUE
Thursday, April 12, 1973.

Paul Naschy's hunchback Gotho loves a sweet girl named Ilsa, who's nice to him even though he works at a morgue. She's sick with consumption but he keeps bringing her flowers every day – even after she's dead. He thinks that she's only sleeping. Kids taunt and throw stones at him. "An unusual love story between a pathetic cripple – who has been cast out by society – and a beautiful dying young girl!" He can't even get a break from the guy narrating the trailer! She ends up at the morgue and when they try to prep her for burial he flips out and kills everyone. Later, Gotho meets a quack scientist who promises that he can resurrect her – but only if Gotho brings him body parts and/or living victims with which the doctor can make a man-eating monster. Gotho finds rats eating Ilsa's corpse and sets them all on fire – for real! Most guys these days can't even be bothered to make plans once they take a girl out on a date.

A girl of 15 is trampled to death in Munich.

24 other girls are also injured when the teens watching a beauty contest in a beer cellar want to leave all at once. They try to get up the stairs en masse. Someone falls. Gravity does the rest.

Creating a crush.

The name of the girl is not known. No other details, either, other than the barest of all possible facts. She might as well have been the spirit of a cautionary tale, for all we know about her. The modern era is nothing if not starved for those.

Everything left to the imagination.

103

No identity. No history. Just a body.

A body beneath other bodies.

In Indochina, the Pentagon says that they've searched and searched, but have found no evidence of any prisoners of war still alive in captivity.

1,359 Americans. That's how many are listed as missing.

Bodies beneath other bodies.

They've got 153 Americans working in Thailand for the POW recovery effort, searching for U.S. airplanes that may have been shot down.

Looking for the remains of airmen who didn't make it out of Indochina.

Precautionary tales.

Near Racine, Wisconsin, the Coast Guard finds a boat overturned in the waters of Lake Michigan.

Four teen boys, missing since Tuesday. They found their car parked near a boat ramp. One boy's parents believe that the kids were running away from home and dumped the car by the lake.

They'll find the last boy's body on May 5.

Swept off a pier by unusually large waves. Pulled out to the depths of the lake.

At least they know now.

LA MORTE NEGLI OCCHI DEL GATTO
Thursday, April 12, 1973.

Constitutionally lovely Jane Birkin arrives at a Scottish castle to meet her relatives but doesn't have much time to get to know them because they're all being murdered. In one particularly vivid sequence, a guy gets his throat cut by a black-gloved killer and is then fed to hungry rats. A big fat cat watches it all unfold. Serge Gainsbourg shows up as a police inspector; by 1973, Serge and Jane are about midway through their notorious love affair. Some nice touches include blood-spattered cobwebs; a glittering straight-razor poking its way through the door, trying to open the latch (a tension-building technique that will show up a few years later in *Suspiria*); and this v. nize big froofty orange cat who don't do any killing but sure thinks them rats look like a pretty good snack for later!

In Mountain View, California, a NASA Convair CV-990 on a research mission collides in mid-flight with a Navy Lockheed P-3C Orion on a training mission.

They've been mistakenly directed to land on the same runway. After the Convair unknowingly descends onto the Orion, they plunge – lethally locked together – onto Sunnyvale Municipal Golf Course and explode on impact in front of the eyes of shocked golfers. Black smoke billows everywhere.

It happens less than a half-mile away from the final approach to Moffett Field.

Almost home.

Only one person – naval radar operator Petty Officer Third Class Bruce Mallibert, 22, a naval radar operator, survives the massacre, falling 120 feet from the broken tail section.

A bystander covers him with a parachute as the flames rise higher. Thinks he's dead. Mallibert is covered in burns and shot through with fractures.

He's then almost run over by a responding emergency vehicle.

A faint pulse is found.

Pilots can be seen clawing at the windows. Trying to get out of the burning wreckage.

They don't make it.

Speaking in 2016 about the accident, Mallibert (whose coma from the accident lasts for 93 days) says, "Yes, I'm paralyzed – but, hey, there are many people in the world who are worse off than me."

"I choose not to be a victim."

A year after the crash, Mallibert calls up the air traffic controller who accidentally set the airplanes on their collision course. Tells him not to torture himself over what happened. That he made a mistake. That life goes on. That he forgives him.

The air traffic controller later commits suicide.

OGGI al REPOSI Il più bel giallo dell'anno!

Il film che vi darà il brivido più lungo della vostra vita

CRUDO, VIOLENTO, VI MOZZERA' IL FIATO

Hiram Keller · Jane Birkin

LA MORTE NEGLI OCCHI DEL GATTO

Venantino Venantini · Dana Ghia

Francoise Christophe · Doris Kunstmann

Luciano Pigozzi

Antony Diffring · Georg Konrad · Serge Gainsbourg

regia di **Anthony M. Dawson**

musiche di Riz Ortolani

una coproduzione
STARKISS · Roma
CAPITOL · Paris
ROXY · Monaco

TECHNICOLOR · TECHNISCOPE

VIETATO AI MINORI DI ANNI 18

Imminente al REPOSI

LA MORTE NEGLI OCCHI DEL GATTO

WICKED, WICKED
Thursday, April 12, 1973.

Shot entirely with a split-screen technique called Duo-Vision, *Wicked, Wicked* stars Randolph Roberts (who a couple years from now will play the second, existentially doomed Chuck Cunningham on *Happy Days*) putting on a monster mask and chopping up blondes in between his handyman jobs at the stately Hotel del Coronado in Coronado, California. He does it because they remind him of a woman who molested him as a child. The characters that people the Hotel are suitably weird and memorable, especially the silent old organist who plays selections from the 1925 version of *The Phantom of the Opera*. The sequel – also in Duo-Vision – was supposed to be called *Evil, Evil*. Here, it's used as much as a narrative device as it is a theatrical gimmick. You could have a whole film festival of movies with titles like *Wicked, Wicked: Author! Author!* (1982); *Boeing Boeing* (1965); *Jamón Jamón* (1992); *Promises! Promises!* (1963); *Piranha! Piranha!* (1972); *Liar Liar* (1997); *Reuben, Reuben* (1983); *New York New York* (1977) and *The Russians Are Coming! The Russians Are Coming!* (1966).

In Cincinnati, a doctor reveals that a woman who gave birth to two girls on March 31 was herself a kind of split-screen spectacle.

She has two uteri.

Two different eggs. Two completely separate wombs. Two cervixes.

At the time, doctors have no record of anything even remotely like it.

In New York City, Mature Enterprises Inc. is

fined $100,000 for "promoting obscenity" by exhibiting the film *Deep Throat*. Judge Joel J. Tyler calls the film "obscene by any legal measurement." Community standards. Of course.

After the film had played in the community at the New Mature World Theatre for 37 solid weeks, that is.

New York, New York: so aroused, they named it twice.

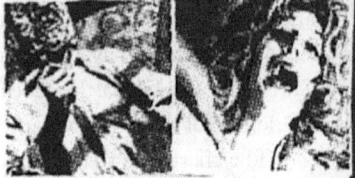

In London, Harry Allen, 51, a security officer for an industrial firm – and formerly England's final official hangman – remarks about Wednesday's decision by the House of Commons to decline the reinstatement of the nation's death penalty, "I am not disappointed. I am not pleased."

He's of two minds on the subject.

THE MAIDS
Thursday, April 26, 1973.

"You haven't seen anything until you see ... The Maids." screamed the ads for *The Maids*. Starring Uschi Digart (it's Digard!) and Tracy Handfoss (that's *Handfuss*!), it's a film that remains desperately rare and unseen, apart from a possible VHS release on the King of Video imprint in Australia. And yet, with a tagline like "They loved their master ... they loved him to death," its intriguing allure qualifies it for a chapter in this book if only because no one else was curious enough to bring this feral film in from the cold. Also starring Angela Carnon, Patrick Harrison, and Roger Taimi. One source says that Serena is also in this film, but is she? Is she really? It may or may not be an adaptation of the French saga of sisters Christine and Léa Papin, housemaids who murdered their boss' wife and daughter with extortionate brutality in Le Mans on February 2, 1933.

In Los Angeles, a man rolls a bag onto a conveyer belt. Out rolls a human head.

Police suspect that the severed head is likely related to four coastal murders afflicting Southern California. Murders for which there are no suspects.

Only bodies.

Four young men, found at area beaches. Murdered, stripped nude and sexually defiled.

Not necessarily in that order.

Two days into the investigation into the multiple murders by Edmund Emil Kemper III, he di-

rects police to dig up the human head that's in his yard. It's already been a week since he murdered his mother, Clarnell Elizabeth Strandberg, 52, with a clawhammer before slitting her throat while she slept. Maybe it's her head. No one knows right now.

"We don't know whose skull this is," says Sheriff Douglas James today, adding, "We'll have to wait for dental x-rays and pathology reports."

"There are numerous girls who were beheaded."

Henry McDaniel, 50, still reels from his en-

counter last night with the thing on his Enfield, Illinois doorstep that's unlike any creature yet reported during the massive wave of high weirdness that was a defining aspect of 1973.

Three legs. Two spindly arms. Huge pink eyes. A grayish color.

Of course, just like any sane, rational Earthling does in a situation like that, he picks up a pistol and fires four shots at it in the yard, sending it fleeing into the Illinois night.

Alien. Terrifying. Alone.

McDaniel knows from dogs or kangaroos – both of which he's had as pets – so it wasn't either of those. As for how he's able to remember so much from such a brief and startling encounter, it turns out that he's got a photographic memory, too.

He remembers everything.

In Buenos Aires, a two-headed baby boy is taken to the Genetic Institute for the Deformed.

According to delivering physician Dr. Raul J. Schwan – who delivered the children prematurely via caesarean at a local clinic in Tucumán – each head operates on its own, even sharing one set of internal organs.

Both constitutions are robust. Both minds remain inquisitive.

Both mouths suckle and nurse.

The violence of the imagination.

BUMMER!
Wednesday, May 2, 1973.

Psychedelic band The Group picks up some groupies and everything goes downhill from there. The Group's bassist Butts abuses and coerces two groupies into showering together, amidst a general overall feeling of oppression and menace. The action is riddled with violence of all kinds in this Sunset Strip time capsule that rather stereotypically equates rock music with total annihilation. At least they got the band's 1970 Ford Econoline tour van right. The strip club scene – in all its multifold misery – is every bit as violent, in its way, as is the killing. Psychic squalor abounds. The nudity is incessant. You should expect nothing less.

In Daytona Beach, another kind of group gets charged with the first-degree murder of a 17-year-old boy from Fresno who worked in an arcade, giving out change.

Six beach bums tied the boy to a table. Tortured him with cut glass. Whipped him with chains.

Sacrificed him to Satan, apparently, in the basement of a rooming house. Roach Haven, they call it.

The devil you know.

"They must have hated this kid like hell because they really tortured him," Police Chief Robert Palmer said.

In Cordele, Georgia, another hated child sits in a courtroom.

Jerry James Ellis, 18, watches as his mother Bonnie testifies about the night last November 28 during which she saw her son come in and shoot her as she sat in the family den in their home in Crisp County, Georgia.

A den for a family that lost three members to Ellis' bloody rampage.

Father stabbed, Sister stabbed. Grandfather stabbed.

Her son struggles with her until she gets away. She gets her daughter Katherine. Takes shelter in the bathroom. As Ellis pounds on the door,

IN THE GAME OF GROUP AND GROUPIES,
(URCHIN CAMP FOLLOWERS OF THE ROCK AGE)

• STARTS •
TOMORROW!

SOUTHWEST DRIVE-IN THEATRES
ACRES DRIVE-IN
3600 West Van Buren • 272 2269

SOMETIMES IT WAS A GROOVE...
BUT SOMETIMES... IT WAS A

BUMMER!

R   COLOR from EVI
A FAR OUT TRIP THRU A HARD ROCK TUNNEL

You Don't Have to
Assault a Groupie...
You Just Have to
Ask..!

A DAVID F. FRIEDMAN
WILLIAM ALLEN
CASTLEMAN
PRODUCTION

BUMMER!

A FAR OUT TRIP THRU A HARD ROCK TUNNEL
in COLOR from EVI   R   RESTRICTED
Starring KIPP WHITMAN • DENNIS BURKLEY • CONNIE STRICKLAND
CAROL SPEED • DIANE LEE HART • DAVID ANKRUM • DAVID BUCHANAN
Produced by David F. Friedman & William Allen Castleman • • • • Directed by William Allen Castleman
Distributed by Entertainment Ventures, Inc.

Katherine – whose throat Ellis has also slashed –
tells her mother, "Mama, Jerry shot me. Mama,
Jerry shot me in the mouth."

The devil you don't know.

On the other side of the door, Ellis shrieks,
"Mama, let me in. Somebody's after me. Somebody's going to get me." They climb out through
the bathroom window.

Honor student. Student body president. Triple
murderer.

No drugs. No alcohol. No motive.

In Buenos Aires, a group of six armed-and-
masked men kicks out the workers before throwing around Molotov cocktails inside a movie
theatre that was scheduled to show the
Argentine version of the rock opera *Jesus Christ
Superstar*. It takes firefighters two hours to put
out the fire that completely destroys the theatre.

The devil, you know.

THE STUDENT TEACHERS
Sunday, May 6, 1973.

Three student teachers share a house with a high
school art teacher who happens to be one of their
boyfriends. They can't get over how incredibly
square all the other teachers are, and they help-
fully point out how the school keeps laying such
a heavy trip on the kids. It's a school that's ob-
sessed with morality, conformity and the terrors
of VD (the music cues have tasteful titles such as
"Eat My Mind," "Venereal Disease Movie," and
"Masked Man Rapes Student Teacher."). With
artful nudity, hints of Vietnam, echoes of the ongoing civil rights struggle, and lots of frightening
rape scenes with a black-clad serial attacker wearing a clown mask. You also get more vintage exte-
rior shots of Southern California, which is always
a beautiful thing. Followed by a sort-of sequel,
Summer School Teachers, in 1974.

A student. Wendy Ann Vick. 18.

Dead in her négligée in a Holiday Inn.

That's how they find the coed from Beloit College
this morning. 18. Shot three times in the head.
Possibly by her boyfriend, David Dauchy, 25.

"It was understood that Dauchy's attentions to
Miss Vick in Milwaukee were not welcomed by
her parents."

Newspapers used to perform such a jarring
high-wire act between printing garish, appalling
headlines and downright outlandish under-
statements. The result was often poetry rivaling
Shakespeare – or the cut-up poetry of Brion
Gysin and William S. Burroughs, certainly.

SUNDAY, MARCH 30
ONLY

They can teach you a lot

Enter
their
course!

SEX-ED LAB

THE STUDENT TEACHERS

WARNING: "Frequent
coarse language and swear-
ing, much nudity," B.C.
Director.

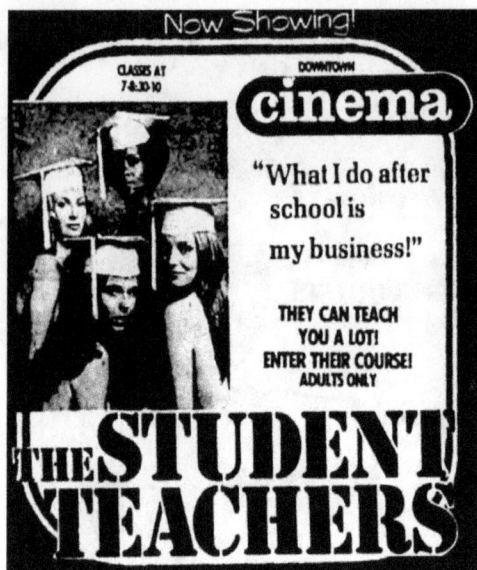

She's remembered as a reserved, quiet and somewhat conservative student.

Dauchy gets 15–25 years in the penitentiary when he's sentenced for her murder in December.

After which, he vanishes from public view into the mists of history and mystery.

One of the advantages of hindsight is that when you see that a killer gets put away in prison – there, high atop a perch of perspective, lo, these many moons later – some level of hope presents itself. For justice. For vengeance? For some semblance of balance, momentary though it may be. But there in the courtroom that winter in 1973 – did justice truly deliver anything even vaguely resembling satisfaction? For the parents, greying and disintegrating on the inside without their daughter? For the killer, who learned too late the effects of a quick decision that satisfied no one?

A father from Gloucester, New Jersey, journeys

to Key Largo, Florida to identify the bodies of his daughters, 16 and 18. The distance between cities is slightly over a thousand miles, although the true distance in these cases is always infinitely longer.

They were found, beaten and shot dead, in a thicket of trees close to Highway 1 by a man walking his dog. They'd been hitchhiking for a week. There are more than 1,700 islands that make up the Florida Keys. It's a wonder they were ever found at all. Ever survived being forgotten. Ever found their way to you, here and now.

The killer or killers remain unknown.

Always more questions than answers.

Never the answers that fit exactly the way you want them to.

The things they don't teach you in school.

THE COLOUR OF BLOOD
Thursday, May 10, 1973.

In this episode of British suspense series *Thriller*, a serial killer escapes police custody after an accident. He encounters a legal secretary who's at Waterloo Station to pick up a man she's never seen so she can give him a bunch of money and keys to a house. The man in question is supposed to be wearing a red carnation. Guess who else is wearing one. 1973 was a big year for mix-ups with psychopaths. The interplay between the killer and the secretary is sterling and tense. Presently it's clear that the killer has no control over his psychotic reactions and soon it becomes pretty easy to tell which person she should give a bunch of money! As with all things *Thriller*, there's a twist in the ending. A bummer – but a *stylish* bummer.

In Wausau, Wisconsin, a man and a woman pick up young men at gunpoint.

Driven to the countryside, the victims are ordered to have sex with her.

She's a small woman. Young. Long black hair. While the confused and hapless kidnap victims are goaded into having sex with her, the man joins in.

When they're finished, the men are driven back to Wausau and freed.

It's happened three times that police know of so far.

In a few days, the couple will be caught. More luckless people will come forward as additional victims of the couple.

Darrell and Florence Lewis. Young marrieds. 25 and 26, respectively. Charged with several counts. Abduction for immoral purposes, in point of fact.

Shortly after Christmas Day, Darrell will be sentenced to an indefinite stay at Central State Hospital in Waupun, Wisconsin.

Florence got probation.

Did she wait for him?

She did.

```
  (7)  News
  (12) News
  (38) Movie —
  (56) Movie —

11:30—
  (4)  Johnny Carson
  (5)  Color of Blood
  (6)  Color of Blood
  (7)  Movie —
  (9)  Color of Blood
  (12) Movie —
```

TERROR IN THE WAX MUSEUM
Thursday, May 10, 1973.

Bing Crosby presents ("presents," he says, as though Der Bingle extended his hand gracefully to bestow unto you only the finest treasures his world has to offer) this story of a bunch of movie stars from one Golden Age or another. They all get together in a turn-of-the-century London wax museum whose statues – played by hot-killers-of-yesteryear Lizzie Borden, Jack the Ripper, and Henri Désiré "Bluebeard" Landru – seem to come to life and do terrible things like murder John Carradine. Yes, the wax figures move. If ever there were a metaphor about the slower, stultifying pace of life in the distant past, wax is it.

It's tornado season. Again. Pair those tornadoes with hail and you've got seven dead in Missouri and Ohio. In McCreary County, Kentucky, three people get the ride of their life when a tornado picks up a pickup truck and moves it 300 feet. "One guy told me kids were flying through the air," Deputy Sheriff Dick Fredritz says. "He thinks there are still kids in the fields. There are too many of them unaccounted-for."

Petrifying. Astonishing. Violence.

Earl Ewin Austin said they'd never capture him alive.

A momentary member of the rarefied clan that is the FBI Most Wanted List, he's captured by The Feds in a resort hotel on the Las Vegas Strip.

Doing something he really wanted to do.

He's been on the run since January 26, when he escaped from the Jackson County Jail and made it out of Missouri. Headed west. 10 years in prison seems like a shorter period of time now than back when time moved at a general crawl and technology didn't double in its advances at an exponential rate. When a person gets out of prison after 10 years now, it's like they're frozen in time. Old methods don't apply anymore. Ways of living and learning change so drastically as to send men immediately back to the pen. Back to making license plates. Back to breaking rocks.

Turned to stone.

In Macon, Georgia, Ray Evans, 23, shoots his fiancée, Vicki Wright, 24, twice in the head before blowing his own brains out.

All because of a broken engagement.

Some people are so deeply stuck in one spot. So inexorably driven to one way of life. So inescapably married to one kind of behavior.

They may as well be statues.

DU NU
Friday, May 11, 1973.

Chen Ping plays a girl who gets raped by a bunch of scumbags with names like "Heroin" and "Crocodile." They give her a venereal disease known as "Vietnam Rose" ("I am a poison ivy!" she laments). Brooding, haunted club owner Lo Lieh shows her how to defend herself, ultimately helping her get her bloody, stabby, incredibly colorful vengeance. Another girl working at Lieh's club shows her how to throw razor-sharp playing cards with deadly accuracy. She becomes a fearsome vigilante known as "The Lady on the Roof" and kills as many of the rapist wretches as she can. Mature audiences in America got to experience the rape-revenge/kung-fu eye-opener as *Kiss of Death*. Immature audiences came mostly for the nudity.

The actor Lex Barker dies today. The former Tarzan was walking down the street on the East Side in New York City, on his way to meet his fiancée.

Heart attack. Just like that.

Sudden. Vicious. Much like Lex Barker – as actress Lana Turner's daughter Cheryl Crane revealed in her 1988 memoirs. While Barker was married to Turner, he incessantly abused Crane. When she told her mother, she forced Barker out of the house – but not before training a gun on him while he slept. Contemplating her future – her family's future – if she pulled the trigger and eliminated him. Divorce proceedings ensued. Suddenly. No stranger to violence visited upon the Turner family, Crane had in 1958 taken a butcher knife and got her revenge on criminal Johnny Stompanato, who was dating and abusing her mother.

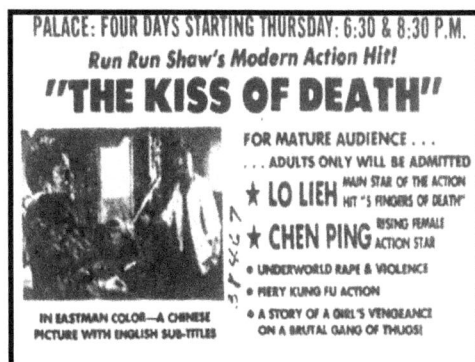

PALACE: FOUR DAYS STARTING THURSDAY: 6:30 & 8:30 P.M.
Run Run Shaw's Modern Action Hit!
"THE KISS OF DEATH"
FOR MATURE AUDIENCE . . .
. . . ADULTS ONLY WILL BE ADMITTED
★ LO LIEH MAIN STAR OF THE ACTION HIT "5 FINGERS OF DEATH"
★ CHEN PING RISING FEMALE ACTION STAR
● UNDERWORLD RAPE & VIOLENCE
● FIERY KUNG FU ACTION
● A STORY OF A GIRL'S VENGEANCE ON A BRUTAL GANG OF THUGS!
IN EASTMAN COLOR—A CHINESE PICTURE WITH ENGLISH SUB-TITLES

In the heart. In the gut. In the kidneys.

Justifiable homicide, they called it.

In San Antonio, Clarence A. "Slim" Lovell – the promising stock car race driver who'd done so well last Sunday at the Winston 500 in Talladega – dies in the city when his pickup ploughs into the concrete pillar of an expressway underpass. "Slim drove the good race and he won!"

That's what it says on his tombstone, anyway.

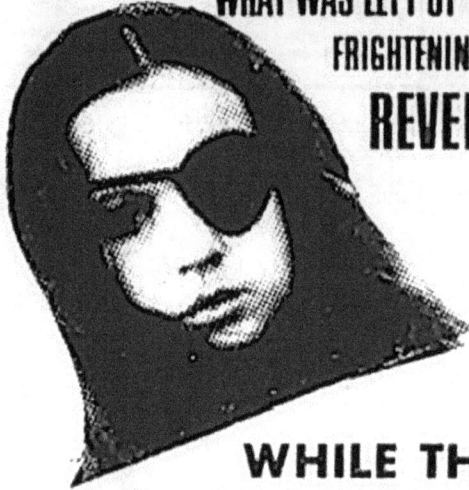

THE MOVIE THAT HAS NO LIMITS OF EVIL!

FIRST THEY TOOK HER SPEECH...THEN HER SIGHT..

WHEN THEY WERE FINISHED SHE USED

WHAT WAS LEFT OF HER FOR HER OWN

FRIGHTENING KIND OF STARRING **CHRISTINA**

REVENGE! **LINDBERG**
_ In Eastmancolor

THEY CALL HER ONE EYE

A CRUEL PICTURE

WHILE THEY LAST
FREE **EYE PATCHES FOR GIRLS —**
THE NEWEST FAD!

THRILLER – EN GRYM FILM
Monday, May 14, 1973.

Frigga (Christina Lindberg, at her most beatifically doomed) gets molested as a young girl by a crazy old bum. She's so traumatized that she's mute for the rest of the film, not to mention her life. Later, as a young lady, she's picked up by Tony (Heinz Hopf, at his most violently repulsive) who absconds with her to the big city, gets her hooked on heroin and puts her to work as a prostitute. He writes cold, heartless letters to her grieving parents. They can't take life anymore so they kill themselves. Tony threatens to take away the heroin that keeps Frigga in thrall. She pisses him off, so he gouges out her eyeball with a scalpel. Scraping together what little money she can after continually dealing with the worst that humanity has to offer, during her free time she learns to handle a shotgun, drive fast cars and destroy with karate. Dressed entirely in black, she systematically tracks down all the ultra-scum who have persecuted and exploited her. They die horrible lingering slow-motion deaths with lots of reverb. She saves the last death for Tony: buried up to his chin, with a rope around his neck tied to a horse straining to reach a nearby pail of food. The soundtrack has some of the saddest, most haunting music and sounds you'll hear this year or any other. At the end of the film, when there's no more vengeance left, all you get is one of the biggest "Now what?" moments in cinematic history as Frigga simply drives away.

In Fresno, California, 32 kids make it out alive tonight after the bus in which they're riding on their way home from Hearst Castle collides with an oncoming pickup truck.

Both drivers die when the twisted wreckage traps them, becoming de facto coffins as everything burns down around them.

The teachers break out the windows of the bus as it burns, saving the children.

Life lessons.

In Seattle, a sniper hiding in the woods near a freeway gets 10 shots off, trying to pick off and kill motorists.

Abraham Saltzman, 54. A property manager at a real estate company in Bellevue. Shot dead as he exits the freeway. He loses control of the car. Plummets 40 feet off an embankment before it's over.

Coming to rest.

70 policemen will search the area tomorrow.

They will find nothing.

They call the sniper's forest hideout a "perfect area."

Even while schoolkids are exploring Hearst Castle and a sniper checks his guns and ammunition, William H. Abernathy, 25, stands atop an 840,000-gallon fuel tank at Portland International Airport.

He has a rifle. He's threatening to shoot straight down into the tank. To blow everything all to hell.

He wants to see his wife and kids. Ex-wife. By noon.

His roommate, Phillip Moss, climbs up to the fuel tank and tries to reason with him. "He just wanted his kids and was at the end of his patience," Moss says. "He told me he saw a lot of people die in Vietnam for no reason, and I told him I did not and that I didn't want to see him die up there for no reason."

Moss goes for Abernathy's rifle. Abernathy snatches it back, pointing it at him.

Phillip Moss reluctantly retreats.

11:59 a.m. Children absent. Wife gone. They never make it. The FBI snipers do, though.

Now what?

They shoot him until he's dead.

That's what.

THE FORGOTTEN
Wednesday, May 16, 1973.

A bunch of crazies in an asylum keep on doing the things that landed them in the asylum in the first place. Doctors aren't what they seem. People can't stop killing each other. Featuring nymphomania, necrophilia and the ravages of Vietnam. Also: popsicles. For once, the "Don't" in the film's alternate, more popular title *Don't Go in the Basement* is fairly crummy advice.

In Luleå, Sweden, enormous flocks of ravens swarm and kill the reindeer herds that have been devastated by an unusually brutal winter.

You wouldn't think such things would happen.

But "travelers" say that it's so. Word reaches Pittsburgh. They print the story – the story – in newspapers from Pennsylvania to Nebraska.

You wouldn't think they'd care.

THE MAKERS OF **LAST HOUSE** ON THE **LEFT**
WARN YOU AGAIN TO KEEP REPEATING...

TO AVOID FAINTING
KEEP REPEATING,
IT'S ONLY A MOVIE
..ONLY A MOVIE
.ONLY A MOVIE
.ONLY A MOVIE
.ONLY A MOVIE
..ONLY A MOVIE...

"DON'T LOOK
IN THE
BASEMENT" R

NOT RECOMMENDED
FOR PERSONS
OVER 30!

...THE DAY THE INSANE TOOK OVER THE ASYLUM!
FULTON MINI DOWNTOWN 781-4354/ STARTS TODAY!
LADIES DAY TODAY UNTIL 5:00 P.M.

But that's the thing about small piercing newspaper blurbs about unusual violence.

What do you choose to believe about that story?

Who gains from that belief?

Or is there no hidden agenda in publishing such an outlandish story beyond a story that, no matter how small, will bring in readers?

Modern myth-making relies on powerful images sinking into your psyche in an oblique way. A home has many doors to enter that reach its living room. Your mind then alters the facts over time. What you tell others about a story you think you remember so well gets further altered and mangled and reversed. It's all in the telling.

There used to be an old insane asylum in those woods. I heard the nurse killed everyone. Let's go check it out. Sure I'm sure.

A flock of ravens is known as an "unkindness."

DEATH WARD #13
–HIS VICTIMS WERE PREY
TO HIS EVERY DESIRE!
CO-FEATURE R
"TWITCH OF THE DEATH NERVE"

NOW SHOWING

TWIN 40 Cinemas I II
UNIONTOWN MALL
AIR CONDITIONED

HELD OVER! AGAIN

RT. 40 438-0024

Any number can play.
Any number can die.

RICHARD BENJAMIN
DYAN CANNON
RAQUEL WELCH
JAMES COBURN
JAMES MASON

THE LAST OF SHEILA

PG

TONITE AT 7:30-9:30

RYAN O'NEAL

"PAPER MOON"

PG

TONITE 7:30—9:30

THE LAST OF SHEILA
Wednesday, May 16, 1973.

A bunch of familiar stars – including James Coburn, Dyan Cannon, James Mason, Raquel Welch and a deeply youthful Ian McShane – take a pleasure cruise for a week aboard film producer Coburn's yacht, bought with money he probably made by bankrolling films like these. It's been a year since a hit-and-run driver killed Coburn's wife Sheila. He gets them all to play a gossip game dedicated to Sheila, during which six different secrets are unveiled in six different ports throughout the Mediterranean. The cards are all printed in big capital letters like YOU ARE A SHOPLIFTER and YOU ARE A HOMO-SEXUAL, which we all know are basically the same thing. Soon, the guests are being murdered and the ultimate secret – the identity of the murderer – is revealed. Written by Anthony Perkins and Stephen Sondheim and based on similar games they and their celebrity friends would play so they wouldn't have to think of mass murder or the Vietnam War or their friends and peers dying in real life.

In the Indian state of Bihar, at least 27 people have been lynched by roving mobs.

Two weeks ago, the skulls of five little boys were found.

In Bihar, people are convinced that a gang of madmen have been abducting children and – at

DAKOTA *Theatre*
223-1877

ENDS TONITE
"DIRTY LITTLE BILLY"

THE
NEXT
MOVE IS
MURDER
Who done it

RICHARD BENJAMIN
DYAN CANNON
JAMES COBURN
RAQUEL WELCH

THE
LAST
OF
SHEILA

Nitely
7:10 & 9:25
Mat. Sun.
1:30 & 3:45

PG

best – forcing them to work as beggars or – at worst – chopping off their heads.

It's even been purported that the children have been maimed to transform them into much more sympathetic targets for generosity.

Speculation and fear and conclusions.

There's no truth so horrible that people can't make even more horrible.

Just ask the Associated Press.

By the time their reports of the situation cross America – published in newspapers from Salem, Oregon to Hazleton, Pennsylvania – the number of lynchings doubles from 8 to 16.

In a day, those frenzied gangs will now be decapitating children.

You know. To make you feel sorry for them.

By the time Reuters spreads the news to Montréal, 36 people have been lynched. Now it's witches and witch doctors that have been poisoning and killing children.

Never mind that a magistrate tells people that the thing that's really been killing those children is food poisoning.

Old women are burned on pyres. Monks are straight-up murdered.

The madness of the mob finds people in crowds and kills them where they cower.

Spurred on by spurious rumors.

tonio directed this obscure slice-of-death drama. I wonder if Javier ever sat through it. Apparently Seberg did the film because she needed the money. Who wouldn't! In 1979, she dies of an overdose because of years of being hassled by the FBI on account of her support for the Black Panthers and other leftist groups. "Forgive me. I can no longer live with my nerves," said the note found next to her body in the back seat of her Renault, parked near her Paris apartment. She was found days after her suicide.

The Watergate hearings start today.

They're on all the radio and television networks, which cover them exhaustively through 1973 into 1974. So shocking is the unfolding level of corruption uncovered at the highest echelons of the American government that 85% of Americans watch the hearings in part or in full over the coming months.

LA CORRUPCIÓN DE CHRIS MILLER
Thursday, May 17, 1973.

Supernally luckless Jean Seberg plays a vengeful woman who hates the man who abandoned her capriciously one day, leaving her to live with stepdaughter Chris in a lonely old mansion out in the Spanish countryside. Coincidentally (?), someone is roaming the same countryside, murdering people. In one scene, the killer dresses like Charlie Chaplin and commits murder like he's in a silent film. A drifter stops by to pick up some money doing odd jobs. Psychodrama commences thereat. The mistaken-identity angle is particularly tragic here. Javier Bardem's uncle Juan An-

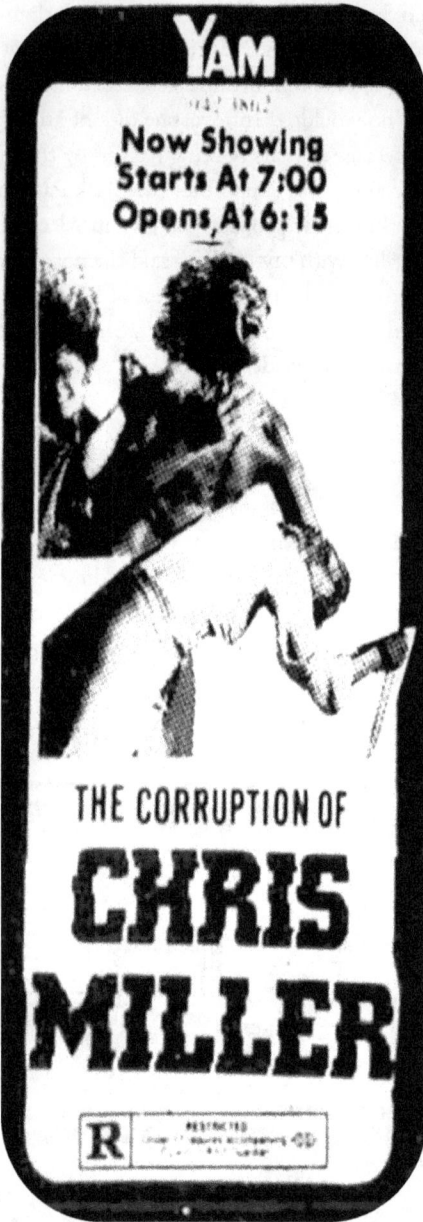

YAM

Now Showing
Starts At 7:00
Opens At 6:15

THE CORRUPTION OF
CHRIS MILLER

R RESTRICTED

It seemed inconceivable that President Richard Milhous Nixon would somehow be connected to five crooks who tried to break into the Democratic National Committee headquarters at the Watergate Complex to plant listening devices and somehow torpedo the opposition's chances of winning against Nixon, who was in 1972 elected by an overwhelming majority.

"What did the President know, and when did he know it?" asks Tennessee Senator Howard Baker next month during the hearings.

Deep Throat knows.

It is the very soul of irony that gives the inquiry into arch-moralist Nixon's corruption an informant named "Deep Throat."

W. Mark Felt, revealed in 2005 to be Deep Throat, sees the writing on the wall. He resigns from his post as Deputy Associate Director of the Federal Bureau of Investigation a week before Baker asks the investigation's most pivotal of all possible questions.

Someone had to ask it.

FUGITIVES
Friday, May 18, 1973.

Three escaped convicts – two men and a woman – break into a home where they find a couple of girls lounging around. They proceed to ravish the girls as jazz blares behind and above and below them. With Rick Cassidy (July 22, 1943 – December 23, 2013) and Cyndee Summers (September 27, 1949 – November 15, 2009), two of pornography's earliest stars. Cassidy, a bodybuilder, found his way to adult films after a stint in the Navy during Vietnam. After it was revealed in 1985 that Traci Lords, his co-star in *New Wave Hookers*, was underage, he left pornography and retired, becoming a real estate agent in Pennsylvania.

In California, Governor Ronald Reagan and his associates walk back a plan to close out state hospitals for the mentally ill. Apparently, patient rolls are withering as those hospitals continue a slow slide into what Reagan points to as irrelevance. Purportedly, local facilities can do a better job than the six hospitals currently operating. Purportedly.

Meanwhile, in Carson, California, a man released from Camarillo State Mental Hospital shoots his wife and three children to death with a .22 rifle.

They find his body at the foot of his son's bed.

In Minneapolis, two teens gun down a young engineer on the interstate as he steps out of his car to see why he was being shot at. Other cars get hit by gunshots as well. Deputy Police Chief Carl Johnson says that there's no motive for the shootings that he can find.

"Other than insanity," he says.

In Stuart, Florida, ex-sheriff's deputy Gerard Schaefer is charged with murdering two teen girls. Authorities suspect that he's killed others about which they're currently unaware. In 1995, he's stabbed to death in his cell, arguing over a cup of coffee.

He's committed to Florida State Hospital at Chattahoochee today for a month of observation.

Who knows how many other people could use a month of observation in a mental hospital in 1973?

Edmund Kemper finally gets an attorney.

He needs one because he's facing eight counts of murder. Victims include multiple co-eds, his mother and her friend. He was so good at killing that he finally had to call the police from a payphone in Pueblo, Colorado and tell them what was really going on.

He's 6'9." Weighs 280. At 15, he murdered his father's parents. Spent five years at Atascadero

NOW SHOWING

THE FUGITIVE

ADULTS ONLY   RATED X

OPEN 10 A.M.
TO 12 P.M.

ALSO SHOWING
"THE STUNT"

RIVERVIEW
FOLLIES
☆ ☆
MOVIE ARCADE, BOOK STORE
ADULT ENTERTAINMENT!
AMUSEMENT CENTER
635 SOUTH FOURTH   Phone
LOUISVILLE, KY.   585-3827

State Mental Hospital.

"No longer a danger to society," they say.

Last September, psychiatrists gave him a clean
bill of mental health.

¡Los antiguos ritos del Vudú africano y los secretos de la magia india, con todo su morbo y erotismo, en el Londres de nuestros días!

LA REBELION DE LAS MUERTAS

PRESENTADA EN **VISTARAMA**

DIRECTOR **LEON KLIMOVSKY** PRODUCIDA POR PROFILMES, S.A. EASTMANCOLOR

PAUL NASCHY
ROMY
MIRTA MILLER
MARIA KOSTY
y VIC WINNER

LA REBELION DE LAS MUERTAS
Friday, May 18, 1973.

All the black masses and cartoonish Satanism in the world couldn't hide the fact that this is a film that at its essence is consumed with fears of death and losing honor. Welcome to Spain! Paul Naschy plays Krisna, an Indian guru (they're never from Bangladesh or Bhutan in these films) that summons women from the dead and commands them to kill his enemies to restore his honor and otherwise do his bidding. You never see evil gurus sending their slaves out to do their dry-cleaning, though. He also plays Satan, and Krisna's malformed brother, too. 1973 was a big year for Paul Naschy; he was really good at resurrecting audiences to do his bidding and go to his films. Besides *La rebelion de las muertas* and *El jorobado de la Morgue*, he was also in *El retorno de Walpurgis* (Curse of the Devil), *La orgía de los muertos* (The Hanging Woman), *El espanto surge de la tumba* (Horror Rises from the Tomb), *El gran amor del conde Drácula* (Count Dracula's Great Love), *Disco rojo*, and *Las ratas no duermen de noche* (The Man with the Severed Head), all of which would make a great film festival on their own. As Cine Salamanca in Madrid gravely noted at the time, "The cinema is allowed to warn the public that the film is terribly torturous, and because of the nature and development of its

¡Los antiguos ritos del vudú africano y los secretos de la magia india, con todo su morbo y erotismo, en el Londres de nuestros días!

¡Asesinaba a todas las mujeres para servirse de ellas después de muertas!

LA REBELION DE LAS MUERTAS

Director LEON KLIMOVSKY

PAUL NASCHY · ROMY · MILLER · KOSTY · WINNER · VIC LAWRENCE

Director LEON KLIMOVSKY

PRESENTADA EN VISTARAMA

gloomy and bloody scenes, it is not indicated for the sensitivity of certain people."

Josef Schwammberger is in limbo today.

On May 4, West German officials serve an extradition order in La Plata, Argentina for Schwammberger, a commandant of multiple forced-labor camps in Poland. He's also wanted for his murder of a Polish rabbi in 1942 on the Jewish Day of Atonement.

He's lived in Argentina for over 24 years.

If only they can find out where exactly he is in Argentina.

By 1973, the criminal and the inhumane have found fertile ground to put down roots and live the lives about which their many victims could have only dreamed.

When one dream begins, another ends.

On August 6, Hermine Braunsteiner Ryan of Queens, New York becomes the first Nazi war criminal extradited from America to Germany. A Majdanek concentration camp guard nicknamed "The Stomping Mare," she whipped and trampled female prisoners to death. Repeatedly.

Her case makes headlines in newspapers the world over.

Consider Ravensbrück guard and SS dog handler Elfriede Rinkel, picking up the newspaper and reading about Hermine. Elfriede immigrated to San Francisco in 1959 and married a German Jew, whom she'd never once in over 40 years of marriage told about her Nazi past.

Perhaps these reports of winds shifting and arcs bending cross the mind of Gestapo agent Walter Kutschmann as he marries his Argentinian wife this August in Buenos Aires. Maybe they even reach Syria, where Adolf Eichmann's assistant and Drancy internment camp commandant Alois Brunner now works for the Assad regime. Conceivably, Sobibór concentration camp guard Hermann "Preacher" Michel catches a news report through the static of a tabletop radio in Egypt and for a split-second is grasped by a moment of mortality.

Conceivably.

Picture the Croatian Hitlerite Jakob Denzinger – a naturalized American citizen as of only last year

– safe and comfortable in his suburban Akron, Ohio home. An executive in the plastics industry. A Cadillac. A Lincoln. Invested in petroleum. Real estate. Somehow, his work as a Nazi guard and exterminator at multiple concentration camps was left off of his professional résumé. Auschwitz. Buchenwald. Mauthausen. Plaszow. Sachsenhausen.

Plastic is what shields his portrait on his tombstone from the elements.

Possibly the news also finds its way to Brazil, where Auschwitz "Angel of Death" Dr. Josef Mengele lives in deteriorating health. High blood pressure. Imbalances. Strokes. Powerless to stop the slow disintegration of his own body.

August 25. Klaus Altmann. Imprisoned in Bolivia. To be extradited to Peru. Tax evasion. Currency smuggling.

Serious offenses.

The Supreme Court of the Plurinational State of Bolivia, however, does not believe that he should be extradited to France.

France. Where Klaus Altmann is more widely known as Klaus Barbie.

The Butcher of Lyon.

In 10 years, France will finally get him. Bolivia's dictatorship – the one in which Barbie becomes a Lieutenant Colonel in the Armed Forces – falls. Their protection no longer functions. In 1991, he dies in prison. In Lyon.

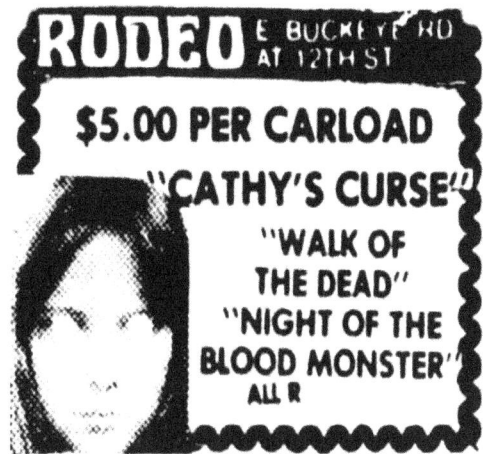

Cancer of the prostate. Cancer of the spine.

Cancer in general.

THE LEGEND OF HELL HOUSE
Wednesday, May 23, 1973.

Haunted house "meller" (*Variety Magazine's* slang term for "melodrama") in which an old rich guy hires three occult buffs to hang out in the late Emeric Belasco's mansion, known as "Hell House." Wide-eyed Pamela Franklin plays the psychic medium. Roddy McDowall ridicules everyone for their boring naïveté. Clive Revill plays the doctor who tries to make sense of the supernatural but bad spirits really hate it when people are all condescending and analytical like that so things don't go particularly well for him. Highlights of Belasco's wackiness include addiction, bestiality, vampirism, sadism, cannibalism, necrophilia and other clichés. You get an idea of where the filmmakers were coming from when they hired occult expert Tom Corbett to come up with this preamble: "Although the story of this film is fictitious, the events depicted involving psychic phenomena are not only very much within the bounds of possibility, but could well be true. Tom Corbett, Clairvoyant and Psychic Consultant to European Royalty." The house is not amused at any of their attempts to cast out its corny evil and slaughters as many of them as it can. *Of* course!

Pansye Youngblood, 66, of Rome, Georgia, dies when she steps out of her car onto her driveway.

The car's open door knocks her down. It's still in gear. It drags her beneath it, crushing her as it rolls over her in front of her house, coming to rest in a ditch.

Pvt. Roland Frost Jr., 32, dies in Portage, Wisconsin when he stops his car in the middle of Highway 51-16 at 1:20 in the morning. A car traveling the other way hits him when he gets out of his car.

No one knows why he stopped. In the middle of the road. In the dead of night.

Fitness enthusiast Jack LaLanne's daughter Janet, 21, loses control of her car west of Augusta, Michigan on Interstate 96. It rolls and rolls and rolls. Passengers in the car survive.

Scarred for life.

They don't know why she apparently lost control of the car.

"Apparently" is a euphemism like "sensational" or "I'm fine." It says nothing. Conveys anything. Sometimes everything.

There's a Jack and Janet LaLanne Scholarship Award for deserving students that excel in performing arts and athletics. To be given in perpetuity.

A legend is forever.

So is wondering why a car moved a certain way, or why someone didn't.

What life would be like if they had.

FOR THE SAKE OF YOUR SANITY, PRAY IT ISN'T TRUE!

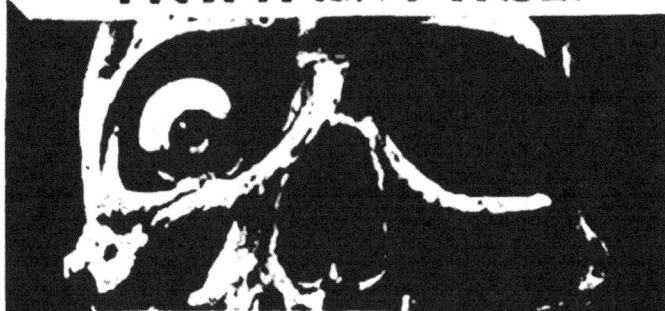

The Legend of HELL HOUSE

PAMELA FRANKLIN, RODDY McDOWALL [PG]

Plus "VAMPIRE CIRCUS"

Starts WEDNESDAY · FIRST RUN
PRESTON · CLARKSVILLE · VOGUE
DRIVE-IN   DRIVE-IN   NEW ALBANY

ONNA JIGOKU: MORI WA NURETA
Wednesday, May 23, 1973.

Sachiko, accused of killing her mistress, gets blackmailed by a couple in whom she foolishly places her trust. They decamp with her to a dark and dour hotel in the woods – hence the film's English title *Woods Are Wet* – take advantage of her by candlelight and make her do all sorts of nutty things. The director censors the nudity with chunky black boxes, sometimes needlessly. The hotel's leering owner pontificates about how humans are dumb for stifling their inner beasts, but he's just flat-out bonkers, so why even listen to someone like that? An unforgiving, deathlessly cynical view of human nature that ends on a note that's both bleakly violent and violently bleak.

In Phoenix, a woman, 29, kills her daughter, 5, and shoots both her two-year-old and nine-month-old in the head before shooting herself. She's found by her husband.

He'd gone out with the neighbor.

All they wanted was to go see a movie.

Her husband, a specialist in the Army, dies almost two years later, in 1975.

No reason given.

In Young Township, Pennsylvania, there's a new shopping center going up on the site that was formerly the home of the Starlite Drive-In Theatre. A department store. A food market. A discount store. A drugstore. Over time, these urban renewals will change the face of America in its small towns, seemingly overnight, while no one thought – or knew enough – to watch.

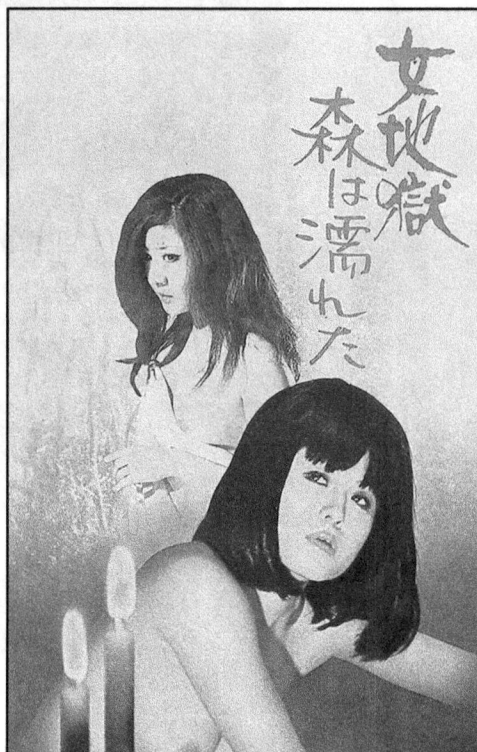

In the Zip City area of Ft. Lauderdale in Florida, a small tornado lifts up Melvin P. Campbell Sr. as he tries to make it down to the storm cellar. A sound like a freight train roars in his ears.

His wife holds on to him.

Holds on to his hands and arms. Keeps him from being torn away from her. She saves his life, then and there.

"I was as close to being blown away as I have ever been in my life," he says.

PIGS
Wednesday, May 23, 1973.

Director Marc Lawrence's real-life daughter plays Lynn, who stabs her cinematic father to death after he rapes and abuses her. The made-up *Los Angeles Times* headline screams DAD RAPES DAUGHTER, DIES OF KNIFE WOUNDS, which was probably news to the *Los Angeles Times*. Breaking out of an insane asylum – and borrowing a nurse's uniform when its owner strips and runs off to have sex with a doctor – she meets up with her director father, who plays Zambrini, a farmer who feeds people to his pigs when he isn't running his grimy diner. If any man reminds Lynn of her rapist father, she kills him and Zambrini cleans up the mess by feeding the corpses to his pigs. "They got used to eating human flesh. I gotta do it. I'm sorry," explains Zambrini, only slightly distressed by his growing awareness of where his life ended up. The film's off-kilter soundtrack uses everything from reverb to bluegrass to some of the most psychedelic jaw-harp music you'll ever hear, and the disorienting camera angles are alternately gory and dreamlike. *Pigs* lived a long healthy life in America theatres due to a series of title changes and new edits; it was reviewed in 1984 for *Variety* as *Daddy's Deadly Darling* at the Liberty Theatre on 42nd Street in New York City.

In Donalsonville, Georgia, Seminole County Sheriff Dan White tells everyone that the fugitives wanted in the murders of Ned Alday, his three sons, brother and wife will get a fair shot at justice. "My people don't want violence, and I'm in a position to know," White says, adding, "We're all neighbors and we love one another. All we ask for is a fair and impartial trial with a good jury that would give justice."

Nor does he fear that his neighbors will rise up and take matters into their own hands.

Even though the offer is on the table.

"They're mourning the loss of their loved ones," he promises.

The massacre on May 14 at the family farm was the most violent in that region in almost a century.

Justice prevails – for some – even now, decades after the judge handed down the sentences.

The last of the killers – Wayne Carl Coleman – is, as of 2022, still serving a life sentence. Another died in prison; a third died shortly after release. The ringleader, Carl Junior Isaacs, is executed by lethal injection in 2003. He ordered a last meal of pork and macaroni, carrot salad, fruit punch and chocolate cake.

At the last moment, he refuses it.

The execution marked the first time in state history that Georgia officials allowed the victims' families in to witness it.

Norman Strait saw Isaacs and two others traveling the highway before the murders. He watched them through the scope of his hunting rifle.

Later, Strait reflected, "I guess I should have shot that son-of-a-bitch right there. It would have saved a lot of lives."

From now until this June, the Michigan Chem-ical Company will accidentally mix up hundreds of pounds of PBBs – a chemical used in the flame retardant FireMaster BP-6 – with livestock feed additive destined for farms throughout the state. Nutrimaster, the milk-producing supplement that was meant for the livestock, has package labels that are incredibly similar to the package labels of FireMaster. Much like the scandal that befell Petchow Chemicals, Inc. They'll finally start to announce the scope of the problem next June. An entire year from now.

30,000 cattle. 1.5 million chickens. 1,470 sheep.

And 5,900 pigs.

All contaminated with PBBs, exposing countless Michigan residents to the poison in these animals, the effects of which on humans are still not completely understood.

I still have no idea what's going to happen to me.

137

THE KILLING KIND
Thursday, May 24, 1973.

Terry Lambert loves his mother. Terry Lambert can't get it up. Terry Lambert almost raped a girl. His mother Thelma blames the girl who got raped by a bunch of his buddies. He falls for Lori (Cindy Williams, only a few years away from becoming Shirley on *Laverne & Shirley*). He calls up Tina, the girl that he almost raped. She flirts with him over the telephone. Lists all the guys she's loved before. Guys who actually *could* get it up. He's furious. He graduates from killing animals to attacking women. All the while, his mother Thelma dotes on him. Takes countless photographs of him. Hangs them up around the house. He almost drowns Lori. His mother calls her a tacky whore. Thelma takes photographs of him showering. After he strangles her half-to-death, he finally realizes that her son is a total psycho and does what she knows she must.

Out in the Arizona desert, 12 rail cars filled with 500-lb. bombs catch fire as they roll down the track, creating a stunning spectacle of fire and disaster near the scenic mountain pass known as Texas Canyon. It's the second time it's happened this month. Possibly intentional. But that's the nature of a bomb: to explode. All that it's doing is fulfilling its innate purpose; looking for its destiny amidst all those countless could-be smithereens.

In other bombshell developments.

They're selling the car in which Bonnie Parker and Clyde Barrow were ambushed and killed 39 years ago today in a hail of more than 200 police bullets.

It's estimated that $10 million dollars has been made by exhibiting the 1934 Ford Deluxe to an endless stream of the curious and the appalled, sticking their fingers in the holes like Doubting Thomas once did to Christ Almighty.

Most people in this day and age know about those characters from Arthur Penn's 1967 film *Bonnie and Clyde*, in which a hernia-inducing stretch of credulity presented Warren Beatty's murderous Clyde Barrow as suffering from impotence.

Former Dallas deputy sheriff Ted Hinton is the only one of the six policemen who fired on that car that's left alive and can authenticate it. There have been many cars known as the "Bonnie and Clyde Death Car" over the years. Several court cases have attempted to clear up the confusion. The real one – the one up for sale today – finally winds up at Whiskey Pete's Casino in Primm, Nevada, where you can see it to this very day.

A brown stain on the car's upholstery has been certified by a doctor as blood.

In case you had any doubts.

THE SEX PROPHET
Friday, May 25, 1973.

The opening notes of Ravi Shankar's "Tala Rasa Ranga" introduce the sinister guru Rava as he counsels couples with relationship issues. The opening credits are written on pieces of paper that catch on fire because they're set too close to the fireplace! Presently, the couples are seduced and corrupted by his metaphysical claptrap. Woe betide them all! "Listen to me, you piss-complected afterbirth of a Mongolian gangbang!" Rava's moronic assistant Igor yells at him during the shocking twist ending. The film reportedly has an alternate title of *Sin Mystic*, although I haven't seen a screening date anywhere to that effect. There was a racehorse named Sin Mystic trotting around at the same time, fêted and celebrated everywhere from Des Moines to Sioux Falls. I think I'd rather have the horse.

Tomorrow will be the last day anyone sees 20-year-old Rosa Vasquez alive.

They'll find her in some underbrush near Golden Gate Park in San Francisco on Tuesday. Strangled. Stripped. Thrown deep into the shrubbery by someone possessed of great strength. Authorities think that she may be one of the long-unsolved Santa Rosa Hitchhiker Murders of 1972 and 1973.

It's been slightly over two years since Frank Losole underwent a heart transplant at Stanford University.

Riding his motorcycle to South Gate, California. He's taking in the Indianapolis 500 this weekend. It's a time for living life. For seeing the world.

AARDE CINEMA AIR COND.
2021 SANSOM ST.
LO 3-9818 (CONT. FR. 12 NOON)
"Where the Action Is"
PENNA PREMIERE
2—ADULT TREATS—2

THEY WANTED FUN ...
THEY GOT ACTION
"SEX PROPHET"
12.00, 2 00 4.00, 6.00, 8.00, 10:00
PEOPLE ON A JOYRIDE OF LIFE
"JOKERS ARE WILD"
1:00, 3 00, 5 00, 7 00, 9 00, 11 00

CINEMA X EAST
FIRST DAYTON SHOWING
She'll Make You an Offer You Can't Resist, But Should!
...LOVE YOU TO DEATH
ADULTS ⊗ ONLY
PRODUCED AND DIRECTED BY
FRANK MILLOTTI
ORIGINAL STORY BY
DAVID WHITE
PLUS: "SEX PROPHETS"
ESCORTED LADIES FREE — SUN. and MON.
COLOR

CINEMA X EAST

2121 E. THIRD
254-9371

DAYTON PREMIERE SHOWING

"SEX PROPHETS"
PLUS
"BENNY BUNGLES IT"

ESCORTED LADIES
ADMITTED FREE — EVERY MONDAY

As hijacker Chingis Yunusogly Rzayev continues his assault on the cockpit, on-board cop Vladimir Yezhikov shoots him in the back.

With his dying breath, Rzayev detonates slightly over 12 pounds of dynamite.

Their distress call ends mid-message. The jet becomes a disintegrating blur on radar screens before disappearing.

Everyone dies.

You knew that already, didn't you.

For second chances.

A lifetime of heart damage befell him after he contracted rheumatic fever. You wouldn't think it to look at him now. "I swim. I shoot pool a lot. And I'm going to take up scuba diving."

"You can't let someone else live your life for you," he says.

Every day counts. He's got approximately 687 of them left to live. He dies at age 40 in 1975.

But no one can see that future for him. He probably wouldn't have wanted to know, even if it could have been shown to him.

An unfulfilling prophecy.

Above southern Siberia, near the Chinese border, the crew of a TU-104 Aeroflot passenger jet transmits a message to air traffic controllers about the bomb-carrying hijacker who's trying to change the jet's course.

ROAD SERVICE
Wednesday, May 30, 1973.

Parents Marc Stevens and Andrea "More More More" True and daughter Helen Madigan are a hypersexualized family suffering through their daily bourgeois dilemmas when a couple of stranded motorists show up. There's a serial "raper" running around who's assaulted 32 women ("That's more flavors than Baskin-Robbins!"). Suspicion falls on one of the motorists. Andrea becomes distressed when it turns out that the mechanic from the garage who'd come out to help the stranded motorists isn't the raper after all. "Lady, are you sure you don't need any tires? Belts? Hoses?" It'd be real interesting to see if anyone will ever cop to composing the film's jaunty and burbly electronic soundtrack. Who would care either way anymore? The best thing about the twist ending is the sad trombone accompaniment. Way to drive the point home!

124 fires are started throughout the state of California in the space of 24 hours. Caused by lightning strikes. Fresno. Tuolumne. Madera. Mariposa. Yreka. Electricity falls incessantly now until there's only flames and ash and renewal across the land.

The bombs that exploded in that Arizona train on Thursday did so because of a reason other than sabotage, authorities reveal. That reason is never divulged.

Some people don't want to believe that nature wants to take its own course.

Sex like lightning, sex like fire, sex like there's nothing else on Earth but cosmic forces bringing two people together to make them feel like they've tapped into something transcendent and beautiful and all-consuming.

Some people simply want to believe other things.

During a storm dripping with thunder and lightning, Esther Cochran, 73, is strangled with a cord in her Pinellas Park, Florida trailer. Neighbors thought they heard a choking sound emanating from her trailer shortly after midnight.

Thought they were imagining things. Went back to sleep.

A week later, the medical examiner will reveal that she had not been raped, but instead "sexually assaulted" in some other way.

She and a series of other older women have been set upon and murdered recently in the area. The killings may be connected. They remain unsolved. There's reportedly evidence – hair, a fingerprint without a match, a cigarette butt – taken from some of the crime scenes. Where that evidence is right now is unclear.

Her daughter, Marie Simmons, visits her in the Memorial Park Cemetery often, where she tells her about her problems.

Unanswerable questions.

In the Dallas suburb of Garland, scientists tell Marie Harris that the protoplasmic blob she found in her backyard is simply a slime mold and that its growing, pulsating form is something that should clear up in a few days by itself under the hot Texas sun.

"I'm glad it's not going to come tumbling into my house," says Harris.

You never know what kind of slime is going to enter your life.

TERMINAL ISLAND
Friday, June 1, 1973.

It's strange how sometimes you can look at an actor in their early roles and see that there's something exceptional about them, despite the size of the role or the words coming out of their mouths. Tom Selleck in this film, for example. Selleck plays Dr. Norman Milford, condemned to Terminal Island for mercy-killing his terminal wife. Terminal Island is where all the killers and reprobates are imprisoned after America does away with the death penalty. No guards. No barbed wire. No walls. Only an endless ocean surrounding them and a patrol boat lurking offshore, waiting to machine-gun escapees into oblivion. One group of crooks tries to do away with a competing group of crooks to take their guns and women, but then of course it all goes downhill from there. The women know how to do things like make bombs and poison darts, which makes them incredibly valuable to the script. Did you know that wild mustard has high sulphur content that can be used to create improvised explosives? I learned that from Tom Selleck! Some poor guy in an outhouse gets blown away by one of their homemade bombs. "That dude just took his last crap," sneers another prisoner, delivering one of the best lines of any film of 1973.

In Springfield, South Carolina, investigators try to decipher the reasoning behind the suicide of Norma Hill Chavis, 37.

On Thursday, her '72 Ford smashes into a guard rail on a bridge on U.S. Highway 3. Two tires blown out. Barreling 200 yards down the highway until coming to a screeching stop.

And then things get really strange.

People come up to help. Chavis is in the front seat. Seen convulsing and twitching.

Then, three gunshots from a .22 revolver.

And then one final shot.

"I won't say flatly one way or the other it was positively suicide," says Coroner Joe A. Dickey, adding, "But from all indications, I think foul play could be ruled out."

No reason. No motive. No explanation.

Other than the facts, that is.

270 miles above Earth, where questions asked remain unanswered, the astronauts on Skylab 1 are seen on television, somersaulting in zero gravity.

IT SLASHES! IT SMASHES! IT RIPS YOU APART!

IT'S THE BLOODIEST WEAPON OF THE MARTIAL ARTS!

TRIPLE IRONS

Watch it outdo Kung-Fu!

THE BLOODY BUTCHERS!

MEN AND WOMEN... BLACK AND WHITE... TAKEN FROM DEATH ROW · CONDEMNED TO DEVIL'S ISLAND U.S.A. WHERE LIVING IS WORSE THAN DYING!

TERMINAL ISLAND

State Police Investigator Larry Coffman says. "And then strangled."

Sandra Jean's killers are members of a local chapter of The Pagans biker gang.

During her trial, when asked if Sandra Jean were alive when she was left behind on that logging road, Grant says, "No, she wasn't. She just lay there."

Mytrice hadn't seen Sandra Jean for a year. Her husband, possibly living in South Carolina, had been absent even longer

Off in their own worlds.

They're smiling.

They're flying.

They're laughing and weightless and free.

270 miles beneath Skylab, in Norfolk, Virginia, Mytrice Harrell weeps and screams when shown the body of her daughter Sandra Jean, 18, beaten and bloodied by three girls now charged with – and ultimately convicted for – her strangulation murder.

Linda Carol Grant. 23. Pamela Jean Blair. 20. June Ann Reed. 16.

She was found May 25 on a lonely logging road in Southampton County. Two weeks after she turned 18.

"It looks as if she was beaten with a belt buckle,"

IN PERSON
FRIDAY NIGHT ONLY! Southutch Drive-In

Lovely Lynn Borden, star of THIS IS A HIJACK will be appearing IN PERSON at the Southutch Drive-In before showtime and during intermission to meet those attending & to sign autographs!

THIS IS A HIJACK
Friday, June 1, 1973.

"What would you do if you were in a plane with a hijacker with a gun with only a few drops of gas left and a nose wheel that won't come down? Ever wonder what you would do?" Oh, all the time! Adam Rourke plays a real dummy who loses too much money gambling. His mob overseers rope him into hijacking his rich boss-man's jet that's carrying a million-dollar fortune so he can pay off his gambling debts. Lead heavy – and yes, he might as well be made of lead, that's how heavy he is – Neville Brand really has fun tormenting the wealthy cowering types on board, making them sing and grunt, ravishing their foxy girlfriends while they stew and/or seethe. Scenes of friction between local Ft. Worth cops and FBI agents anticipate everything from '80s action movies to reruns of *Matlock*. It's typically topical exploitation madness, with priceless shots of an era that was already bygone the day the film opened in Wichita. Co-star Lynn Borden showed up at the Meadowlark Twin Drive-In Theatre premiere to sign autographs and hang out with weird, wild and wonderful Wichitans. A thing like that makes a lasting impression. Just like a hijack does.

In Waynesboro, Pennsylvania, the Red Run Drive-In Theatre – which has hosted Methodist church services for the past 20 years – says goodbye to its flock when the church board announces its departure. The reason? The theatre keeps playing those X-rated films that are all the rage these days.

Can't talk about movie on plane

Guilt, association, et cetera.

In Rome, Georgia, the adult film *The Dirty Mind of Young Sally* – held over for a second week – is advertised thusly: "It strikes like a tornado."

Across America, weather patterns all year have led to tons of tornadoes striking at the nation's heartland. "We can't say why the world's weather is out-of-whack this year," says Allen Pearson, Director of the National Severe Storm Forecast Center in Kansas City. Whenever tornadoes head east, Georgia falls squarely in the path of all that windborne death and annihilation.

Everything goes straight up.

In Argentina, engine problems complicate the hijacking saga that involves a Colombian jet. After seven stops, 14 people are all that are left aboard the four-engine Electra that was taken over on Wednesday by two kids in masks.

Where do you go from there?

Near Rio, a Sud Aviation SE-210 Caravelle crashes and explodes after the #1 engine stalls on landing approach. It plummets into the jungle embrace of the Amazon city of Sao Luiz. 23 people die instantly.

On impact.

FILE IT UNDER FEAR
Saturday, June 2, 1973.

In this film taken from the British television series *Thriller*, a madman goes on a rampage, killing young women in a nameless British hamlet. Suspects and suspicions abound. The frowzy/dowdy/frumpy (circle one or more) local librarian finds herself trapped one night in the library with the maniac who makes her file *everything* under "fear." Townies continually hit her with a very specialized type of violence: the passive-aggressiveness of their perceptions of The Librarian as Old Maid. What a bunch of assholes. Taut, tense, twisted and terrifying, it's a pulse-pounder until the final moments, after which you'll want to head to your local library to just get a little peace and quiet.

It's a banner day for kids running out into the street from between parked cars in Ventura County, California.

Skull fractures. Shoulder fractures. Internal injuries. These are the things parents are always afraid will happen to their children.

All those kids survive.

It's surprising how infrequently these random violent events occur in a life. The Roman Stoic philosopher Seneca once wrote, "There is nothing so wretched or foolish as to anticipate misfortunes. What madness it is in your expecting evil before it arrives!"

Of course, when it does arrive, it's a real pisser.

But it's a thing that you deal with – as all good stoics must – and then you go on to the next

Terrifying events of murder leave librarian (MAUREEN LIPPMAN) to believe that she is the next victim in ITC Entertainment's thriller, "File It Under Fear."

File It Under Fear

thing that happens before the thing after that, which is itself followed by yet another thing that happens.

It's not just the kids *between* the cars who are in peril. In Wilson, Oklahoma, two children die when tornado-borne winds topple a tree onto the car in which they're sitting, crushing them in the back seat.

Businessman Theodore N. Vail once wrote, "Real difficulties can be overcome; it is only the imaginary ones that are unconquerable."

In Plainview, Texas, eight people die when their car collides with a fertilizer truck. It spins like a tornado before coming to rest on the side of the highway.

"Let us be of good cheer," James Russell Lowell once said. "However, remembering that the misfortunes hardest to bear are those which never come."

That is, until they do.

KHOON KHOON
Saturday, June 2, 1973.

In this Indian rip-off and/or remake of 1971's *Dirty Harry* – it's so close an homage that Warner Bros. sues production company Eagle Films in August – a tough cop in Bombay chases down a sniper who can't help himself from killing people. Dirty Harry clone Anand (played by Mahendra Sandhu) isn't too thrilling – nor is his constantly leering comic relief partner, who uses police binoculars to spy on women undressing – but that's a good thing because Danny Denzongpa is a real revelation here as the unhinged baby-stabbing psychopath, embracing a range of extreme emotions from fury to fear to egomania. Sometimes all at once! Imagine all that Bollywood dancing still going on even with all those violent repulsive murders happening at the same time. What troupers!

In Resistencia, 500 miles north of Buenos Aires, two sleep-deprived long-haired hijackers pack up their $50,000 ransom, pile into a pickup truck thoughtfully provided by police, and drive off into the night.

SAM Colombian airline Commander Hugo Molina heaves a relieved sigh as their guns – which have been trained on him for the better part of 30 hours – leave, too.

The hijackers are also globetrotters. Molina says that it was almost as if they "had taken a map of South America, placed a finger almost anyplace and said, 'Let's go there.'"

Paraguay. Ecuador. Peru. At each stop, a few more passengers are allowed off. In Aruba, the ransom money arrives.

Originally, they demand $160,000 and the liberation of some 140 prisoners languishing in the anguish of Colombian jails. Before they go, the hijackers promise to kill the stewardesses and flight crew if something happens to them. They tell them that they'd kill their families, too.

Non-negotiable.

On Friday, Francisco Jose Solano Lopez Dominguez, 31, is caught in Asunción, Paraguay after having spent $12,000 of his half of the ransom. He's a former pro soccer player. Eusebio Borjas, 27, is the other hijacker.

Still in the wind.

They'd told everyone that they were working on behalf of the Marxist National Liberation Army faction in Colombia. It turns out that they wanted the money for themselves.

After 1973, they're heard of no more.

Got out while the getting was good.

THE WEDNESDAY CHILDREN
Wednesday, June 6, 1973.

"Wednesday's child is full of woe," goes the old nursery rhyme – something that plays out with exceptional strangeness in this horror show about neighborhood kids being neglected by their horrid bourgeois parents. A sinister bearded hippie farmhand teaches them a spell that "transfers" all the thoughtless adults to some nameless elsewhere – only for him to realize too late that he's created an army of childish supernatural dickweeds who have him in a predicament that's screwed up six ways from Sunday. A preacher man tells the kids, "You're only children! You can't decide anything!" Says you! The hippie counters with "Everything in every store will be yours. Free. Isn't that what freedom means? Everything free?" I don't know – does it? Director Robert D. West was a Universalist-Unitarian minister who taught film at John Carroll University in Cleveland. With an ominous soundtrack that's way more rockin' than you'd ever expect.

In Blackpool, England, Jimmy Clitheroe – the comedian and vaudevillian who played *The Clitheroe Kid* on BBC Radio for 14 years – starts drinking on the day of his beloved mother's funeral. Brandies. Many brandies. They chase sleeping pill after sleeping pill. Barbiturates.

They find him in bed.

Dead to the world.

When he was born, he was what used to be called a "forceps baby." Forceps babies are extracted during some births using obstetrical forceps, which look a little like salad tongs.

STRAND-WADSWORTH
335-0741 AMPLE FREE PARKING
FILMED IN WADSWORTH AREA
TOM KELLY·MARJI DOOBELL
THE WEDNESDAY
CHILDREN
COLOR 2·00·3·45·5·30·7·15·9·00

When Clitheroe was delivered this way, the forceps accidentally damaged his thyroid gland. As a result, he never grew taller than 4'3".

He looks like a child for all 51 years of his life. From vaudeville halls to film roles, he wears his constant costume – even on radio – of short trousers, schoolboy cap and blazer.

Benito Mussolini's son Vittorio is in London, coördinating the publication of a book about the affairs of Il Duce.

"My father was not like Hitler," he tells reporters. It's all merely a misunderstanding, you see. "For 20 years before that alliance with Hitler, he did many good things for Italy."

As with any good comic worth his weight in laughs, Jimmy Clitheroe had a catchphrase.

"Don't some mothers 'ave 'em!"

YASAGURE ANEGO DEN: SÔKATSU RINCHI
Thursday, June 7, 1973.

Female Yakuza Tale: Inquisition and Torture might outwardly seem like just another Yakuza crime drama – with all the annihilation of the individual that that implies. It stars Reiko Ike – who previously thrilled you as the vengeful valkyrie in *Furyô anego den: Inoshika Ochô* – who returns here as the Inoshika Ochô character in yet another cinematic testament to revenge and balance. They call these films "pink films," but maybe someone was watching an old faded print when they saw this because it's nothing if not filled to overflowing with rich red blood, blood, blood. Most Americans didn't know what they were in for when they saw it in theatres under the title *Naked Free For All*. Here, she gets revenge on the people who've tortured her and framed her as a maniac killer; the deeper she goes into finding them, the more she finds herself embroiled in clan warfare. The sequence where Ochô finds the daughter of the dead clan leader strangled and electrocuted in the insane asylum is especially grim. With more slow-motion murders than you can slowly shake a stick at, much nudity, heroin smugglers using doped-up prostitutes as disposable drug mules, and mental patients as figures of sorrow and ridicule.

In Albany, New York, the State Court of Appeals rules that the law that gives copkillers the death penalty is unconstitutional.

It's the culmination of a process that has wound its way through the courts for years, spurred by the case of a man who killed two policemen in 1969.

It's enough to make you want to hire someone with sharp and pointy implements to do what the courts won't.

Vengeance is the thread that runs through the '70s cinema like garrote wire. A man murders his way through the evil that men do and is judged by popular opinion to be right in that his ends – his *results* – justify his means. A community fights back against ominous odds or criminals that endlessly exploit the system. The state becomes too bogged-down with bureaucracy, too slow to move, too wrapped up in its own laws to act as an effective servant of the people.

In point of fact, there is no justice system.

There is a legal system, though.

Clashing with this narrative in '70s cinema is a distinctly post-Vietnam attitude: that the good guys don't always win. The conclusion of a struggle remains perilously in doubt.

That good people die for nothing, in the end.

They pulled a man's body from the Allegheny River in Pennsylvania today. He was 60. No one had seen him since Wednesday morning.

Elsewhere on the Allegheny, they're dragging the river looking for a boy who drowned in the afternoon. He was 17. He'd been swimming with friends.

In Santa Cruz, a star-like object is found by astronomers. It's almost 10 billion light years from Earth and recedes from us at 90% the speed of light.

They call OQ172 "one of the brightest objects known." A quasar. The most distant object currently known. "Our universe seems to be expanding," Dr. E. Joseph Wampler says, as the body of a boy sinks deeper into the rising waters of the Allegheny River.

HIGH PRIESTESS OF SEXUAL WITCHCRAFT
Friday, June 8, 1973.

Georgina Spelvin plays Ellen, whose sailor son Wayne has returned from the high seas and is now looking for love. When she isn't dominating her ineffectual, spiritually withered husband, she recommends that Wayne talk to young Sally, a neighbor girl. They get along famously. Later, his suspicions aroused – so to speak! – he finds out that his mother is in reality the High Priestess of Sexual Witchcraft, inducting young Sally into whatever infernal nonsense she has planned. The poster for the film is a real eye-opener, with the perfectly-balanced Priestess splayed and writhing, her explicit nudity hidden by the implicit ramifications – so to speak! – of a big dripping black candle, the flame of which is positioned over her throat, importantly signifying what a red-hot orator she is. So to speak. It must have been distinctly weird to see this film in New York City's adult theatres and notice, in the opening shots, a skyline so profoundly altered by the Twin Towers, which opened on April 4. Includes a bald flasher, family frolics (in the uncut version), and bongos playing behind the Satanic shenanigans that pretty much show how square these people really are at heart. The final title card says "The End?" and should be included in a film festival of existential blockbusters that end with a question mark.

In Orlando, two people die when a broadcasting tower – once billed as the tallest structure on Earth – collapses.

When you hear workers screaming the word "headache," you know something bad is going down.

the movie place... where couples go...

FRIDAY & SATURDAY
10:30 P.M. ONLY!

PUSSYCAT CLUB

COLOMA, MICHIGAN
468-7231

THIS WEEKS SHOW
"HIGH PRIESTESS"
WITH
Georgina Spelvin

1,484 feet of metal and cable and death – over 22 stories taller than the Empire State Building, formerly the standard by which all colossal spectacles were judged – plunge to the ground.

Eugene Hobby, 21, is installing coaxial cable 40 feet up when the tower collapses. "I just grabbed hold of a piece of that tower and held on," he reveals from his hospital bed. "It was like the sky coming down."

"A noose around my neck."

That's what security guard George O'Leary says about his family.

"My family is a noose around my neck and someday I'm gonna kill them all."

That's what the neighbor remembered him saying.

By Sunday, the decomposing bodies of O'Leary, his wife and five children are found in their home in the Dorchester neighborhood of Boston. He shot them all. Right before he sat down, took an overdose of drugs and died.

The only survivors are O'Leary's eight watch-dogs and his 14-year-old daughter, who was staying for a week at Boston City Hospital. She promptly went straight back to the hospital after finding out what her father did.

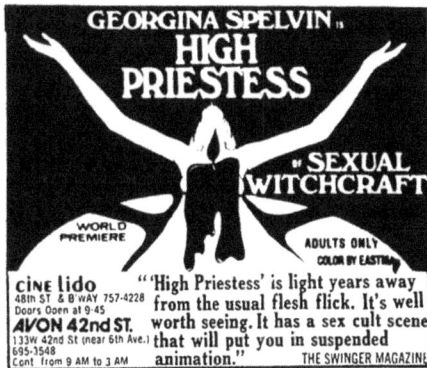

In Mount Vernon, a Penn Central express train from New York City rams a commuter train. Running behind schedule. Someone dies. 119 go to the hospital. Many are pinned beneath debris in the sweltering June weather for excruciatingly long minutes until they're rescued.

An engineer runs from the front of the car, screaming to everyone who'll hear him, "We're going to crash! We're going to crash!"

The violence of gravity.

CAPITOL

MAÑANA, TARDE
¡ESTRENO!
LA QUINTA ESENCIA
DEL ESCALOFRIO...

¡GRITOS DE MIEDO INCONTENIBLES!
¡ATAQUES IMPETUOSOS DE VESANIA... PSICOPATAS
SEXUALES... BELLAS MUJERES ATERRORIZADAS!

GRAN GALA DEL TERROR

LA CASA DE
TERCIOPELO
(THE VELVET HOUSE)
Y
EL ESPECTRO
DEL TERROR

EASTMANCOLOR

(Autorizado para mayores de 18 años)

EL ESPECTRO DEL TERROR
Saturday, June 9, 1973.

Maria is a stewardess. She gets stalked by Charly, a deranged and damaged Vietnam vet who moonlights as a photographer and occasional strangler of women. The point-of-view of the film switches back and forth between Maria and Charly, who owns a lot of weird crappy dolls, suffers through flashbacks starring whistling bombs, and finally snaps. The sound design becomes especially important throughout – various assorted noises include a jarring Wild West piano, sinister bubbling liquids, and piano strings plucked to nerve-wracking effect. Charly ultimately captures Maria and the finale is one of those downbeat '70s endings that Spanish cinema tended to use when they wanted to talk about what it was like to live under a dictatorship but couldn't find the words. Ultimately, it's a film about how people handle fear itself – and the level of strength that's forged within a person when they come out the other side of a terrifying, violent experience.

At Florida Technological University in Orlando, Professor Laurence Wyatt teaches a course titled "Death and Dying." This semester's lesson? 60 students. All dead. All told to look deeply into their own lives and take from their lives as they are now lived lessons that inform how they might approach their own deaths.

A field trip to a funeral home. Writing their own obituaries.

A deathless sense of perspective.

"What it showed them," says Wyatt, "Is that they're wasting their lives. Things that suddenly became important were things they could be doing now."

Of course – Cold Wars and winding roads of life-not-yet-lived notwithstanding – in the larger scheme of things, the question remains: so what really *is* important?

Ultimately. Ultimately.

Wyatt continues, holding forth on the short-sighted, short-term, sold-short priorities of 60 students who barely know their ass from a tree. They value things like driver's licenses, seeing the world, and not facing death.

The usual.

"We tell kids Daddy went away, or the dying relative that we'll go fishing as soon as he's up and about. These are lies. It's a way to dismiss an unpleasant reality by saying, 'Oh, it's too morbid to discuss'," Wyatt says, philosophically fuming.

What do the dead students think of it all?

"It was the most interesting course and I'm not even an English major," one croaks.

No one knows Janice Marie Young's name today.

All they know is that she's dead. A runaway, pushed in front of a speeding car by Lawrence Dorn, 24, after an argument on the streets of St. Petersburg, Florida. It takes 42 years, a tirelessly curious younger brother, and the advent of DNA evidence testing for Janice, eternally 15 years old, to get her name back.

PRIMA VISIONE

ORFEO: Oggi

Una inedita storia di amore,
sensualità, passione
e turbamenti

DEVIAZIONE

MARIA PEKY · ARAMIS NEY

Vietato anni 18 · Scope · Colori · Astor

With a knife in one hand and a broken soda bottle in the other, she possessed few things before she died except for a habit of telling people different things about her identity so she didn't have to go back to her adoptive family in Newport News, Virginia.

Dorn is eventually freed and not charged with her death because police couldn't prove that he meant to harm her when he shoves in front of that oncoming car. The composite sketch of the unknown girl, offered up by the police, reveals little in the way of her appearance apart from the barest of details. This is partly because her body was so destroyed by the car that struck her; partly because police artist sketches so rarely capture the fury in the eyes of a person coming at you with a broken bottle. It gathers no leads. Presents no clues. Offers no hope.

Dead ends.

In Aurora, Texas, an enigma of an entirely other variety pits two different UFO investigation groups – the Midwest UFO Network (MU-FON) and the International UFO Bureau (IU-FOB) – against one another. They're at odds because of the legendary crash of a flying saucer in 1897 in Aurora that may or may not have left the corpse of some alien or other buried in Aurora Cemetery. Each group possesses different examples of evidence. Each group casts aspersions on the veracity and validity of the other's evidence. Some of the metal is tested at North Texas State University by physics professor Dr. Tom Gray, who says that the metal that is recovered from the area is 3/4 iron, but isn't magnetic like iron. "We cannot draw any conclusions," he says.

Most of the older residents of Aurora know some of what happened. Few of them saw the ruined body of a pilot that purportedly died in that crash.

They wouldn't know its name even it had one.

Adelaide, Australia police search feverishly for 11-month-old Darren "Jason" Shannon, stolen from his grandparents' home by his estranged father John "Barry" Shannon, 25. He's chased down by his father-in-law A.H. Hindle as he flees with the child.

Shortly thereafter, John is killed in a head-on car crash. Baby Darren, however, is not found in the wreckage of his father's vehicle.

In fact, he's never seen again.

It's as though the child simply flew away.

NO ONE ADMITTED! WE WON'T LET YOU IN AFTER THE FEATURE BEGINS! A LOVE STORY THAT TURNS TO DIABOLICAL HORROR... It's A SHOCKER!

SO SAD ABOUT GLORIA

COLOR
PG
DEAN JAGGER
LORI SAUNDERS

You Must See "Gloria" From the Beginning!
CAUTION! MAY BE TOO SHOCKING FOR PRE-TEENAGERS
The Terror Of Psycho!

SO SAD ABOUT GLORIA
Tuesday, June 12, 1973.

Rick picks up his niece Gloria from the nuthatch, where she's spent the last year-and-a-half because she watched her dad die. Apparently, she's recovered from her fear of death. Apparently! She dreams of a man in a cape, all dressed in black, holding an axe. Better than dreaming of a big snake wearing a vest rolling a big donut, I guess. Her dad left her loads of money. They go home, but nearby, a lady gets killed by an axe-murderer – not to be confused with an axe murderer, which is a killer that really hates axes. Gloria gets a new horse. On the trot, she meets up with a writer named Chris Kenner. They fall in love. Marrying after a whirlwind romance, she starts having visions of murderousness once again but everyone tells her she's bonkers. One day, while she's alone making dinner for herself

and Rick, the masked axeman runs in. Back to catatonia it is! The end? Shot in the Ozarks, it's a film that much of the crew started on after coming off last year's Arkansas opus *Encounter with the Unknown*, produced by the same people. *So Sad About Gloria* has at least one major plot point in common with *The Night God Screamed*, but likely this is merely a happy coincidence in which we the audience benefit all the same yesterday, and today, and for ever.

"They didn't know what hit them," Fire Commissioner Joseph Rizzo said about the two Philadelphia firemen who died in an explosion at a plant that manufactured printers' ink. Robert Malley, 37, and John W. Welsh, 33.

While trying to break through a cement wall to fight the fire, the firemen let in the air that feeds the fire that makes the wall explode onto them in the narrow alley. Debris strikes other firemen and a policeman, injuring several.

Flames and black smoke tower over the city, darkening the moonlit sky. The scent of violence drifts to all parts of the city, smoke and burning ink combining to create a signature odor by which tonight's inferno will always be remembered.

THE ROMANCE OF "LOVE STORY"
THE TERROR OF "PSYCHO"
"SO SAD ABOUT GLORIA"
Lori Saunders • Dean Jagger
Plus Selected Short Subjects
Today At 1, 2:50, 4:40, 6:30 8:15 and 10:05
VARSITY
6610 DELMAR

BREVARD
DRIVE-IN THEATRE
EAU GALLIE · 254 1361

A STORY OF
TERROR!
7:00 & LAST

A STORY OF
LOVE!

8:55
"LET'S SCARE
JESSICA TO
DEATH"

PG "SO SAD ABOUT GLORIA"

12/5

The sense of smell is almost unassailable in terms of long-term memory. A sudden whiff of something can summon up memories long thought dormant or suppressed. The scent of perfume, of fire, of sweat and of sex – all these things bring back experiences and histories and memories when breathed in once more.

Think of how much of your life is guided by smell.

What does death smell like to you?

Saenger
THEATRE

TONITE 7:00
SAT. 1:00 AND 7:00
ADM. 1.00-1.50

3 BIG ACTION ON WHEELS SHOWS
"THUNDER IN DIXIE"
AND

THE ACTION IS GO...
HELL ON WHEELS
TECHNICOLOR

SHE-DEVILS
on Wheels
IN BLOOD BLINDING
COLOR

MARTY ROBBINS
JOHN ASHLEY · GIGI PERREAU · CONNIE SMITH
...THE STONEMANS

SUNDAY-MONDAY-TUESDAY
"SO SAD ABOUT GLORIA"
Don't Miss One Of The Most Realistic And Chilling Ax Murders Ever Recorded On Film. . .Has The Romance Of "Love Story" And Terror Of "Psycho". Rated R

SEXUAL AWARENESS
Thursday, June 14, 1973.

Ocult Films presents this seamy tale of occultists luring in new recruits to have sex in their sect. A cultist named Jerome seduces the first girl while "Life Stories" by psych-rock group Cynara plays in the background and she repeatedly tells him that it can't be real. A metaphysical film. You know you've got a hell of a cult going on when guys named Jerome can join. "You will obey only the will of the master ...obey...obey...obey..." the cult leader says as he zaps another chump in the forest while "Mermaid Song" by Cynara plays. I wonder if the guys in Cynara know about this film. "Silver Tongue" by Humble Pie plays during the threesome scenes! The cult leader is a real blowhard and keeps bugging people to have sex on his altar. This is what's known as an altar ego. A detective comes in during one of the guru's preening meditations on otherworldly claptrap and accuses him of holding women against their will. The guru offers him one of the girls to keep quiet. The detective gets taken over and indulges himself. Imagine a world so small!

In Jacumba, in southeastern San Diego County, two children suffocate in an abandoned refrigerator at their aunt's home. Their mother is taken to the hospital.

In shock.

So many children died from becoming trapped after hiding in abandoned refrigerators that the Refrigerator Safety Act of 1956 passed and mobs of people would hunt for junked refrigerators, taking off the doors and destroying the locks and latches. The construction of older refrigerators made them impossible to open from the inside,

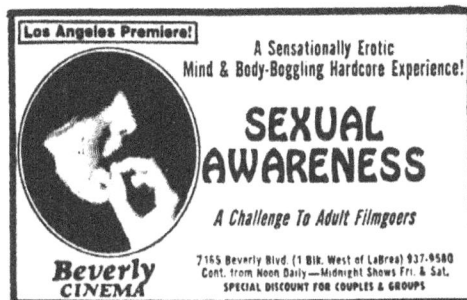

and they were doubly deadly because the airtight seal meant that it was difficult to hear cries of distress from the outside.

The way we lived before we knew any better.

They're getting the last of the passengers out of a stalled cable car that's been suspended 650 feet above the Sandia Mountains of New Mexico.

Lightning struck the cable car yesterday as it traveled through a storm, knocking the cable car off its guidelines. Freezing it in its tracks.

Marian Morrow is three months old.

She's with her family, up there, stuck in the storm. "The darling of the tram," they call her. "She was marvelous," beams her mother. "She never cried unless she was hungry."

Desperate rescue workers bring baby formula and other supplies while the trapped group sits and waits. And dances. And sings. "We made up stories and told jokes," says Mrs. Ron Caraglio.

"We went through about all the dirty jokes we knew."

NIGHTMARE CIRCUS
Wednesday, June 27, 1973.

Also known under its more evocative title *Barn of the Naked Dead*, this violently nihilistic film stars Andrew Prine as a character destroyed as a person by abuse. He's so shattered that he takes out his rage on a group of unsuspecting showgirls that stumble into his desert web. Easily dismissed as regrettable trash, *Nightmare Circus* can be viewed as an allegory about the implosion of the nuclear family – well, post-nuclear – in America in the '70s. Consider the radioactive and mutated father; girls, like desire itself, hidden away in a barn and endlessly beaten down because of massive overwhelming guilt; issues of control, issues with mother, and issues for which there seems no resolution for the damaged individual except inflicting pain, pain, and more pain. With Chuck Niles – the absolute soul of jazz as a disc jockey for more than four decades in Southern California – as the showgirls' agent, assault by snake, and a disturbing and bracing soundtrack by the underrated Tommy Vig. Unforgettable.

"Duke is a wonderful dog, very gentle – but he is very frightened of storms."

That's what Mrs. Rolando Rodriquez tells the press in Miami after her German Shepherd jumps onto a city bus to get away from the sound of thunder.

Duke leaps into the driver's seat and grabs driver A.L. Rivera's hand in his mouth when he tries to pet him. 25 passengers – and the driver – hurry out. "A dog took over my bus," Rivera exclaims to a passing fellow bus driver.

Beautiful victims to a monstrous wildman!

TERROR CIRCUS
PLUS! *Flesh Feast*

R

Terror Circus at 7:10 10:15
Feast 8:50

"66"
CENTRAL & COORS N

Police arrive. See what happened. Are duly astonished.

Says one cop, "If you've got a dog on the bus, I guess the best thing to do is to keep him there."

Outside the town of Farmington in Stanislaus County, California, it's Bob Ramont's 23rd birthday. He's herding cattle on his horse. Fires race up and down the Sierra Nevadas.

A bolt of lightning kills him. Kills his horse, too.

The epitaph written on his tombstone says simply, "A Cowboy."

In Commerce City, Colorado, Marine Sgt. Abel Kavanaugh loads a bullet into his .25, puts the weapon to his temple and pulls the trigger.

He wanted out. His superiors want him back in Camp Pendleton 60 days after the medical leave he's needed since returning from his years as a POW. He's the second former returning POW to have killed himself recently.

He shot himself at his father-in-law's home.

There's a statement in there. Something that goes beyond words.

He's one of eight former POWs accused by Col. Theodore W. Guy of collaborating with the Cong while in captivity. Guy claims that they were traitors. Says it as loud as he can, even while other POWs are being welcomed home with joy and sadness and fervor. The U.S. government tells Guy to take back the charges. He eventually does, but not in time to save Marine Sgt. Abel Kavanaugh. Guy will suffer a slow death from cancer, dying in 1999.

Joseph Remco is the attorney for another POW in the group. "I don't know if the others can take it or not," he confesses.

The violence of identity.

They put William Workman into a psychiatric hospital today.

The former carpenter, 43, apparently bought into the more superficial aspects of the Christ narrative and tells a judge that he's "God's son" and that he "had to take matters into (his) own hands." It was only yesterday that he murdered seven people with a .22 rifle in and around his home in Palos Hills, a suburb of Chicago.

Both of his parents. A pregnant neighbor. Her 12-year-old daughter. Three other friends of the family – an old married couple and their 47-year-old son. He wanders around the neighborhood during the night. Shooting. Just like that.

When the police arrive, he goes home. Just like that.

The cops urge him to surrender. They toss him some tear gas. He walks out, carrying a beer. He tells anyone who'll listen that he's going to kill others while he's locked up. That he'll even kill himself.

It takes him a while to die. Eight years later, on July 6, 1981, a prison guard making his rounds finds him dead in his cell.

Natural causes, they say.

There's a William Workman High School in City of Industry, California. It must have been strange to hear the case of the slightly-more-murderous William Workman brought up to anyone at the time in the Class of '73.

Cases like the Workman murders were, largely and overwhelmingly, buried in the mouldering newspaper morgues of communities who suffered through those times of violence. Never to be spoken of again. Secrets carried to the grave.

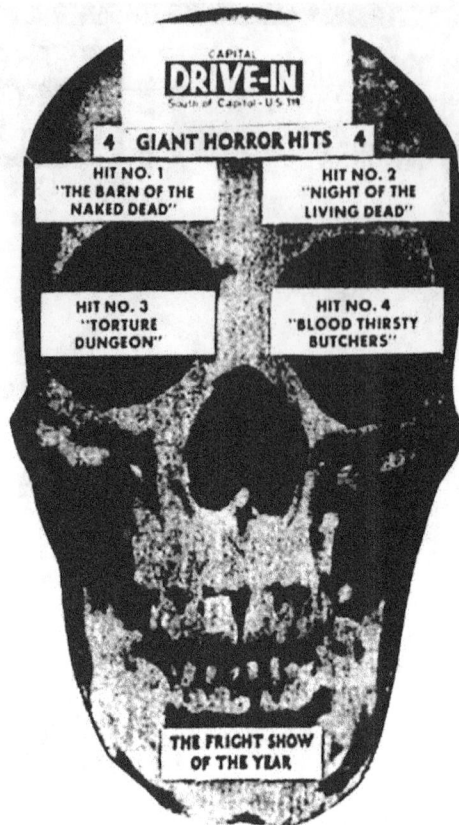

Crimes against polite society.

Against civilization.

LAS FLORES DEL MIEDO
Thursday, June 28, 1973.

Ray and Liz live in a mansion out in a lonely part of the country. Tony, a stranger, comes over and wants to consult with them about the nature of fear. His brother jumped out of a window to his death so he's already vaguely vexed. Liz is a famous medium and got so rich off her psychic gifts that she's retired but she's also kind of bored. She and Ray delve deep into the depths of divination to help Tony out. They do all kinds of experiments with spiritualism and telepathy and generally freak each other out a whole bunch. Liz is in psychic contact with a pisser of a ghost named Helen, who communicates with her via her painting. Presently, a love triangle manifests. Ray shoots Liz and Tony, then himself. Then they show up back in the same mansion where they started. So did they die, or didn't they? A neat plot twist at the end makes this one of the deeper and more esoteric entries in the canon of the cinema of violence, and was pretty damned hard to find until recently. One character reads a Bible psalm which says, "My heart rejoices for thou wilt not leave my soul in Hell." Yeah, but does that mean you have to hang out with *these* dummies for all Eternity?

> A loving father
> Tender and kind
> What a wonderful
> Memory you left
> Behind

That's what it says on the gravestone of John Zygmaniak. He died in February of a heart attack. He was only in his mid-50s. The loss devastates the Zygmaniak family, a tight-knit Polish family who had already suffered and

survived the horrors of land-thieving Nazi occupiers during World War II.

Today, his son Lester, 23, is indicted by a grand jury in Monmouth County, New Jersey.

Lester killed his brother George. Shot him point-blank in the head with a sawed-off 20-gauge shotgun while he lay paralyzed in his hospital bed. George's body was so ruined because of a motorcycle accident at the family's home on June 17. Neck snapped.

"All I am is a head," George said.

He asked Lester to do it. Begged him. Didn't want to be a burden on the family. Didn't want to be crippled for life.

The moment before Lester pulls the trigger, he tells his brother, "I love you, George. God bless you, George."

A "mercy killing," they call it. Motivated by kindness. Motivated by altruism. Motivated by the kind of love that transcends fear.

There are flowers on the Zygmaniak gravestone.

I wonder what kind they are.

Two books, newly published: *Crash* by J.G. Ballard and *Rendezvous with Rama* by Arthur C. Clarke.

One deals with the peculiar blossoms that grow out of injuries gathered by purposefully crashing motor vehicles for erotic effect. The other involves a massive interstellar craft explored by Earthlings in 2131 as it hurtles toward the galaxy that is Large Magellanic Cloud. A lonely alien flower is picked by one as a souvenir on his way out of the machine.

Sometimes having an unreal future is better than the reality of right now.

"Une Histoire d'O, mais vécue par l'auteur." Le NOUVEL OBSERVATEUR

2nd WEEK

18 ANS Adultes

LA PUNITION

KARIN SCHUBERT · GEORGES GERET COULEUR

LA PUNITION
Thursday, June 28, 1973.

In this streamlined slice of porno chic, Karin Schubert plays Britt, a prostitute who doesn't do exactly as her pimp dictates. This leads her to be spirited away to a mansion off in the nowheres. Her room has only a bare mesh bedframe and a bunch of bondage devices so she can be "punished" by seemingly anyone who trots on by. She's kept constantly nude, cowers and cries a lot, and is whipped so severely that she's draped in ribbons of blood. An expressive, immersive and depressing tribute to the lengths to which people will go just so they don't have to be bored and alone.

Sandra Lee Kavanaugh weeps.

She weeps as she announces her intention to sue Col. Theodore W. Guy of Tucson for his accusations of treason he'd levied against her late husband, Marine Sgt. Abel Kavanaugh, who killed himself with a gunshot to the head yesterday. News services from coast to coast pick up her story. Amplify it. Carry it for weeks.

"I do not plan to let this end with his death. I blame Colonel Guy and The Pentagon for his death," she announces, emphasizing, "Without their insistence on pursuing those fictitious charges, my husband would be here today."

She's two months pregnant with Kavanaugh's child.

"He was outraged at the charges," she says. Those charges include "disrespect toward an officer, disobeying an order, and insubordination." Guy was the highest-ranking officer in the Viet Cong prison camp at which Kavanaugh and seven others mentioned in Guy's charges were held.

"He went to Vietnam and the North Vietnamese kept him for five years. Then he came home and his own people killed him," she says.

She dies in 2002 at age 50.

On her gravestone are two words.

His Wife.

DIE ZÄRTLICHKEIT DER WÖLFE
Friday, June 29, 1973.

Kurt Raab gives one of the most gut-wrenching, compelling performances in all of 1973 as Inspector Fritz Haarmann, a character based on early 20th-century German serial killer Fritz Haarmann. Raab entices and coerces young males home to his threadbare flat, does unspeakable things to them, bites their throats out, then chops them up and sells the meat to the lady running the bar down the road. The neighbor downstairs gets suspicious of all the comings-and-goings-on but the cops blow her off. When too many people go missing, they finally realize something's going on. Director Uli Lommel, who wasn't even 30 when he made *Die Zärtlichkeit der Wölfe*, really paints a depressing picture with this one; Raab co-wrote the screenplay and Lommel's longtime friend, the director Rainer Werner Fassbinder (who also produced and co-edited the film), shows up in a supporting role as a shlubby dirtbag. Raab's luminescent baldness and desperate penetrating gaze are visions on par with Max Schreck's Nosferatu or Peter Lorre's Hans Beckert (in M, the 1931 film also based on Haarmann's crimes). Post-World War I Germany was positively flooded with maniacs, a roster that included perennial psychotics such as Karl Denke, Carl Großmann, and Peter Kürten.

At the unfinished Harbor Bridge leading to Jones Island in Milwaukee's inner harbor, construction workers feel the scaffolding beneath them begin to shake and buckle. The cables holding the platform to the side of the bridge snap. They'd been rubbing against the side of the bridge during all the work and had, consequently, frayed from the friction.

Three of the men die when the wreckage takes them straight down.

One man, Raymond Firari, 19, survives. He holds on to the large iron jacks used for the scaffolding's support. Holds on for dear life. He pulls himself onto a large beam as he watches his co-workers fall.

Worker Dennis Jaehnke's widow says, "He was brave. He wasn't afraid of anything." His brother Douglas, 20, watches the bridge collapse. Treated at the hospital for shock, he later has to identify his brother's body. Trancelike in obligation.

It's a young construction crew, made of working-class men. Men brimming with promise. Men with places to go. Men with their whole lives ahead of them.

Killed by a fall.

There are bloodstains that mark where they fall on that hot Wisconsin day. Chances are, everyone that knows what happened there – whenever they pass that spot, even after those stains have long faded – will always look, always remember. Always wonder.

Wonder about what could have been.

"She smiled at us and went out the door."

That's what Donald Jolly, 57, recalls about his daughter Rita, 17, after she goes missing tonight in West Linn, Oregon. At 7:30, she goes out for a walk and never comes back.

Not a runaway. Not a troubled child. She's just gone. Near-perfect grades at Clackamas Community College. A loner. An independent thinker.

Also a mystery. For as long as anyone can remember.

By 1979, there's some suspicion that Ted Bundy might have done away with her, but detectives didn't have time to ask him in 1989 if he did or did not before he's executed in Florida.

Donald Jolly writes a letter that he passes out to anyone who might know what happened to Rita Lorraine Jolly.

"The price of senseless violence everywhere is paid in mourning and sorrow, often never known to the hard and uncaring ones who may have caused a lifetime of melancholy memories for the survivors."

THE SEX VICTIMS
Saturday, June 30, 1973.

Derek Robbins directs this short film about a lorry driver who encounters an eerie naked blonde on horseback, swannin' about the shrubbery. He pursues her through the countryside on his own horse and catches her. They have sex. He then finds out that she knows a pal of his. Of course it turns out that she's connected to his friend in the most depressing of all possible ways. The jazz-and-menacing-synth soundtrack is particularly strident given the subject matter, and the shots of the working-class outlands in Britain in 1973 are exceptional. Also features an early role for esteemed British actor Alun Armstrong, who plays the scummy friend here; he later went to a career playing cops and other authority figures. A sad, mystical film that usually screened in British cinemas before feature presentations like *She Should Have Stayed in Bed* (originally titled *Let Me Love You*).

There's a total solar eclipse today.

The moon passes between the Sun and the Earth for a total of seven minutes and four seconds. There won't be another one that lasts that long until 2150.

If there's anyone left then to know what to do when it happens.

As far north as France and as far south as the Cape of Good Hope in Africa, people labor under the temporary illusion of darkness. Seven scientists from the Los Alamos National Laboratory, University of Aberdeen, Paris Observatory, and other seats of higher learning board an early version of the supersonic Concorde jet to hurtle 1,300 miles per hour through the skies and chase the eclipse, artificially extending its life to last over 74 minutes. Astrophysicist Pierre Léna's memoir – *Racing the Moon's Shadow with Concorde 001* – publishes in 2015.

Others look up and wonder when the darkness is going to end.

In Virginia Beach, Virginia, the sun shines on the bodies of two 19-year-olds as a worker at the beachfront motel in which they'd been staying opens the door to check on them after they didn't check out.

Lynn Seethaler of Pittsburgh. Janice Pietropola of Verona, Pennsylvania. Described as "very nice and attractive" by people at the motel.

Strangled. Shot in the head. Raped. Stabbed in the neck with a wine bottle.

Desperate for leads, detectives even ask Jack Paul Reale, the Vietnam vet who's already killed several people, if he had anything to do with it. The investigation stretches into October.

The police have no leads. The darkness in which they labor remains total.

Until April 8, 2019.

Ernest Broadnax. 80. Arrested in New York City. A suspect in even more killings around the Virginia Beach area at that time.

In 1998, investigating Police Captain William Haden spoke about the case. "I have always

RED HOT AND SEXY!
SANDRA JULLIEN
(of "I AM A NYMPHOMANIAC")

She should have stayed in bed
COLOUR x

THE SEX VICTIMS x
AND
COLOUR

referred to them as 'my girls'...I still don't know why this case was so personal."

"There is no way I can describe that to you."

SLAUGHTER'S BIG RIP-OFF
Sunday, July 1, 1973.

Jim Brown returns as the vengeance-and-mononym-seeking Slaughter and this time he's up against Ed McMahon as Duncan, a crook who chases a lot of women and is the latest face of The Mob. They still want revenge on Slaughter for all the chaos and carnage he caused in the previous film. A vicious circle. Slaughter's trusted companions from the first film – played by Don Gordon and Stella Stevens – are nowhere to be found. Maybe they got slaughtered. You even get to hear Ed McMahon have sex. Haven't you always wanted to hear Ed McMahon have sex? I wonder what Carson thought of this one when he saw it. With generous amounts of nudity, an unbeatable opening sequence during which a biplane strafes Slaughter's garden party, and Don Stroud playing a sadistic fixer and all-around racist asshole. Buy the soundtrack – featuring songs with titles like "People Get Up and Drive Your Funky Soul," "Transmogrification" and "Sexy, Sexy, Sexy" – by Godfather of Soul James Brown & Godbrother of Someone Fred Wesley on Polydor 8-Track!

The United States Drug Enforcement Administration is launched today in Washington, D.C.

In London, doors to the British Library open for the first time.

Sometimes, you have to step back and enjoy the peace that comes with balance.

Wherever you can get it.

TEENAGE TRAMP

Wednesday, July 4, 1973.

Kim gets mixed-up with a bad crowd. She decides to take her deadbeat boyfriend Skip with her to cool out with her artsy bourgeois older sister Hilary – but not before Kim gets groped and molested by the van driver with whom they've hitchhiked. The only problem with her brilliant plan is that her brutal possessive Mansonesque ex Maury (David Sawn, who also wrote the screenplay for this terminal bummer) and his clutch of nude hippie reprobates have followed her. They commandeer Hilary's home, trash the place and chatter hep patter – and then things get really depressing. "You think you're so hip – like really part of the scene or something! Well, let me tell you something, baby – you're just as uptight and straight as the rest of them!" Kim yells at the abusive Maury, who just laughs and laughs. The scene where Maury tries to stage Hilary's suicide by force-feeding her liquor is especially stark. With Astrodelic Sound Effects by Jerry Oddo.

Frank Larry Matthews, 28, skips out on an unheard-of $325,000 bail in New York City.

He's now the most-wanted fugitive in the history of the Drug Enforcement Agency. They've put up a $20,000 reward for his capture, a figure rivaling the reward once put forth for the apprehension of John Dillinger.

Just in time for Independence Day.

Narcotics are Frank Matthews' stock-in-trade. He was supposed to show up with 14 others to answer heroin and cocaine trafficking charges, along with ever-popular income tax evasion charges to the tune of a cool $7 million. The newspapers call him "Super Fly" or "Pee Wee."

They say that he controls the heroin trade from Atlanta to Cincinnati to Baltimore to Brooklyn. They call him the "kingpin" of all the black drug dealers in these here United States of America.

They also say that he made so much money from "the dope trade" that he opened up his own bank to work through it all.

Maybe he went to see *Teenage Tramp*. Hiding in plain sight.

He's never seen again.

That you know of.

Over at the Southland 75 Drive-In in Dayton, Ohio, a fireworks van explodes.

A man and his two sons, lighting pyrotechnics during an Independence Day celebration at the theatre, set off one that only lifts a few feet into the air before it blows up prematurely. 20 feet away from the family fireworks van. Puking out sparks that ignite the entire shebang.

The family escapes, coming away from their near-death experience with a spellbinding story to tell over the years.

"They were just lucky, I guess," one fireman says.

Would you rather be lucky, right, or free?

LA MORTE HA SORRISO
ALL' ASSASSINO
Wednesday, July 11, 1973.

Ewa Aulin plays Greta von Holstein, who comes
back from the dead courtesy of an ancient Incan
formula given to her by her hunchback brother
Franz, who's coincidentally her lover. She falls
in love with another man – a doctor played by
Klaus Kinski – and dies in childbirth. Years later,
a black carriage hurtles down the lane in front
of the doctor's house. It crashes and impales the
driver on the wreckage. Greta shows up in the
back of the carriage, an amnesiac with no idea
what the hell is going on. The doctor's new wife
Eva immures Greta behind a wall because she's
so damned jealous. Here come the deaths! People
are bumped off left and right as entertainingly as
possible. Greta can't make up her mind if she's really a radiant beauty or a hellish walking corpse
from beyond the grave. This life – *such a struggle!* Director Joe D'Amato sure does come off as
cynical about relationships, repeatedly shooting
close-up after close-up of eyes as though these
shots might be the only truth he can drag out
of his actors. At one point, a pretty bouquet of
white flowers turns into a mean murderous cat
in mid-air! The film showed up on late-night
television across America as *Death Smiles on a
Murderer* for the better part of 15 years. Lucky us!
Includes murder by boisterous demonic cat; a pin
plunged into an eyeball; and stylish, sleazy and
slightly confusing action throughout.

Lon Chaney Jr. will die tomorrow.

He's only 67. You'd think that all his years
immersed in the supernatural and otherworldly
might give him an inkling of a hint of a notion
that he doesn't have much time left to live. If he

SUNDAY

L.A. PREMIERE
TODAY AT 3...
The dead come back to life...
But the bodies don't stay alive for very
long... in...

"Death Smiles
On A
Murderer"

CHANNEL 13

The Station That Plays Favorites!

knew, what would he do? Look Death square in
the eye and smile?

You can't go visit his grave, though. He donated
his body to science.

He continues to rise from the dead on a regular
basis, however, on all the late-night horror shows
that have broadcast on television across America
since the '50s.

In 1973, these shows exist at the apex and zenith
of their popularity. Their hosts are celebrities
in an alternate cosmos devoted to mischief
and mockery and monster movies. Late-night
network variety shows like *Saturday Night Live*
– the ones that will eventually help spell their
death knell – are only a few years away.

These are their names.

BOB WILKINS (on Creature Features, KTVU-2 in San Francisco)

† † †

CHILLY BILLY (born William Robert Cardille; on Chiller Theater, WPXI-11 in Pittsburgh)

† † †

COUNT GORE DEVOL (Richard E. Dyszel; on Creature Feature, and Saturday Chiller, WDCA-20 in Washington, D.C.)

† † †

COUNT SHOCKULA (Ernest R. Bennick Jr.; on Shock Theatre, WGHP-8 in Winston-Salem)

† † †

THE CREEP (Louis Ferraioli; on Creature Features, WNEW-5 in New York City)

† † †

DR. CADAVERINO (Jack DuBlon; on Nighmare Theater, WITI-6 in Milwaukee)

† † †

DR. E. NICK WITTY & EPAL (Alan Milair and Willard Lape, respectively; on Monster Movie Matinee, WSYR-3 in Syracuse)

† † †

DR. PAUL BEARER (Ernest R. Bennick Jr., on Creature Feature, WTOG-44 in St. Petersburg)

† † †

DR. SHOCK (Joseph Zawislak; on Scream-In, Mad Theater and Horror Theater, WPHL-17 in Philadelphia)

† † †

DR. VOLAPUK (Larry John, on Nightmare Theater, KCPX-4 in Salt Lake City)

† † †

THE FRIENDLY FEARMONGER (Charles W. Kissinger; on Fright Night, WDRB-41 in Louisville)

† † †

MAJOR MUDD (Edward T. McDonnell; on The Major Mudd Show, WNAC-7 in Boston)

† † †

SEYMOUR (Jerry Vance; on Fright Night, KHJ-9 in Los Angeles, and on Seymour's Monster Rally, KTLA-5 in Los Angeles)

† † †

SHOCK ARMSTRONG (Paul C. Reynolds; on Shock Theatre, WTVT-13 in Tampa)

† † †

SIR CECIL CREAPE (William R. McCown; on Creature Feature, WSM-4 in Nashville)

† † †

SIR GRAVES GHASTLY (Lawson J. Deming; on WJBK-2 in Detroit)

† † †

They only truly die when we forget them.

I hope Death smiled on Lon Chaney Jr., too.

Death is downright giddy today when an out-of-control Varig Flight 820 from Galeão International Airport in Rio de Janeiro crashes on approach to Orly Airport in Paris. Smoke in the cabin from a fire that someone accidentally set in the lavatory trash bin – a factor that eventually leads many airlines to tell you before your flight takes off that smoking is not allowed on board, including in the lavatories. The fire kills many of the passengers on the way down. Smoke inhalation. Carbon monoxide poisoning.

It lands in fields of lettuce and onions. Flaps down. Landing gear down.

Burning. Burning all the way down.

Of 134 passengers and crew, 10 crew members and 1 passenger survive. Farmers pull as many people as they can from the wreckage. The jet almost crashed into Paris itself. It could have been much worse.

It can *always* be worse.

Pilot Gilberto Araújo da Silva is hailed as a hero throughout France for his bravery and nerve in landing the jet and saving lives even in the face of terrible peril. He goes on to command a Varig freighter on January 30, 1979, flying from Japan to Los Angeles with a fortune in Brazilian abstract paintings by the artist Manabu Mabe.

Never to be seen again.

JACK THE RIPPER
Friday, July 13, 1973.

Det. Chief Supt. Charles Barlow (Stratford Johns) and Det. Chief Supt. John Watt (Frank Windsor) dust off the timeworn Jack the Ripper case and try to figure out what the hell really happened all the way back in 1888 with those murders in the Whitechapel district of London. Using the facts at hand, as well as newly-discovered evidence in the case, their acerbic humor and typically British sense of understatement resurrects the magic of their mid-'60s BBC One series *Softly, Softly*. In the process, they present an early example of the police procedural genre that's become one of the cornerstones of dramatic television. Episodes "The First Two," "Double Event," "Butchery," "Panic," "Suspects" and "The Highest in the Land?" are shown in 50-minute segments, with some evidence re-buffed and some theories – like the Loch Ness Monster being a suspect – debunked.

Friday, July 13, 1973.
In Belfast, the mother of a prison warden loses four fingers in a letter bomb explosion. The offending note is addressed to her son. Irish Republican Army factions are blamed. In East Belfast, a boy is found strangled. Unidentified.

Friday, July 20, 1973.
Bruce Lee dies at age 32. The autopsy indicates death from brain swelling – possibly caused by an adverse reaction to the medication Equagesic, later suspected to be caused by heatstroke. He only wanted to make his headache go away. On a stone book at his grave are engraved the words "Your Inspiration Continues To Guide Us Toward Our Personal Liberation." Near Amarillo, Texas, land artist Robert Smithson, 35,

BBC-1

11 0	Golf: The 1973 Open Championship.
12 55	Llangollen Eisteddfod.
1 25	News; Weather.
1 30	Mary, Mungo, and Midge.
1 45	Golf: The 1973 Open Championship.
4 15	Play School.
4 40	Jackanory.
4 55	Daktari.
5 45	News; Weather.
6 0	Nationwide.
6 45	Disney Carnival.
6 55	Top of the Pops.
7 30	Star Trek.
8 15	The Blackpool Tower Circus.
9 0	News; Weather.
9 25	Jack the Ripper.

dies in an airplane crash at Marsh Ranch with two others while surveying sites for his work *Amarillo Ramp*. His landmark 1970 land art *Spiral Jetty*, installed on the northeastern shore of the Great Salt Lake in Utah, remains as much an integral part of the earth as he is, now.

Friday, July 27, 1973.
At Oklahoma State Prison, rioting inmates kill 3 and hold 19 others hostage. They've taken over most of the prison by now. A mere five prisoners set in motion the upheaval that would see over 1,000 inmates join in the chaos. Presently, a second group takes control of the prison from the first group. You never hear about the riots that go easy.

Friday, August 3, 1973.
They're looking for the boys who set the fire last night at the Summerland leisure center on

the Isle of Man. 50 to 53 people died. They're not really sure how many. That's how horrific the fire was. It happened when the boys were smoking and accidentally set the shack in which they were hiding on fire. The building materials of Summerland burned swiftly. Only when flames became evident did anyone try to evacuate. 3,000 people. Locked fire doors. Firemen still 20 interminable minutes away. A crush to get out through the front doors. Trampling. Inhalation of a chemical brew created by all those scientific advances, mingling and melting into one miserable suffocating vapor of death.

Friday, August 10, 1973.
DJ Kool Herc invents hip-hop tomorrow at his sister's back-to-school party. 1520 Sedgwick Avenue in the Bronx. Breakdancing. Rapping. Just wait. You'll see.

Friday, August 17, 1973.
Near Route 30 in Kingston, Pennsylvania, a man's car almost collides with a massive animal resembling a gorilla with red, glowing eyes and ears that taper to points. It flees screaming "like a man in pain." If you're in Dawson City in Canada's Yukon Territory, go see riverboat captain Dick "River Rat" Stevenson. He's inventing the Sourtoe Cocktail today. He found a man's severed big toe preserved in a jar of salt in a trapper's cabin near the headwaters of the Sixtymile River. The toe – and several like it, over the decades – will be used as a garnish for whatever drink you like. Be sure that you don't swallow it. Then you'll really see things.

UNA SECRETARIA PARA MATAR
Friday, July 13, 1973.

Lee Remick plays Eleanor Sims, who gets raped on her wedding day and laughed at. Consequently, she can't stand to be touched by a man. She gets a job as a secretary to a tycoon who's in charge of making super-secret electronic whatsits in Montréal. Cory, a smooth dude with an eye for Eleanor, gains her confidence but in truth he's an industrial spy who really wants what her boss has. She witnesses him murdering an old nightwatchman and immediately she's plunged into 24 stories of terror. Knife-happy Cory hunts down the increasingly terrified woman in an empty locked-down high-rise so he can keep her quiet and/or have her as his trophy in this loose retelling of Richard Connell's reliably suspenseful story *The Most Dangerous Game*. Finally, he finds her, approaches her slowly, and with a sudden motion, she … CONTINUED NEXT WEEK.

This just in from the National Transportation Safety Board in Washington, D.C.: Roberto Clemente and everyone else who died in that New Year's Eve airplane crash perished because their aircraft was overburdened with cargo and underqualified pilots.

Too much. Too soon.

The airplane itself is in terrible shape. It sits idle for four months before Clemente's group starts it up, trying to bring relief to Nicaraguan earthquake victims.

Four engines on the DC-7.

The left inboard engine fails on takeoff.

The right inboard engine is worn-out and weak.

The left outboard engine? Damaged after the aircraft topples into a concrete ditch while taxiing on a runway earlier that December.

It's amazing they got as far as they did for as long as they did.

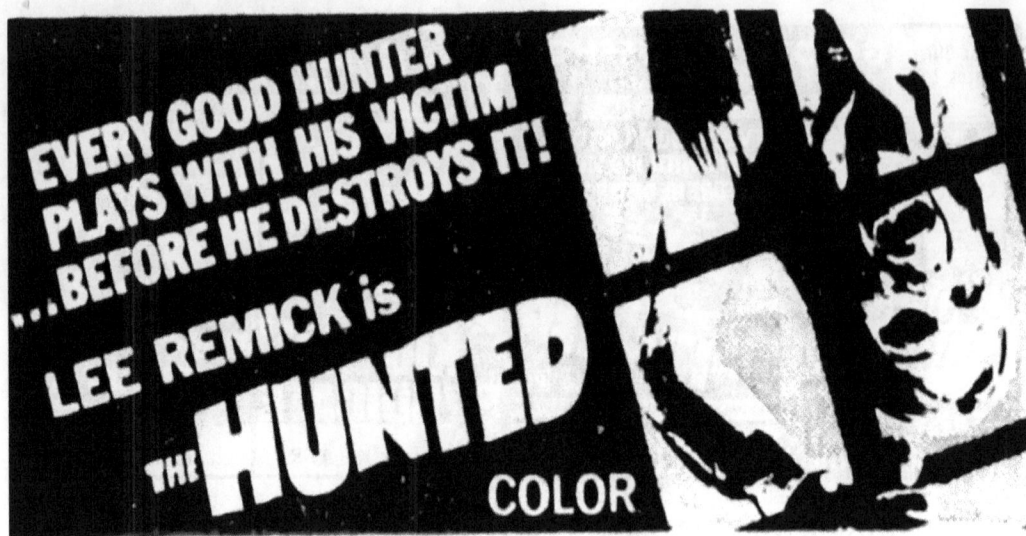

EVERY GOOD HUNTER PLAYS WITH HIS VICTIM ...BEFORE HE DESTROYS IT!

LEE REMICK is THE HUNTED

COLOR

LEE REMICK IN THE HUNTED CO STARRING MICHAEL HINZ · AN ATLAS FILMS RELEASE **PG**

In Hawaii, Mr. and Mrs. Maurice Bailey finally disembark from the South Korean fishing ship that saved them after finding them drifting on the open ocean in a rubber life raft for 118 days.

A whale sunk their yacht while they were sailing to New Zealand.

When they get back home to London, they're going to build another boat and do it all over again – whales notwithstanding. Notwithswimming, certainly.

You find violence in the strangest places sometimes.

THE BRIDE
Monday, July 30, 1973.

Barbara takes her lover David to a fancy new-fan-gled house she's building in the country. Barbara wants David to marry her, but he knows that marrying her means he has to hang out with her dad – who's also his boss – and *that* guy is basically slow poison. He's a really noxious fuddy-dud-dy who grouses all about those wacky kids these days. They get married anyway and Helen, one of David's ex-girlfriends, shows up. He trots off with her and they have sex! What an asshole! Barbara catches them, grabs some scissors and hacks away at his arm, which spatters her wedding dress with blood, blood, blood. She rages, smashes up the wedding cake – gee, thanks a lot, Barbara! – then deserts everyone. Helen secretly shacks up with David while Barbara is missing. Her old man consoles David and tells him about the time Bar-bara tortured her pet chicken. Gee, thanks a lot, Dad! Helen finds bloody birds, a bloody skeleton, the bloody dress – bloody hell! – in that house in

the country and takes off, completely freaked out. Then everything gets really nuts!

In Seal Beach, California, the body of one of Randy Steven Kraft's victims is found, barefoot and abused, beside the 7th Street on-ramp of the 405 Freeway.

At least they think it's one of Kraft's victims.

Kraft, one of several so-called "Freeway Killers" operating in Southern California throughout the '70s, has competition in 1973 in the world of mass murder. The Toy-Box Killer. The Hitchhiker's Killer. The Thrill Killer. The Want Ad Killer.

Sensing a pattern.

The Highway Stalker. The Campus Killer. The Co-Ed Butcher. The Torso Killer. Killer Petey. The Monster of the Andes. The Lady Killer. The Butcher Baker. The Dating Game Killer. The Killer Clown. The Alphabet Killer. Charlie Chop-Off.

In London, after 12 years' worth of legal tor-ment, the High Court orders the Distillers Com-pany to pay $50 million in damages to more than 400 English victims of the birth defects caused by thalidomide. The chemical-and-whisky con-sortium had for years marketed the drug thalido-mide as something to give expectant mothers re-lief from morning sickness. It's money to be held in trust and distributed over time to the families of the many thalidomide babies who were born missing eyes or arms and could never fend for themselves otherwise.

Cold comforts.

Double murder? Murder-suicide? No one knows.

They, like so many other victims of violence, fade into a haze of vanished secrets and lost time over the years.

At least they didn't die alone.

Two teens, aged 15 and 13, are found in the woods of Leet Township, Pennsylvania, on a lonely stretch of land the locals call "the old Davis estate."

Both teens, each with a history of running away from home, are found by a man and his 10-year-old son out picking berries.

Not quite "the talk" most parents think they'll have to have with their children.

It's probably something that boy still thinks of – if he's still alive – especially when he remembers how close they were to his age. Finding one dead body – let alone two – is something that sticks with you, if you ever experience such a thing.

Both teens – a boy and a girl – had been missing for months.

Their clothes hang loosely on their bodies. They're almost completely skeletonized when they're found. Each died from a gunshot to the head.

THE SINFUL DWARF
Wednesday, August 1, 1973.

Olaf the crippled piano-playing dwarf works for his drunken ex-cabaret singer pimp mother Lila, procuring young girls at their boarding-house. He lures them with wind-up toy poodles (!) and shoots them up with heroin until they're addicted and pliable. They then whore them out to undiscerning dirtbags who take advantage of them. One young lady who gets a room with her writer husband gets kidnapped. It turns out that she was the wrong young lady to kidnap. The procurement business goes right down the drain with the usual horrifically depressing and depressingly horrific results. Alan R. Howard, writing in the *Hollywood Reporter* in December, calls *The Sinful Dwarf* "...among the ugliest movies ever made ... its soul rotten through and through." Conversely, this was the film that – when screened at the New Beverly Cinema in Los Angeles to a packed house after the 2007 death of owner Sherman Torgan – showed the Torgan family that they should keep the theatre open. Not a dry seat in the house. Sordid and unsettling in a way that few films ever really are.

In Aiken, South Carolina, a doctor is sterilizing pregnant women.

Clovis H. Pierce is that doctor.

Sterilization is a condition of his when it comes to delivering babies of welfare mothers. He's the only obstetrician in a town of slightly over 13,000 people.

His avowed rationale for these sterilizations is to reduce the welfare rolls. He threatens to take one woman, Marietta Williams, to court if she

HARRY NOVAK PRESENTS

ABDUCTED BRIDE

HER UNWILLING YOUNG BODY FLAMING INTO A CRAZED, UNCONTROLLABLE PASSION

A VALIANT INTERNATIONAL PICTURE *In* COLOR

doesn't sign the consent form to sterilize her before delivering her child.

"I wouldn't marry again," she says, tending to her child, who has remained sick with chronic malnourishment since birth. "Who would want me, knowing I cannot have any children?"

In 1972, 16 of 18 babies delivered in Aitken by Dr. Pierce were born to black mothers who were sterilized immediately thereafter.

A witness testified in patient Shirley Brown's lawsuit against Dr. Pierce. "He came in and he hadn't examined me or anything. I was laying on the table. And, he said, "Listen here, young lady." He said, "This is my tax money paying for something like this." He said, "I am tired of people going around here having babies and my tax money paying for it." He said, "So, if you don't want this (sterilization) done, you go and find yourself another doctor"."

In 1975, Shirley Brown will be awarded $5 in her suit against Dr. Pierce for her coerced sterilization.

Five dollars.

A jury of five women and one man rules that her civil rights were violated. Just not that seriously.

Five dollars.

Dr. Clovis H. Pierce has over 60 years' worth of experience with "conditions of pregnancy and delivery." He graduated from Vanderbilt. As of 2022, he practices obstetrics and gynecology in Greenville, South Carolina.

THERE WAS A LITTLE GIRL
Wednesday, August 1, 1973.

Ken has been divorced from his wife for a decade. One day, his former stepdaughter Sharon (Lyllah Torena) comes to visit. It turns out that she's a real maniac when it comes to sex. Knock it off, Sharon! She tries to seduce him, and then his new partner, chainsmoking drunkard Rita – in the shower, no less! It's getting real old, Sharon! Scenes of Sharon bopping around Hollywood Boulevard are a real treat, especially when she passes by the New-View Theatre. It's showing *Save the Tiger*, which came out in mid-February, so you have a general idea of when this film was shot. The New-View became a Pussycat Theatre, the basement of which housed notorious ground-zero punk venue The Masque. You also get a rare glimpse of the long-gone Por-No Theatre, where she gets followed by a tubby shutterbug whose shirt doesn't even cover his disgraceful gut as the jarring electronic soundtrack blares on. Director Gary Graver – a cinematographer for Orson Welles and John Cassavetes – stocks the streets of Hollywood with feckless, fuckless men who are demonstrative and obvious wackos; his son Sean shows up in one scene, pushing over a guy who steals his 25¢ fire engine ride. It's hard to believe that Miceli's Italian Restaurant and that newsstand on Cahuenga across from the old Bijou Theatre have been around in Hollywood for as long as they have. Nostalgia can be a kind of pornography all its own, from time to time.

Elsewhere in Hollywood, Charles Bukowski writes poetry.

Today, he separates from his longtime lover, the poet and sculptor Linda King.

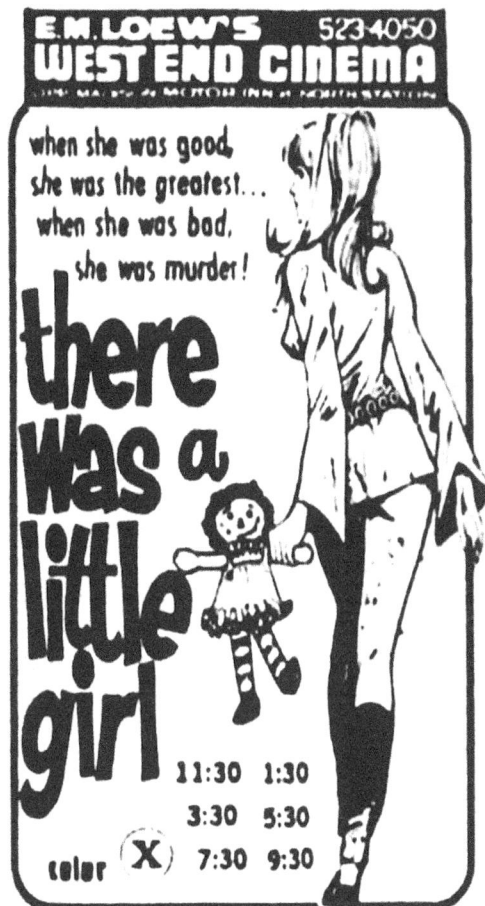

Speaking to the *San Francisco Chronicle* in 2009, she recalls, "It wasn't that he had other women. It's that he always wanted me to know about them, always wanted to tell me all the details about what they did together. Who does that unless they really want to make you mad?"

At the United States Penitentiary in Leavenworth, Kansas, a "maniac killer" stabs unarmed prison guard Wayne Lewis Selle, 39, to death during lunch. Warden Loren Daggett doesn't know who the killer is. His face was covered with a t-shirt when he was last seen sprinting with murderous intent toward Selle. It happens in Cellblock A. Where they put the more problematic prisoners.

There are only so many places someone like that can be.

Selle leaves a wife and three children. "Wayne wasn't the tough type," his widow tells the press from their home. "He was firm but easy-going. He loved children."

Korea. Vietnam. Leavenworth.

40 inmates operating on behalf of prison religious group Church of the New Song (CONS) instigate actions to disrupt the prison. It's been a week since the last prison riot almost annihilated Leavenworth. Between the black militants in Cellblock A, the white militants taking hostages, and the Chicano militants setting fire to things, it's a wonder more people haven't died.

Selle's killer is revealed to be William Hearst, who kills himself awaiting trial.

Did Hearst remove the shirt from his face when the knife slipped in?

Did Selle see the face of his assassin?

East German leader Walter Ulbricht dies today, aged 80. First Secretary of the Socialist Unity Party of Germany. Chairman of the State Council.

Creator of the Berlin Wall.

There hasn't been anyone shot trying to make it over The Wall since April 27.

Peace in our time.

GORDON'S WAR
Thursday, August 2, 1973.

Gordon comes back home to Harlem after a tour in Vietnam. Gordon's old lady died of an overdose. Gordon sees what heroin has done to the community that seems worlds away from the way he left it. Gordon has three friends from Vietnam – and now they're going to war with all the drug dealers in Harlem. As these soldiers get closer and closer to the men at the top of the drug supply chain – fighting through small-time temporary losers with names like Spanish Harry and Luther The Pimp – that goal seems less attainable the deeper they go. As the staunch and principled Gordon, Paul Winfield transmutes the disillusionment and cynicism surrounding his experience with the War into hope and pragmatic violence as he realizes that he and his fellow war dogs have something worth fighting for in Harlem. That they can truly make a difference there – as opposed to futility of the war in Vietnam – is something that changes them. Transforms them. For good. Forever. The actors who appeared in *Gordon's War* showed up later in the most interesting places. Director Ossie Davis continued to be the greatness that was Ossie Davis; diva and singer Grace Jones shows up in a bit part, nude and resourceful; and Gilbert "Spanish Harry" Lewis was in the first season of *Pee-wee's Playhouse* as the original King of Cartoons. Switch out heroin for opioids and Vietnam for Afghanistan and you could remake this film today fairly easily.

"He hollered out, "Kar-r-ren ..." and bang! He shot her."

She dies. The 33-year-old killer, Brian Gebarski, calls out from his window perch, "Kathy, this one is for you." Another gunshot. She dies, too.

"Then he hollered out, "John, here's one for you." He hit John Dahm in the head."

John Dahm was his best friend.

Stanley Kurz waits, plastered against the wall directly under the window through which the shots blasted in and killed his daughters on July 24. It's his son-in-law that's doing the killing. Kurz's testimony in a Milwaukee court today is deeply shocking, inescapably riveting and constitutionally tragic.

Kurz pushes his wife and grandson into the house directly opposite the killer's vantage point, saving them when they come out to see what all the noise is about. Firing. The killer keeps firing into the house.

Gebarski shouts, "Now I got rid of the rest of them, I'm going to wipe you all out." He'd ambushed his wife Karen and the rest of the family while they're in the backyard putting up a swimming pool for the summer.

When apprehended, Gebarski vacillates wildly in his murderous rationale. "I shouldn't have shot them. It's against God's law." Then he says, "I shot them because they deserved it."

He killed them because his wife had filed for divorce.

In Santa Rosa, they're questioning a man named Voorhees, who stands 6' tall and weighs in at over 300 pounds, about sex slayings and attacks in Colorado, Virginia and Canada.

In Santa Cruz, the issue of Herbert William Mullin's sanity arises in the mass murder trial that's transfixed California for months. Over three weeks in and around Santa Cruz, he killed 10 people. Before that, three others. His public defender maintains that Mullin, a "psychotic schizophrenic," killed his 13 victims as "human sacrifices needed to save California from earthquakes."

The definition of insanity.

188

BABY BUBBLES
Friday, August 3, 1973.

Agent Baby Bubbles – a member of G.A.S. (Girls Against Slavery) – goes undercover to bust two guys running a phony modeling agency. They're secretly using drugs to addict women and get them ready for prostitution. She's called Baby Bubbles because she comes off as a simple bubble-headed doofus – she's also called a "mental deficient" with a body "that would make a rich man drool" – but as ever, underestimation is a flaw as fatal as any murder. Some scenes are repeated; given the essence of the subject matter, which at its essence is fairly nightmarish, it's understandable that trauma would be relived on a regular basis. Debussy's *Prélude à l'après-midi d'un faune* (Prelude to the Afternoon of a Faun) appears liltingly on the soundtrack, which is immediately elevated because of it, and Eumir Deodato's serene-yet-funky hit *Also Sprach Zarathustra* (2001) also shows up, which is somewhat enterprising on the part of the filmmakers because it had only hit the American charts by late March. The narrator mentions that all this goes down on April 27, so maybe that was really the date they filmed this. Who knows? Who would care? It hurts to be thorough, sometimes. It hurts so bad.

Dean Arnold Corll murders his last victim today.

James Dreymala. A teacher's son. Riding his bike and looking for empty bottles to recycle for a little cash. His killers drive him to Corll's den of tortures. Corll's accomplice David Brooks shares pizza with him. Right before the end. Defiled. Strangled. Disposed of in the boat shed where so many of Corll's other victims are discovered.

A "squalid den of vice and iniquity."

RATED X
ADULTS ONLY
NO ONE UNDER 18 ADMITTED
Turn Me On · · ·
I'm All Yours!

FIRST SHOWING IN MICHIGAN
"BABY BUBBLES"
Plus
"TINA MAKES A DEAL"
Also
"CONNIE AND FLOYD"

GLOBE ART THEATRE
OPEN 9.45 a.m
J520 Grd River at Trumbull
832-7555

That's what they've resorted to calling the chronic seediness of the Broadway Central Hotel in New York City. Hunkered down on the twilit outskirts of Greenwich Village, eight stories of the storied hotel implode and fall down tonight. Four people die.

They can't find them yet, but they're dead all the same.

19 people, some of whom are police and firemen, are taken to the hospital for treatment. 100 people are instantly homeless. Welfare residents.

As if things weren't bad enough in New York City.

Like a samurai that has committed seppuku, the guts of the hotel sag onto the streets, leaking the blood of rot and asbestos and carcinogens from an earlier, more innocent time. Two years after its opening in 1870, financier and robber baron James "Diamond Jim" Fisk Jr. is shot down at the hotel by former business cohort Edward Stiles Stokes. Reasons of money. Reasons of love. Unreasonable regardless.

The negative space of the ruin is overwhelming. It turns out that one of the basement walls was altered illegally, leading to the building's fall and demise.

In a few hours from now, hundreds of theatergoers were supposed to fill the playhouses of the Mercer Arts Center, situated on the other side of the Hotel. Ultimately, New York University will build a 22-story dorm for law students where the dust and the sadness now linger. It's only a broken husk now.

The kind of body that makes rich men drool.

NIGHT WATCH
Friday, August 3, 1973.

Rich hausfrau Elizabeth Taylor hangs out in her London home and has nightmares about the motorcrash that killed her ex-husband Carl one rainy, rainy night, long ago. Her new husband John (the then-dying Laurence Harvey) is a stockbroker. They're at odds because he spends too much time on business and not enough on their marriage. They fight. Liz sees a guy get his throat slashed in the slanty shanty across from their home as lightning flashes. She screams. The cops come to check it out but there's no body. Later, she screams again when she thinks she sees the body of a dead girl in the old decrepit house. It turns out that the wreck that killed Carl also killed his mistress. Intrigue ensues. She freaks out and it turns out that new husband is having an affair on her, too! She can't get even! Originally rated R. What a seamy, seamy version that must have been. The film premiered in Sun Valley, Idaho at the Sun Valley Opera House as part of

the Brut Film Festival. Also at that Festival was the premiere of Laurence Harvey's *Welcome to Arrow Beach*. *Night Watch* was later screened at the Cairo International Film Festival, 17 years since anything even remotely related to Elizabeth Taylor appeared in Egypt since her films were banned because of her support of Israel. The AVCO Embassy press release touting *Night Watch* included Liz's recipe for chili con carne, which we include here for your pleasure and general overall delectation: Take two chopped onions and sauté until transparent in nut oil. Cook 2 lbs. of beef mince in frying pan. Add onions and chili powder to taste. Stir until meat is brown. Add two 16 oz. cans of stewed and peeled tomatoes and two 16 oz. cans of red kidney beans. Cook over low flame for two hours.

The grave of Sgt. Leopold Chouinard is a modest one.

Slate gray is the gravestone that marks his final resting place. Praying hands and a rosary draped across a cross are its only decorations.

There is no hint of the unmistakable agony he endured during the wreck of the Delta DC-9 that tried on July 31 to land in Boston at Logan International Airport. It struck its landing gear on the Boston Harbor seawall and crashed in the fog, killing 88.

He's the only survivor.

They're amputating Leopold Chouinard's legs today.

Doctors at Massachusetts General Hospital labor for hours to sever Chouinard's destroyed legs. They think it'll save his life. He holds on for 133 days. Until December 11.

He's buried in Hope Cemetery in Barre, Vermont.

You should visit him. Feel the wind on your face. Take a deep breath of that cool clean Vermont air. Hear the birds and the leaves and everything else swirling through the world around you. Remember how good it feels to be alive.

You never know how much pain is hiding under someone's gravestone. That's why they make them so heavy.

Too heavy to lift up and see.

WELCOME TO ARROW BEACH
Saturday, August 4, 1973.

It's Korea, not Vietnam, that creates monsters this time around when Laurence Harvey plays a war vet and photographer who lives with his sister amidst a backdrop of remote beach locations that emphasize the loneliness of Harvey's character. Everyone thinks he's so upstanding but in fact he's a brutal cannibal who lures impressionable hitchhikers into his gourmet web. Scenes of him doing his *Peeping Tom* thing behind the camera possess a rare kind of menace that's fleeting yet true. Eerily beautiful Meg Foster plays the hippie who stumbles upon his dastardly secret. You could do worse than to have Meg Foster stumble upon your dastardly secret. Lou Rawls sings the theme song. Imagine pitching this film to Lou Rawls. Harvey dies at 45 of stomach cancer on November 25. He was dying when he made this film. Films made by dying people tend to have such a strange sense of pacing. The film was released later to unsuspecting theatres as *Tender Flesh* to traumatize and perplex audiences all over again.

In the ocean off the coast of Ventura, California, student pilot Bryan Riley Harris, 25, dies as his single-engine airplane disintegrates on impact when it plunges into the sea.

The airplane dives straight down out of a dense fog. It crashes 10 feet from a 24-foot cabin cruiser skippered by Gene Brock, 39.

In 1971, Brock suffered extensive burns from a boat that exploded not far from here.

Near-misses can be as violent as direct hits.

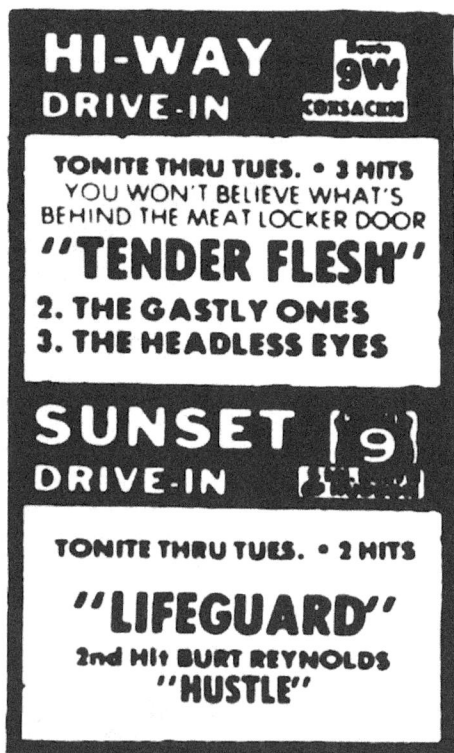

HI-WAY 9W DRIVE-IN CORSACK

TONITE THRU TUES. • 3 HITS
YOU WON'T BELIEVE WHAT'S BEHIND THE MEAT LOCKER DOOR
"TENDER FLESH"
2. THE GASTLY ONES
3. THE HEADLESS EYES

SUNSET [9] DRIVE-IN

TONITE THRU TUES. • 2 HITS
"LIFEGUARD"
2nd Hit BURT REYNOLDS
"HUSTLE"

It's a different kind of violence. The effects are lifelong, instructive and multifold.

Mr. and Mrs. Stanley Hilt of Chillicothe, Ohio, borrow a truck and travel to Northwest Missouri State University to pick up their daughter's belongings.

Their only daughter.

Teresa Sue Hilt, 22, a beloved multilingual singer. Wanted to be a music teacher. Stripped and strangled. Face down in a shredded bed. Stabbed multiple times.

Near the heart.

The killer put a sheet over her. Cleaned up the

A nice place to visit...but no place to live.

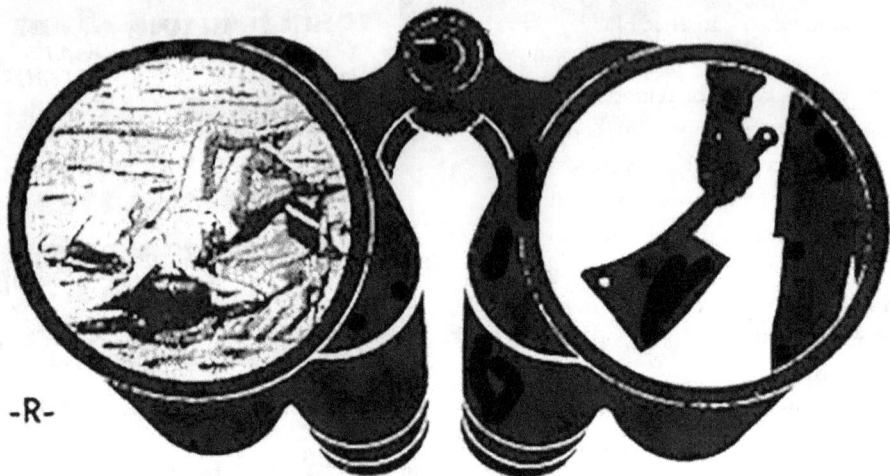

-R-

WELCOME TO ARROW BEACH

PLUS

CHAMBER OF HORRORS

Come Early
And Visit
Our Snack Bar

TODAY!

OPENS
7:30
1 SHOW
STARTS
AT
8:30

IF YOU HAVE
HEART TROUBLE
"DON'T COME"

Thunderbird
Drive-In Theatre
812 GREENSBORO ROAD

abc
THEATRES

ES-74-6

```
TACONY-PALMYRA BR. TWIN DRIVE-IN
At The Bridge, Route 73, Palmyra, N J
TA 9-3000
TACONY TWIN DRIVE-INS
Two Separate Drive-In Theatres
AT ONE LOCATION
TWO Complete Shows to Choose From!
Tacony-Palmyra Red—
Tacony-Palmyra Blue
TACONY TWIN DRIVE-INS
2 Theatres—1 Location
NOW PLAYING AT TACONY BLUE
AMUCK (R)
MEAT CLEAVER MASSACRE (R)
TENDER FLESH (R)
At The Bridge, Rte 73
Palmyra, N.J.
NOW PLAYING AT TACONY RED
KENTUCKY FRIED MOVIE (R)
TUNNEL VISION (R)
SHAMPOO (R)
At The Bridge, Rte 73
Palmyra, N J. TA 9-3000
Box Office Opens 7:30 PM
Elec. In-Car Heaters Opt
Swap 'N' Shop Flea Mkt Every Sunday
```

apartment. Put the knife that killed her into her hand as she lay lifeless on the floor.

Detectives say that the killer may have suffered from a condition that causes the hair to fall out. Hilt was recorded on tape earlier this year, complaining about greasy-haired man. She loathed him but he kept trying to manhandle her anyway.

It may have been the killer's hair that was found in her mouth when she died.

In the waters off Ocean Beach on Fire Island, New York, a strangely strong undertow drags three people out to sea to their deaths. 25 people are injured.

They're injured because, in the words of the local police, "Our biggest problem was having to rescue people who were trying to rescue other people."

Echoes of violence, haunting and glancing off those who keep going.

The ones who keep living.

In Rome, Italy, three lions run away from the circus.

They're heading toward the beach at Ladispoli. Running free. Running away. As fast as they can.

"Friendly but misunderstood," the press calls them. "I am looking out of my window and there is a lion looking back at me," one woman tells the police over the telephone.

Whether she called to tell them out of fear or pride, we know not which.

The lions reach the beach. They sit down amid a crowd that had some fleeing of their own to do. They're cleaning their paws as their trainers come to take them home.

Circus workers say that the friendly lions came up to people "only to be petted."

Well, what did you expect?

THE STONE KILLER
Thursday, August 9, 1973.

Charles Bronson stars as a New York City cop who accidentally shoots a kid and gets bounced off the force. He gets a job with the police department in Los Angeles and manages to find out when a big Mob hit is going to go down. Mafioso Martin Balsam wants revenge because a bunch of Mafia dons got wasted in 1931 and apparently he's real good at holding a grudge. As ever, the Mafia is on the cutting edge of things because they're hiring freshly-damaged Vietnam veterans as disposable killers. With an unusually heavy level of on-location filming throughout New York City and Los Angeles; cynical Norman Fell as Bronson's point man in Los Angeles; John Ritter is a dumb young cop; otherwise-fatherly Ralph Waite as a racist scumbag detective; and brutal murders, exhilarating car chases and a complex Roy Budd soundtrack that ranks among his finest. I wonder how handy with a gun Charles Bronson was in real life.

In Pasadena, Texas, they're pulling out bodies that have been buried in and around the home of Dean Arnold Corll.

It takes all day. They're up to 17.

His longtime accomplice, Elmer Wayne Henley, shoots him stone cold dead last night as he's about to kill him and two others he's captured. "You won't do it!" Corll taunts as he comes at Henley, who holds a .22 pistol in his hand.

Then – just like that – he does it.

The young men that Corll and his accomplices defiled and murdered over the past few years will

IMPLACABLE FEROZ INMISERICORDE

¡Sus ojos quedarán atónitos ante tan terrible venganza!

CHARLES BRONSON

AMERICA VIOLENTA

con MARTIN BALSAM

PRESENTADA EN CINERAMA

Los persiguió con saña, seguro de su maldad

ultimately add up to one of the largest cases of mass murder in American history. As recently as 2022, one victim nicknamed "Swimsuit Boy" remains unidentified. A short boy. Brown hair. Found next to a shirt emblazoned with a peace symbol.

A massacre diametrically opposed to the Mafia's murders, fueled by lust, annihilation and insatiability.

What they must have thought of one another when they read the newspapers.

You can read about the details of Corll's rampages elsewhere. When you get to what Corll did with the slim glass rods he'd stockpiled, you'll wish you hadn't.

I'm going to be three years old this year. What's murder? All I want to do is hang out with my mom and dad.

Shenandoah National Park Ranger Roy Cleveland Sullivan, 61, nurses the wounds caused by the lightning that struck him on Tuesday while on patrol.

He's hit by lightning seven times over the course of his 36-year career.

Maybe eight. But who's counting?

He watches a gathering storm cloud follow him as he tries to escape it. As though it has a mind of its own. Just when he thought it was safe to get out of his Park Service truck, he says, the lightning hit him. He sees the bolt of lightning burst out of the cloud and come for him. A bolt of electricity five times hotter than the surface of the sun radiates down his left arm. Down his left leg. Knocking off his still-tied shoe. Leaping over to his right leg and blasting out.

He was on fire.

Sullivan pours the five-gallon can of water he

keeps now for emergencies like this over his head to quell the second-degree burns. "It was the hottest one of all," he says about this latest blast.

Sullivan thinks, "God spared me for some good purpose. I know what it is, but it's between God and me, and nobody but us will ever know."

He shoots himself in the head around 3 a.m. at his home in Dooms, Virginia on September 28, 1983.

Engraved on Sullivan's tombstone is this epitaph: "We Loved You, But God Loved You More."

God sure has a funny way of showing it.

COME DEADLY
Friday, August 10, 1973.

A stocking-faced maniac wearing clunky white gloves runs around raping and murdering female members of an acting troupe and it's up to Detective Winston Rains to go undercover and join the cast (performing, in a nice flourish of superficial irony, *The Taming of the Shrew*), stop the maniac and save the nubile thespians in this loose and psychosexual re-telling of *The Phantom of the Opera* (they even use Bach's *Toccata and Fugue in D minor*, The Phantom's organ theme). One poor girl gets assaulted twice – just when she thought she got away! They all keep on rehearsing. No one even takes a personal day. The killer's final admission of guilt blames everything from molestation to inadequacy and is far more revealing than you might think. "Please, God – *I didn't mean to kill 'em!*" The end?

There's a boy named Larry somewhere in New Mexico, calling for help on his father's CB radio.

Amateur ham radio enthusiasts around the nation hear him crying as he tells them that his father has collapsed and died at the wheel while driving. That their truck overturned while on a hunting trip, jamming both doors shut. That he can see the lights of helicopters searching for them in the Manzano Mountains area throughout the week.

The battery in his father's car starts to die.

Police suspect that it's all a hoax. Others who have heard the child crying disagree.

No one ever finds them. For all anyone knows, they're still out there, ready for a passing airplane to find them while looking for another lost family.

Disappointment and violence are distant relations that remain close.

Consider the case of Kathy Fiscus, fallen into a deep well in San Marino, California in 1949. Newscasts kept people enthralled and hopeful until it was painfully apparent that she hadn't made it out alive. Conversely – Orson Welles' magnificence notwithstanding – that we didn't really get invaded by Martians in 1938 was difficult to grasp for those fearful fleeing folk that were ready to do what they had to do in order to survive.

Hoaxes. Lies. Gratuitousness.

At 2 a.m., someone drenches the stage, seats and balcony of the Fox Theatre in Oakland with gasoline.

Built in 1927. 3,300 seats. 50 firemen battling the inferno through the small dark hours of the morning. A 2-alarm fire. $30,000 in damage. $186,016.41, as seen through a five-decade long prism of inflation.

Acid melting the carpets.

The stark, striking simplicity of details. Sometimes that's all you can see through the haze that surrounds you.

The stage, Assistant Fire Chief Renzo Balassi says, "suffered particularly severe damage."

Why would someone act like that?

Oggi "grande prima" al cinema **TORINO**

C.I.A. CINEMATOGRAFIE INTERNAZIONALI ASSOCIATE presenta una realizzazione di RODOLFO SABBATINI

FREDERICK STAFFORD

LA RAGAZZA DI VIA CONDOTTI

con la partecipazione di MICHEL CONSTANTINE

e con **FEMI BENUSSI** **ALBERTO DE MENDOZA**
con **PATTY SHEPARD** (nel ruolo di Simone) **CLAUDE JADE**
Regia di **GERMAN LORENTE** sceneggiatura di ADRIANO ASTI · GERMAN LORENTE
MIGUEL DE ECHARRI

EASTMANCOLOR · Colore della Itoco Film

UNO DEI PIU' GRANDI SUCCESSI DELLA STAGIONE

VIETATO AI MINORI DI ANNI 18

LA RAGAZZA DI VIA CONDOTTI
Saturday, August 11, 1973.

Private eye Sandro Mattei – here played by an extra-cynical, luxuriously macho Frederick Stafford – finds his wife Simone dead in bed, strangled by a mystery lover. She's no stranger to violence – their opening scenes together involve him pinching her face shut to wake her up, and then holding her head under water in the bathroom sink to rouse her from her alcoholic stupor. "Poor little bitch," he mutters. He finds a photograph on the floor near her body. In it is a man on a motorbike and a woman in sunglasses in the background. A clue! His photographer mistress Tiffany enlarges the image. They discover that Laura, the woman in the image, works as a stripper in a Rome nightclub. Sandro gets threats written in that way where you have to cut out a lot of different letters from the newspaper and paste them all on a piece of paper so people know you're serious because you spent a lot of time on it. He tells

Tiffany, "You always look on the bright side of everything. A gumshoe like me only sees the dirt, the dregs of society – the failures, the perverts, the scum!" Gee whiz, mellow out already! A love triangle expands to a love rectangle and all sorts of nefarious deeds and drugs and violence ensue. Covetousness and possessiveness – as presented by the multiple photographs that drive the story – are prevailing themes. One of the most nihilistic films of 1973, it holds only the barest photon of hope at the end. Stafford dies horribly and violently in 1979 during a mid-air Rallye/Piper collision above Lake Sarnen, Switzerland.

In Redwood City, California, Ruth Hoffman throws a party for everyone she knows.

She's in a room at Sequoia Hospital. Dying – even while they celebrate – of bone cancer.

It was only this past Mother's Day that she got the diagnosis. Terminal.

"We all have to die. I was ready then. I still am, and I wanted to have a party for my friends," she says.

Her family weeps in the hall. Some remain sorrowful; others are stoic. "This is rough on us, but it makes my mother happy and she really digs it," says her son Don, 24.

In the hospital room, Hoffman cradles her grandson and sings him a lullaby as her friends stream in and out of the hospital room, enjoying the punch and cake on hand.

Making memories.

A friend observes with admiration, "She makes other people stop and think."

Film producer William McGarry stops and thinks.

Thinks he hasn't seen his ex-wife, the actress Peggy Castle, in some time. Thinks he should go see her at her Hollywood apartment. Doesn't know what to think when he finds her dead on the sofa, aged 45.

Castle, famous for her roles as sirens and other women in westerns like *The Yellow Tomahawk* and thrillers like *Invasion U.S.A.*, will be found to have died of cirrhosis.

Elsewhere in Los Angeles, a man visits his friend. Tells him he wants one dollar. Isn't going to leave without it.

The man, Charles L. Murray, 50, is found on the doorstep shortly thereafter.

Shot dead in the head. By his friend.

You can't choose your family, but you can choose your friends.

UNA VITA LUNGA UN GIORNO

Tuesday, August 14, 1973.

Mino Reitano's character falls for beautiful Ewa Aulin's character. He finds out that she's a real sick character and needs hospital treatment. A heart condition. He offers himself up to a bunch of rich dissolute assholes who want five murderers to hunt him so he can get the money to pay for her care. A condition of the heart. He gets a ton of money if he gets away. He gets assassinated if he doesn't. Also, he doesn't get any money. He dodges all the killers only to find himself in a surprise ending inside a surprise ending! Just like life!

In Hawaii, they're ordering an end to the bombing campaign in Cambodia.

For the past 160 consecutive days, American forces have dropped bombs on opposition forces throughout the country. The Hawaiian directive marks the end of years of military assaults on Cambodia starting in 1969. Possibly upwards of 150,000 Cambodians die during these years.

The last bombs are scheduled to fall at 11 a.m. in Cambodia.

That way, they could really see it coming.

The final survivors of violent events always present a certain fascination.

Think of General George Armstrong Custer's horse Comanche, last free survivor of The Battle of the Little Bighorn in 1876, living out the rest of his life drinking beer and leading parades until dying of colic in 1891. Florence Beatrice Green, the last veteran of World War I, dying

in West Norfolk, England in 2011 at age 110. Teruo Nakamura, the final Imperial Japanese Army holdout, brought back to Taiwan from his encampment on the island of Morotai, Indonesia in December 1974.

In spite of everything – to spite everything, maybe – someone has to survive.

Someone has to make it out.

Somewhere. Somehow.

HAPPY MOTHER'S DAY, LOVE GEORGE

Wednesday, August 15, 1973.

Johnny (Ron Howard, four months away from starring in *Happy Days*) shows up at a New England fishing village. Down at the café, waitress Ronda – played by the deathlessly great Cloris Leachman – takes his order. He wanders around town and finds his way to a home owned by Ronda's sister Cara, played by an exceptionally bonkers Patricia Neal. Cara's nubile daughter Celia (Tessa Dahl, Neal's actual daughter) comes out and is smitten with Johnny. Cara catches her mooning over him and gives her what-for before haranguing her son Porgie and his "tramp" wife Yolanda. Johnny wanders around some more and gets hassled by police chief Roy, who tells him that there have been a string of disappearances so he's got to hassle him as a matter of police policy. It turns out that Johnny is really Ronda's son and he's here to find to find out the identity of his real father. Ronda's dating Eddie the chef (Bobby Darin), who doesn't like the fact that Johnny has abruptly appeared in his life so he breaks up with her and beats up Johnny! Later, it's revealed that Cara's husband George was stabbed to death in his front yard. The ultimate suburban nightmare. Later still, all kinds of wacky skeletons come dancing out of their closets and various characters go crazy and kill even more people. You know. The usual. Directed by Darren McGavin – making an appearance in an old photograph as poor dead George – it was the final film for singing actor Darin, who dies on December 20 after open-heart surgery. Maybe Ron Howard thought of this film when he played organ in that band on *Happy Days* and Potsie sang "Splish Splash." The editing turned out so weirdly that some actors listed in the credits aren't even in the film.

Douglas Riege probably didn't think he would be clutching at his throat today as his heart beat so hard that it filled him with heat and confusion and fear.

Feeling the life ebb out of him in Brando, Manitoba.

On a golf course.

He dies today when he gets his ball caught in the rough. His club hits a tree and snaps. The shaft flies back and drives itself into his throat.

He probably had all sorts of plans as to what he was going to do after his golf outing. Dinner. Attend to business.

Maybe call Mom.

Violence cancels all plans.

More precisely, it gathers them all up in one pile and impales them on one of those spikes made for the collection of receipts and memos. Everything streamlines. Everything narrows. It happens quicker than a thought – beyond thought, beyond belief – when something sharp comes straight at you. Tearing up your plans. Pinning them down and making a mockery of your control, your dominance, your civilization.

Violence is a dagger aimed directly at the heart of the civilization you've built for yourself in all the years you call a life.

Kimberly York shoots her boyfriend Donald McPherson with a .22 rifle in their home.

Arguing over another woman. He probably

thought it would all blow over. You never really think these things will escalate to the degrees that they do.

York calls the police after she kills McPherson.

She shoots him in the face.

And near the heart.

NO, IL CASO È FELICEMENTE RISOLTO
Wednesday, August 15, 1973.

Humble civil servant Fabio Santamaria is out at the lake fishing one day when he accidentally witnesses Professor Eduardo Ranieri assaulting a girl. In a shocking burst of cinematic action, the camera spirals around the scene, closing in as he eventually catches and beats her to death. The girl's dead eyes lock with Fabio's. The Professor tells him to keep his trap shut but of course Fabio is too honest for that – so then The Professor tells the cops that it was *Fabio* who did the killing and that *he* was the witness! *Che bastardo!* He hides behind a veil of respectability and Fabio is merely a lowly peon – so who do you think the cops will believe? Fabio has to find a way out of it before he gets life in prison for a murder he didn't commit. Hideously piteous everyman Enzo Cerusico acts up a storm as the increasingly desperate, put-upon Fabio – a man who only wants to go fishing, listen to the game on the radio, live his simple life and not be hassled with things like this. It's a film that's more about actual crime, violence and the legal system than most police melodramas.

People who do all the "right" things in life sometimes find themselves on the wrong end of things.

It's like getting crushed between two railroad boxcars.

People often make hyperbolic statements like that. They want to emphasize how they're feeling about a certain thing. The more dramatic the description, the more intimate the connection becomes between them and you, no matter how brief.

A shared moment of emotion.

How often do you really consider such things?

How many times have you thought at length about getting crushed between boxcars at any point in your life?

"Sonder" is an emotion defined as a realization that everyone you encounter during your day – even if only for a fleeting and solitary moment – constantly and continually lives as full and complicated a life as you do.

An aspect of compassion.

Sonder means that people feel similar feelings as yours; they have similar troubles, issues and adventures as you do over your life.

Every single person.

Like Brian Jaeckel. He's dying today.

He works for the Milwaukee Railroad. He's only 32. He got caught between colliding boxcars while working in the Menomonee River Valley in Wisconsin. It takes a 20-ton jack to pull those boxcars apart, so surely had they collided, practically fused together as they are with weight and momentum.

With gravity.

In Kaukauna, north of Milwaukee, a nine-year-old girl is crushed by a tractor on the family farm. She's playing on it with her brother. When it goes into gear, she goes under the wheels.

The population of Kaukauna at the time is slightly over 11,300 people.

Everyone would know.

Everyone will talk.

No exaggeration.

the BLACK ALLEYCATS

SO CUDDLY BY DAY... SO DEADLY BY NIGHT!!

COLOR X
PLUS 2nd X HIT
"LOVE ELIXIR"

ROCHESTER DRIVE IN

THE BLACK ALLEY CATS
Friday, August 17, 1973.

Four women (including perky brunette Sandy Dempsey, previously in *Little Miss Innocence*) get gang-raped and decide to find the vile scum who did it so they can make them pay. They learn martial arts and sharpshooting, and get matching black leather outfits with the growly cat from the film's title card emblazoned on the back. Masked and deadly, they recruit another Alley Cat from a girls' finishing school where all sorts of nude wrestling and wacky antics transpire. Another creep has sex with one of the Alley Cats while she's drugged. He and his wife have a good laugh while they try to blackmail her with photographic evidence. Time for more vengeance. A more politically-charged adult film than most – they're trained to harness their own power by a black man; they rob from the rich who steal from the poor – it was an X-rated film that wound up getting edited down to an R-rating so they

could show it at more theatres. Not to be confused with *The Black Bunch*, an X-rated film that was also presented around the same time by Entertainment Pyramid Inc. and easily confused because both films were often paired on the same bill, reused taglines and had the same director, Henning Schellerup.

An early-morning stroll. No one's out. Nothing's around. It's only you, the air, and the night to hold you.

Until you come home. Then everything goes wrong.

Harry S. Wells, 78, is visiting family in Silver Spring, Maryland. He leaves the front door open so he can get back in without having to wake anyone up. 40 feet away, there's a house that looks exactly like his family's house. Middle of the night. Honest mistake. Anyone could have made it.

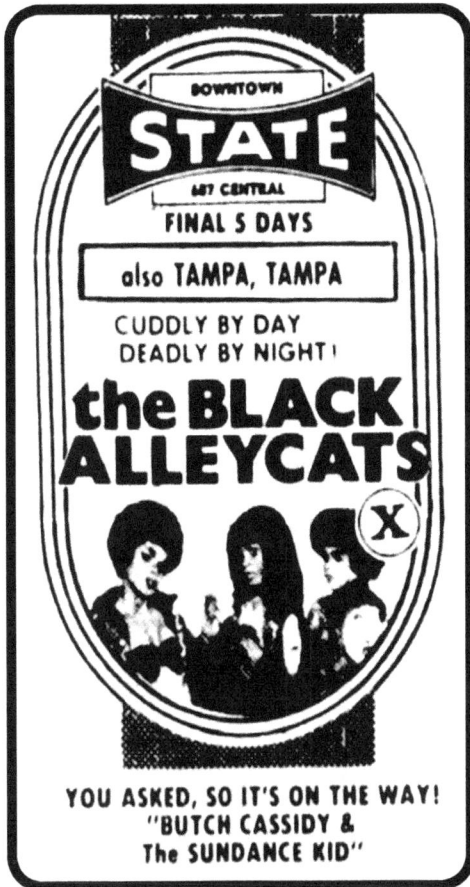

James Lee Bailey Jr., 35, quietly loads the shotgun and approaches the door that, at this godawful early hour, is making entirely too much noise.

Harry thinks that this is his home. He can't understand why the door is now locked. He jiggles the handle. Maybe it's stuck.

The noise he makes is unbearable to young James.

Now the night is electric. Warm clear air erupts with fire and tension and fear.

James Lee Bailey Jr. pulls the trigger on that shotgun. The round rips through the door. It hits Harry S. Wells directly in the chest.

He dies in the hospital in the early hours of this morning.

The sun rises. The sun sets.

In Miami, Victor Hartman, 85, recovers at Jackson Memorial Hospital after being shackled in a swimming pool pumphouse.

In Miami. In the summertime.

His landlady, Bonnie Wilkie Blanchard, 55, has been paid for this rather austere form of room-and-board by Hartman surrendering his Social Security check to her. $186. Each and every month.

For years.

Security.

Ms. Blanchard, of course, has only the kindest rationale for his entrapment.

She says that she keeps him locked in the pumphouse so he won't fall in the pool.

To make him feel totally secure, she's put a leather belt around his waist. That belt is connected to a 10-foot rope.

Wrapped around his neck.

Neither thing is just.

Both things just are.

WARLOCK MOON
Friday, August 17, 1973.

Two lovebirds (plucky Laurie Walters, later Joanie Bradford of *Eight Is Enough*, and fresh-faced Joe Spano, later of *Hill Street Blues*) visit a remote tuberculosis spa with a haunted past. A hunter clues them in to the sordid story of the place but they're still drawn to it. A cannibal cult lurks somewhere nearby. Flowers die and then bloom again. There are not one, but two axe-murderers. Try watching this dreamlike film with the sound turned off. You won't regret it. A defining theme of American independent cinema involves the rot going on behind the façade of the so-called "American Dream." *Warlock Moon*, with its cults and its cannibals and its consumption, never gets credit for its insightful views on how that "Dream" corrupts love and consumes true dreamers.

Night swimming.

Sharon Elaine Holmes lives in Sarasota, Florida. Camping with her parents at Oscar Scherer State Park, near Osprey, she decides to end the night with a relaxing swim.

Today, they shot the 11-foot-long alligator that devoured Sharon Elaine Holmes.

It had become so accustomed to humans, after years of being fed and marveled at by them, that no one thought it was particularly dangerous anymore.

They find Sharon's body on the banks of the river. Guarded by the alligator.

Her left hand. Her left arm.

Inside.

Her father had heard her screams. He tried to pull her out of the water.

She was being pulled back down into the waters by something.

Something he didn't understand until it was too late.

Sharon Elaine Holmes becomes the first known fatality of an alligator attack of the 20th century.

She was 16.

She was born around the same time as the alligator that killed her had found its way into a creek flowing through Oscar Scherer State Park.

People who say that there are no such things as coincidences can be such assholes sometimes.

RODEO
294-3532
5101 Nogales Highway

LAST NIGHT — IN COLOR
"DEVIL'S NIGHTMARE" (R)
— PLUS —
"DEVIL'S GARDEN" (R)

— STARTS TOMORROW —
a horrifying tale of the supernatural

WARLOCK MOON

Starring Laurie Walters, Joe Spano and Edna Macafee
Produced by Bill Herbert · A SWEET BLINDNESS PRODUCTION

from
Enchanted Filmarts ≡ color PG

SKY-VUE DRIVE IN THEATRE
64 EAST ● OPEN 6:00

TONITE Thru SUNDAY

THE FILM MAKERS CO
presents

FORCED TO
USE THEIR
GUNS AND
BODIES
TO SATISFY
THE MAN
WHO
OWNED
THEM

THE
DIRTY
DOLLS

At 7:30 - 10:20

ALSO

Willing young coeds

Swinging Sorority

IN COLOR

ADULTS ONLY

At 6:00 - 9:00

None Under 18 Admitted

THE DIRTY DOLLS
Sunday, August 19, 1973.

Psychotic Johnny Feral has a Mansonesque messiah complex. He also has an all-girl gang that goes out and does crimes for him. One fateful day, they pull a diamond heist by themselves and take a couple of hostages with them back to their lair. Johnny goes nuts. What incompetence! No witnesses! The girls hassle a lady hostage into joining their orgy. Meanwhile, Johnny's sister Dee Dee – an impressionable teen crook herself – begins to wonder if he's totally lost his mind. In a shocking turn of events – he has! They fight and what happens next leaves nothing to the imagination – especially if you'd already read the posters on your way into the show. "Sex-starved girls ... forced to use their guns and bodies to satisfy the man who owned them! He even seduced his own sister!" screamed the posters trapped behind glass and suffering the agonies of two-dimensional existence at a theatre near you.

In California, detectives think that there's a link between the Dean Arnold Corll mass murders in Texas and a Los Angeles film producer who often traveled to Dallas to find new males to be in his hardcore smut films. They decline to name the producer, however.

27 bodies so far. The biggest mass-murder case in 20th-century America.

That they know of. That's the thing.

They can't stop digging.

On Wednesday, Dallas police announce that they've uncovered a "homosexual ring" related to the murders.

A ring? Oh, you've made me so happy.

Beyond the headline and the lack of more illuminating news, that's as far as it goes. Apart from the story being splashed across the front pages of countless small-town newspapers from one end of the country to another, that is.

They'll never stop digging. They have no choice.

DNA tests will, over the decades, identify most of the victims of Corll and his accomplices. His name and crimes will constantly be resurrected. Revived. Revivified.

Going over the same ground with a double-edged sword.

DNA evidence – a kind of Department of Post-Crime – offers the promise of some bare semblance of justice to victims' families. The only problem is that they may be long-dead by the time that justice arrives.

Next year's poster for *The Texas Chain Saw Massacre* asks, "Who will survive, and what will be left of them?"

Maybe there's no sense in asking.

Claude Lanzmann is hard at work today on the genesis of *Shoah*, an epic nine-and-a-half-hour documentary interviewing both perpetrators and victims of The Holocaust. It's a film that will consume the next 11 years of his life.

Lanzmann maintains that to try to explain someone like Adolf Hitler is "obscene." Pointless.

That there is no sudden epiphany after nine-and-a-half hours, when the darkness finally lifts and you're delivered into the light.

That there won't be an explanation for the violence, even after you've sifted through the dirt and dust of it all.

That all there is to do sometimes in life is to pick up the pieces.

PETS
Tuesday, August 21, 1973.

At the intersection of "seamy," "sleazy," "hoity" and "toity" (and yes, an eight-way intersection is as crazy in reality as it sounds) lie these three stories linked by the presence of naïf waif Candice Rialson (as Bonnie) exploring the concept of possession and the countless ways in which people give themselves over to someone or something. Also: boobs! By which of course I mean the bores whose lives are so intellectually bankrupt and emotionally barren that keeping someone captive on one level or another holds some kind of allure or illumination. Also: breasts! Some characters: the Black liberationist who uses Bonnie to help her kidnap a rich white dude; the rich white dude who wants Bonnie as the star attraction in the nightmare circus in his basement; and the lesbian painter who needs Bonnie as her muse and focus for all her pent-up hostility. Depravity runs deep through the veins of *Pets*, which was doubtless one of the more profound cinematic experiences involving this year's field of sex films that concentrate on the climax and not the journey.

At Stanford University, experts predict the existence a new class of robot slaves.

In five or ten years, those robots will take over the harmful jobs that tend to kill humans. Humans like Camilo Chica, 42, killed today in a gas explosion at the Matheson Company's industrial gas bottling plant in Newark, New Jersey after accidentally pouring hydrochloric acid into a cylinder that was meant to store sulphur dioxide. Humans like the 12,000 fireman from across America that are today fighting the forest fires caused by either arson or carelessness that have annihilated 175,000 acres throughout California, Idaho, Washington, Oregon and Montana. Humans (?) like the unknown helicopter pilots chased away by shotgun blasts from a farmer in Union County, Illinois. Hovering over a herd of his cattle. Shining a light down onto the anxious animals. Motor eerily quiet.

Robots do the dangerous menial tasks so that men – men! – can be freed up to do the jobs that require much more advanced brainpower.

At today's International Joint Conference on Artificial Intelligence, Jason – a machine not of the killing variety – purportedly will be improved by its creators so that it works by remote

control. Have a vocabulary of 30 words. Become a teaching tool for children.

You know. Like a pet.

"If a robot goes astray, it will dramatically illustrate the error in computer programming and so help students understand how computers work," says its maker, the mathematician L. Stephen Coles.

If a human goes astray? Consider William Ray Bonner, 25, in Torrance, California when he shoots seven people dead, including his fiancée.

He gets arraigned today for his a rampage this past Easter. Handgun. Shotgun. He shot people he'd known since he was a child. Co-workers at a gas station. People he thought had wronged or slighted him in some unfathomable way.

His last stop is the California State Prison at Vacaville.

To a cage.

aribau cinema

¡El mayor impacto emocional que Ud. habrá vivido en el cine!

¡3.ª SEMANA DE EXITO!

UNA GOTA DE SANGRE PARA MORIR AMANDO
EASTMANCOLOR
SUE LYON · CHRIS MITCHUM · JEAN SOREL
dirigida por ELOY DE LA IGLESIA
una coproducción HISPANO-FRANCESA
JOSE FRADE · P.C.S.A.

UNA GOTA DE SANGRE PARA MORIR AMANDO
Wednesday, August 22, 1973.

Eloy de la Iglesia directs this tale of a bunch of scuzzy red-helmeted bikers and dune buggy enthusiasts who like bullwhips and love rocking the world of various bourgeois families in Madrid on whom they pounce and destroy. Jean Sorel plays the doctor who has a very special kind of therapy for scuzzy bikers. Sue Lyon plays a serial killer with a very specific age-and-sex demographic in mind. Christopher Mitchum plays the head scuzz who blackmails Lyon after catching her trying to get rid of the body of one of her victims. He experiences Sorel's tender mercies and it gets real depressing after that. The futuristic setting – crafted by de la Iglesia and co-writers Antonio Artero, Antonio Fos, José Luis Garci and George Lebourg – showcases characters that are civil, non-threatening and passive, thereby representing the loss of the type of violence that makes humans human. For better or worse. Or worse or worse.

Former Army Corporal Orvil C. Binger, 56, faces an entirely different kind of menace while, against his doctor's orders, he picks up a little extra cash by gathering up stray shopping carts for a Red Owl Supermarket. He's set upon by two boys who pull the carts he's collected off his pickup truck. He chases them. Repeatedly. He's getting more and more exhausted. Later, witness Martin Cvikel says, "These kids have a gang. They pulled the carts off as quick as that poor man put them on." They throw stones at Binger's truck as he drives away.

He dies behind the wheel.

In Buenos Aires, the kids are rampaging for reasons other than just kicks.

The government of Perónist President Héctor Cámpora has banned street rallies. In response, the kids protest the anniversary of the assassination of 16 jailed leftists.

In response, the police fire bullets and tear gas.

Crying for Argentina.

If anything, the youth of Argentina demonstrate for a better tomorrow.

Tomorrow, in Norrmalmstorg – a ritzy region of Stockholm – Jan-Erik Olsson and Clark Olofsson will assault the Kreditbanken. They take hostages. Policemen arrive. One gets shot in the hand. The other is ordered to sit down and sing "Lonesome Cowboy." Olsson calls Olof Palme, the Prime Minister of Sweden. Makes threats. Later, Palme gets another call. It's from one of the hostages. Scolding him for not letting everyone go. Olofsson sings Roberta Flack's "Killing Me Softly" as he waits in the vault. Roberta Flack singing "Killing Me Softly" does tend to calm people down when they're being held hostage. The hostages grow to sympathize with the two thieves. The whole thing unfolds on live television. The great mesmerizer.

The cops use gas on Tuesday to subdue the thieves. Olsson gets 10 years. Olofsson gets freed because people believe that he was simply there to help calm the hostages. "We never felt the boys were a threat to our lives," says hostage Kristin Enmark, 21. "No one did anything to us," she says when interviewed in the hospital, emphatically denying reports that any of the

hostages had been raped.

And that's why they call it Stockholm syndrome, baby.

MILANO TREMA: LA POLIZIA
VUOLE GIUSTIZIA
Wednesday, August 22, 1973.

More madness in Milan as a cop played by Luc Merenda wastes a couple of escaped crooks. Their gang retaliates by offing his police chief – a guy who always helped Merenda get off the hook whenever he played judge, jury, and executioner. People never talk about the men who are pushed so far that they become judge, stenographer and executioner. Busy Richard Conte plays the capo of the criminal gang. Of course Merenda goes after him and everybody around him – violent professionals and violent amateurs alike. All sorts of people die in the crossfire throughout the film, shot through as it is with beatings and car chases and crashes that practically hurtle off the screen and explode in your lap. Luc Merenda looks like the greatest Sears menswear catalog illustration ever. Miss it at your peril.

In Milwaukee, a man of 74 collapses near a TV station's UHF transmitter that shuts off his pacemaker.

In Waco, a boy of 14 drowns when the motorized lawnmower on which he's riding drives him into a pond.

In Galveston, an Apollo 13 astronaut of 39 crashes an airplane and walks away with burns over half his body.

In Houston, a man of 38 who murdered a motel manager during a robbery is sentenced to 999 years in prison.

In Phoenix, a student of 27 is murdered by a man who empties a .38 into him and throws the gun onto his corpse.

ONE MAN AGAINST THE SYNDICATE-
WITHIN THE LAW OR WITHOUT!

CARLO PONTI THE
VIOLENT PROFESSIONALS
RICHARD CONTE · LUKE MERENDA

In Elberfeld, Germany, three people of various ages die when a jeweler's watch museum explodes because of a gas leak.

In Duncannon, Pennsylvania, the 25-year-old, 392-seat Kanon Theatre is being demolished to make way for a new Handy Market.

Which of these brief stories affected you most?

How long did they stay in your mind?

In what way did they affect you?

Why do you think that was?

NADIE OYÓ GRITAR
Saturday, August 25, 1973.

Coming off his hit *Una gota de sangre para morir amando* – released just three days ago! – Eloy de la Iglesia helms this story of classy sugarbaby Elisa (Carmen Sevilla) who accidentally catches her neighbor Miguel (Vicente Parra) dumping his dead wife down the elevator shaft of their apartment building. Miguel catches her catching him and makes her help him get rid of the body or else. Road trip! Stockholm syndrome sets in and Elisa shows him how helpful she can be. It's sort of like one of those films where people go on a long journey to bury a loved one and find out all the secrets they couldn't share while the dearly departed was alive. I guess Barbra Streisand was right about how people who need people are the luckiest people in the world.

1,200 feet underground.

That's almost a quarter-mile beneath the earth. It's where they find the two miners trapped beneath a layer of mud in a mineshaft in Casa Grande, Arizona. The temperature hovers around 120 degrees when they reach the men. Nothing heard from the pair since the earth collapsed in on them. Hoping against hope to find them still alive after eight days.

Why hope against hope? That really sounds so hopeless.

The digging machines that had been used to break through the collapsed ground and find the missing men had coincidentally started a fire inside another mineshaft. It only took a spark and what came out of the pit was a whole new catastrophe.

No one knows how long they lived.

They find one of the men face-up in the mud. He'd died while trying to light one last cigarette.

Not enough time.

In Rome, Italy, the kidnappers of J. Paul Getty III tell negotiators that they're cutting their ransom demands. Also, they're cutting off one of his arms or legs if the money doesn't show up.

They want slightly over $5 million. Down from $17 million. A bargain.

The Getty family says they'll only go in for $250,000.

A bargain.

Last month, the kidnappers offered to mail one of the kid's fingers to his mother so she could feel the warmth of their sincerity.

Joanne Ratcliffe is 11. Kirste Gordon is 4.

Both vanish today from a crowd at a football match at the Adelaide Oval in South Australia and are never seen again.

COMEDIA

Hoy, 10.40 noche

ESTRENO

...Y LA NOCHE SE LLENO DE GRITOS
QUE NADIE OYO...

CARMEN SEVILLA
VICENTE PARRA

NADIE OYO GRITAR

MARIA ASQUERINO   ANTONIO CASAS   GOYO LEBRERO   y la colaboración de TONY ISBERT

Producida y distribuida por OSCAR GUAREDO   con la colaboración de BENITO PEROJO, S. A. y P.I.C.A.S.A. (JOSEF A. ONGINAL)

un film de ELOY DE LA IGLESIA   EASTMANCOLOR

¿Qué puede inducir a una mujer que desprecia a los
hombres a convertirse en cómplice de un asesino?

(Mayores 18 años)

DIRIGIDA POR:
ELOY DE LA IGLESIA

NADIE OYO GRITAR

There's a man seen loitering by the ladies' restroom at the Oval. A man reportedly wearing a brown pantsuit, a brown wig, silver nail polish and patent leather boots.

Also never seen again.

If there was a scream, no one heard it

UN TIPO CON UNA FACCIA STRANA TI CERCA PER UCCIDERTI
Monday, August 27, 1973.

Christopher Mitchum follows up his role as the obsequious psychopath in *Una gota de sangre para morir amando* with his turn here as a gangster's son named Ricco. Most people caught this film under its title *Cauldron of Death*, lured in as they were by the lurid image of a woman melting in that selfsame cauldron. Hippieish Ricco gets out of jail and immediately starts down the road of revenge on a mean machine made of gunshots and karate chops. He does it to avenge his father, a capo who got assassinated by the scurrilously opportunistic Don Vito – played by Arthur Kennedy, scowling his trademark scowl of contempt like there's no tomorrow. Don Vito dumps anyone who gets on his nerves into a big industrial vat of acid. He also has a guy graphically castrated, fed his manhood and tossed into the acid after catching him having sex with his girl. Don Vito also stole Ricco's lady Rosa, played by endlessly nude Malisa Longo. Barbara Bouchet plays Scilla, the grifter who sympathizes with Ricco's righteous plight and helps him out. She even strips in the middle of the street on a foggy night in a scene that's both sexy and surreal. The Italian title translates to *Some Guy With a Strange Face Is Looking For You to Kill You*. An unusually loud film – the gunshots explode like grenades – it has a strangely cynical, resigned aura, and the ending is one of the best of the worst.

They're waiting for Wesley Parker to rise from the dead today.

He's a little busy, though. Lying in state tends to fill up one's social calendar. Besides, he's only 11.

TRIPLE HALLOWEEN HORROR

THREE TIMES TERROR
A TRIO OF EVIL
STRAIGHT FROM HELL!

THE CAULDRON OF DEATH

THE FEMALE BUTCHER

A FILM VENTURES INTERNATIONAL RELEASE

A TRUE TALE OF THE DEVIL IN A WOMANS BODY
Documented in the pages of the Guiness book of world records

The Original!
BEYOND the DOOR

R

NOW AT A THEATRE OR DRIVE IN NEAR YOU
CHICAGO: McVICKERS   LOGAN
                Downtown   North
OUTLYING: SKYLARK MIDWAY HAMMOND OUTDOOR
            Aurora   Dunlap   Hammond
41 OUTDOOR   DELUXE DRIVE IN   STARLITE
Hammond   LaPorte   Osceola
53 OUTDOOR   LASALLE DRIVE IN   31 OUTDOOR
Palatine   LaSalle   Niles, MI.
212 OUTDOOR   CHIPPEWA   VILLA OAKS
Michigan City   South Bend   Villa Park

He lived – or lives, depending on the person with whom you speak – in Barstow, California.

His parents came to the conclusion that diabetes is caused by various devils, and that to feed them insulin encourages them truly and unduly.

Wesley Parker died on August 22.

The mortician and the gravedigger wait to see what will happen. Wesley's dad told them not to bury him.

You never know when a resurrection is going to just kind of "happen."

You have to be prepared.

Jesus said, "I am the resurrection and the life. He who believes in me will live, even though he dies."

It says so, right there on Wesley's gravestone.

How long did the mortician and the gravedigger wait for something to happen? How long do you stick around before something seems unnecessary? How quickly do you leave and feel some level of shame or regret because you didn't stay?

Where is it written what you should do in a case like this?

Near Bogotá, 42 people die in the crash of a Lockheed L-188A Electra. Fog obscures their way. They crash into the side of a hill after take-off.

Five minutes after their ascent.

The airplane, split in half by the impact, spilled forth "pieces of legs and cut and burned bodies scattered all over the hill," according to a local reporter on the scene.

Where is it written what you should do in a case like this?

Terry Roberts Johnson, 20, falls to his death near Taft, California when the star formation that he's constructing mid-air with a team of 10 skydivers is shattered by another skydiver who smashes into them.

Johnson's parachute was operational. He never managed to pull the ripcord.

They think he may have been knocked out on impact.

Where is it written what you should do in a case like this?

It's one thing to be ready to die. To prepare yourself for the eventuality. To make your peace with everything.

What if you're not even there when it happens?

TESTA GIÙ, GAMBE IN ARIA
Wednesday, August 29, 1973.

Andrea (Corrado Pani) is an artist and rebel who hates everything in his life but loves the comfort he gets from his level of social privilege. To free himself from all his bourgeois trappings, he practices yoga – hence the film's title, which translates to *Head Down, Legs in the Air*, referring to the Sirsasana yoga pose he keeps fucking up when he tries to do it. He knocks up his model girlfriend (Marina Malfatti, seen earlier this year as the evil mistressmind in *Il prato macchiato di rosso*), so she has an abortion without telling him. He beats her up and dumps her. So much for transcendence. There's also a maniac stalking Rome, killing intellectuals and professors. Soon, people begin to think that Andrea is the killer. Presently, he trails a man whom his murdered friend had suspected of nefariousness. He gets so paranoid and freaked-out that he strangles the guy – but he's not the killer, he's only some random professor! He realizes he's got to face the madman himself if he's going to get any peace. Never mind that he killed another guy, beat up his girlfriend and brought shame to his yoga guru! One pose at a time, man!

As if recovering from the biggest earthquake in Mexico's recorded history wasn't enough, they're also being flooded today by the worst storms in three decades.

In one apartment building, upwards of 100 people are asleep when the quake hits at 3:50 a.m. They die in an agonized instant when the building collapses in on itself.

Searchers keep finding bodies. The broken and the injured litter the landscape from mountains

to tropics. Veracruz and most of South-Central Mexico felt the temblor, ultimately measured at 7.0 on the Richter scale. In Puebla, the earth opens up and swallows cars. Buildings. People.

All that comes back out is dust.

In a London hotel room, Academy Award-nominated actor Michael Dunn breathes his last.

In amidst everything else going on.

Does he stop breathing at the same time as those earthquake victims in Mexico?

Timing is everything. Sometimes it's just not *your* everything.

Dunn, 39, was only 3½ feet tall and yet he commanded a fascination unrivaled in his era, thanks to his portrayals of everyone from contemplative hunchbacks to sinister scene-stealing genius Dr. Miguelito Loveless on the reliably bizarre television series *The Wild Wild West*.

A program, it should be noted, on which he constantly returned, undeterred by people or ethics that got in his way.

On his way to wherever it was he was going.

In Copenhagen, Jens Jørgen Thorsen vows to forge ahead with his new film *The Sex Life of Jesus*.

Facing criticism and violence by everyone from Pope Paul VI to the furious faithful, Thorsen promises that *The Sex Life of Jesus* will include a nude, bank-robbing Christ on a motorcycle romancing Mary Magdalene in a whorehouse. Yesterday in Rome, Roman Catholic agitators hurl three firebombs in protest at the home of the Danish ambassador to Italy. I bullshit you not.

Imagine being the person picked to give the Pope the memo on this one.

You'd probably wish the ground would swallow you up and take you away.

THE SPOOK WHO SAT BY THE DOOR
Friday, August 31, 1973.

Ivan Dixon – Kinchloe on *Hogan's Heroes* – directs this story based on co-writer/producer Sam Greenlee's explosively honest novel. Lawrence Cook plays nondescript Dan Freeman, a CIA employee who goes back home to inner-city Chicago to teach the downtrodden and oppressed how to use espionage techniques against aggression both naked and three-piece-suited, racism both overt and casual, and exploitation both explicit and implicit. Riots happen and violence rules the day but of course Freeman's endgame is a long one, meant to spur the oppressed to look beyond short-sighted measures like property destruction and stride onward to a truer form of liberation that doesn't depend on others for fulfillment. The Feds tried to confiscate the film and take it out of circulation; the negative survived only because it was mislabeled in a film can. With an absolutely blistering soundtrack by Herbie Hancock. The ultimate film about fighting back.

John Ford – the motion picture director whom Ingmar Bergman called "the best director in the world" and whom Satyajit Ray compared to Beethoven – dies at age 78 today in Palm Springs, California. Stomach cancer.

All hail the master of the long shot.

Even in obituaries, it was shown that he wore a big black patch over his left eye.

To protect his sight.

Meanwhile.

A film director dies that no one has heard of in

decades. Jon R. Pownall, 39, is found murdered in his office in Portland, Maine. Shot in the back of the head.

No suspects. No weapon.

Pools of blood, however, are found by a cleaning lady in the elevator and on the floor of the corridor leading to the elevator.

Since April, he'd worked on a film for a production company called Planet 3 Films. Jim Backus, Margaret Hamilton and some locals were set to star in *The Salem Six*, a film about meddling kids who band together to destroy a factory that spews out pollutants.

Interstate's
abc WACO 753-4031 **NOW** Open 12:45
Spook: 1:00-4:30-7:55
DOWNTOWN WACO MALL   Halls: 2:45-6:00-9:35
No Early Bird!
Adults $2.00 Stu. Card $1.75

BOK-RI LTD

"the spook who sat by the door"

PG   United Artists
Companion Feature
// **"Halls of Anger"** //

A $400,000 life insurance policy. Taken out on him less than two weeks ago.

The beneficiary? Planet 3 Films.

In a couple of years, interior designer Herbert R. Schwartz and his partner Truman H. Dongo are tried for Pownall's murder. Both will be acquitted. A jury rules that Transamerica Life won't have to pay out on that insurance policy after all. In 1981, Planet 3 head Joseph A. Castellucci – and prosecution witness in their trial – is himself arrested for hiring a hitman to kill his in-laws.

Sometimes when you play a long shot, you just lose.

On the obelisk at Pownall's grave are engraved the words "Murdered. We all miss him."

In Gainesville, Florida, eight anti-war activists known rather cryptically as the Gainesville 8 are found innocent by a federal jury. They were accused of plotting violence during last year's Republican National Convention.

Bombs and guns. The usual.

Nobody could prove that they were all in it together, though.

In Hanford, Pennsylvania, liberation of a different sort happens when Sterling McWilliams, 39, jumps out of a second-story window at 3 a.m.

His house is on fire.

Kids were smoking. On the couch. Ablaze, the couch sets a nearby propane tank alight. It explodes.

His wife Joyce, 32, five children – aged 14, 12, 11, 10 and 9 – and their two dogs aren't quite as lucky. The fire flashes through the house, incinerating the tiny bungalow in which they are so completely trapped.

McWilliams tries repeatedly to go back and save someone. Anyone.

The inferno forces him back.

Again. Again. And again.

He dies in 1994. The family gravestone encompasses everyone who died that morning.

Everyone except him.

His stone stands alone.

Imagine something so violent that it haunts you even after you're dead.

THE HOUSE OF SEVEN CORPSES
Monday, September 3, 1973.

John Ireland plays a director making a film about occult-oriented murderousness that happened at various times within stately Beal Manor (doubling for the Governor's Mansion in Salt Lake City). John Carradine plays the caretaker who warns them not to trifle with the powers of the Great Beyond. The striking opening credits depicting those murders are inescapably eerie in their framing and presentation. *The Tibetan Book of the Dead* is read aloud and unspeakable horror is unleashed from beyond the grave, which may or may not be the same thing as the Great Beyond.

J.R.R. Tolkien died yesterday.

A bleeding ulcer and a chest infection do him in. Aged 81.

Like Peter Cushing's wife Helen, the death of Tolkien's wife Edith in 1971 cast a particularly melancholy pall over his life. They had been married for five decades, an extortionately rare phenomenon considering how fraught the world had been with wars and plague throughout the 20th century.

As a reflection of his devotion to his wife, Tolkien had the name "Lúthien" etched upon her gravestone. In his Middle-earth saga, Lúthien was an elf who came to the angelic Valar to beseech them to bring her love Beren back to life after he had died at the hands of great evil.

A four-year-old got shot in the head in Harlem today.

Accidentally. In his stroller. On the sidewalk.

Drinking apple juice.

"They were hitting him with tire jacks and slicing him with straight-edge razors," says one policeman who helps save the luckless killer from a frenzied mob.

Police put themselves between the killer and the rage of the crowd.

Patrolman Lyman Gerrish says, "Me and my partner were absorbing the impact of the blows of the crowd."

In Toronto, The Odeon Carlton – last of Canada's majestic organ-bedecked cinema palaces – heads to wreck and ruin this September 28.

Coming soon.

2,000 seats. Only the faintest fraction of those seats is filled by customers watching movies from Monday through Thursday. Some nights, the theatre looks like a house with seven corpses.

The culprit? The audience itself.

"It's a pity, but people's entertainment habits have changed," says theatre spokesperson Charles Mason. "They watch TV on weeknights now, and the trend is toward smaller theatres with about 400 seats," he adds.

As for that custom-built theatre organ, it's given to the government.

All transcendence in its own time.

CEREMONIA SANGRIENTA
Monday, September 10, 1973.

Jorge Grau directs this quality version of the real-life story of Countess Elizabeth Báthory de Ecsed, in which the Countess' aristocratic husband makes all the villagers think he died and came back as a vampire. He does this so they'll think that it's a vampire that's draining all the young local girls of blood instead of his wife. What a pal. He ends up dead and staked in a coffin and put on trial – even though he's dead! Her ancient hag housemaid does her part to poison her mind, helping convince her that she should be a real asshole and kill all those girls. The Countess (played by Lucia Bosè) is kind of pathetic and dopey, and even after all those bloodbaths she looks like she's maybe in her early 30s as opposed to probably being 35 or 36. When the villagers really figure out what's going on, they wall her up in a windowless room and leave her there. Now no one can see how young all that blood made her! What an incredible waste of time!

In Niteroi, across the Guanabara Bay from Rio de Janeiro, Maria Tomaz Pedro, 27, takes her five children, aged seven months to five years old, to a well 30 feet deep.

One after another, she throws them down that well.

They were hungry. Their father – jobless. That's the explanation we get on page 13 of today's *Milwaukee Journal*, in between a road study and a recycling proposal.

Fold the page and you'd miss it.

Her husband Helio, 27, stops her from killing herself when she comes home after killing her children.

The *Atlanta Constitution*. The *Montréal Gazette*. The *Nevada State Journal*. The *Orange County Register*.

And then, nothing.

Like falling down a well. Into oblivion.

In Plainfield, New Jersey, the Strand Theatre recovers from last night's bloodshed. Nearly 70 kids go nuts on the final night that the Angela Mao film *Lady Kung Fu* screens there.

The local newspaper describes it as a "film featuring Oriental practices of self-defense."

Two cops beaten up. One clubbed over the head repeatedly. Kids smashing windows, pilfering ice cream and slashing the upholstery of innocent chairs.

Policeman Patrick McColgan blames *Lady Kung Fu* for the fracas.

"I think this type of movie, which is predicated on violence, tends to excite these young people," he said, adding, "Drastic steps are going to have to be taken to protect our police officers from being brutalized at the hands of youngsters who have no respect for law and order and are apparently not controlled by their parents."

Conversely, as Chinese philosopher Confucius once wrote, "Few are those who err on the side of self-restraint."

Near Griffin, Georgia, retired millworker Ress Clanton claims he saw a golden egg fall from the sky today, five miles south of town. This may or may not be related to the unidentified flying objects seen recently throughout the vast wide Georgia skies.

Strictly speaking, that's exactly what they are. Objects that are flying that have not been identified.

When that golden egg hits the ground, it vanishes into a billowing plume of white smoke. "I tell you, I believe it to be a piece of brimstone from Heaven come down here to show people how He can burn the Earth with it," Clanton says.

Researchers investigating the earth into which the golden egg descended report that the temperature of the ground was 300 degrees Fahrenheit. They also found higher-than-normal traces of copper and chromium within that earth.

Not that one necessarily follows the other.

That cosmic egg didn't burn its way through the Earth to come out whole inside a well on the other side of the world and spirit away those children to some alien planet where they'd be happy and loved for ever and ever, world without end.

Those are called wishes. You save those for falling stars.

What would you choose?

The fantasy, or the reality?

DRIVE HARD, DRIVE FAST
Tuesday, September 11, 1973.

Race car driver Mark Driscoll (Brian Kelly) gets roped into ferrying Carole Bradley (Joan Collins) back home to New Orleans from Mexico City by driving her husband's sportscar. The car has been bugged by chop-happy machete madman Deek La Costa (Henry Silva, luxuriating in the severe splendor of all his henrysilvaness) and so of course they have to outrun his craziness for 90 minutes, which is just exhausting. Made in 1969 but not aired on NBC until 1973, it was Kelly's final acting role. On November 27, 1970, while driving his motorcycle down Benedict Canyon Road in Los Angeles with galpal Terrie Tanberg, the third gear stuck. They hit some water. Slammed hard into an embankment. Tanberg escaped with a bruised hip. Kelly got a skull fracture; his right arm and leg, paralyzed. He went on to executive-produce *Blade Runner*, which is no small thing.

"I declare my will to resist," continues Chilean President Salvador Allende. "Even at the cost of my life in order that this serve as a lesson in the ignominious history of those who have strength but not reason."

"We cannot tolerate mob violence, whether by well-intentioned citizens or by people trying to disrupt the community," vows New York City Police Commissioner Donald Cawley.

"Workers of my country, I have faith in Chile and its destiny. Other men will overcome this dark and bitter moment when treason seeks to prevail. Keep in mind that, much sooner than later, the great avenues will again be opened through which will pass free men to construct a

"Drive Hard, Drive Fast"
8:00 PM MOVIE SPECIAL
The suspense is stunning, and so is the action as this first-class mystery makes its TV premiere!

Come and see NBC!

13

better society," Allende promises.

Jamie Marquez hears the sound of the engine of the "Flying Pinto" – a Ford Pinto with wings – faltering near the airport in Oxnard, California. He looks on as one wing of the aircraft buckles, then plunges to the ground, parts spewing from its ruined body all the way down. "The plane then struck the top of a tree and crashed into the truck and exploded into flames," he reveals.

"Long live Chile! Long live the people! Long live the workers!" Allende says in his farewell speech.

Right before the bullets tear his body apart.

THE CROOKED ARRANGEMENT
Wednesday, September 12, 1973.

Jim coerces Davey into morning sex and tells him that if he doesn't do what he says, he'll throw him out on the street. Muzak plays while they have sex. After Jim takes off for work, Davey stays in the apartment and talks to Jim's associate Dale over the telephone out of sheer boredom. A mysterious man stroking a little white dog sits in a chair slightly off-camera and drinks as Dale and Davey talk. Later, a telephone repairman comes by and bugs the telephone while Davey's there. Elsewhere, the enigmatic man watches two guys soundlessly have sex while "Freedom of Expression" by The J.B. Pickers and "Welcome to Nevada" by Jerry Reed play. He can't stop stroking that dumb little dog. When Jim comes home with his associate, it turns out that he's mixed-up with drugs, and occasionally violent things happen to you when you're in that business. Director Roger Marks fills the film with interesting camera angles that are at points unusual and evocative, and the film ends on a suitably depressing, downbeat note.

They're flying Samuel Moore's heart in by helicopter today.

He's not getting a transplant. He's giving his heart. Doctors pack it in cold salt to make sure it survives the trip from Oakland, California to the Stanford Medical Center where a recipient is on the operating table. Waiting.

He was shot in the head on Monday.

And here he is today.

In this day and age, some coroners object to using

the organs of murdered people for transplants.

At issue is the moment of death.

Dr. Robert Burns, chief surgical resident at Highland Medical in Oakland points out that the definition of death has not been conclusively reached, even in 1973.

Should a person be pronounced dead when their brain stops – or when their heart stops?

What do you think?

In Atlanta, the co-owner of an adult peepshow dies when TNT rigged to his truck's ignition blows him sky-high.

James A. Mayes Jr., 40, is ripped to shreds by the blast that also tears the roof off of his truck. His partner, William Scarborough, says Mayes "hadn't had any arguments or fights with anyone. I just don't know." Mayes, a technician manufacturing and servicing coin-operated peep-show booths, leaves behind a wife and daughter and the makings of what will be a scandal that involves the Mafia and its control of the business of pornography on the East Coast of America.

For now, police have no leads.

There's nothing they can use.

HEX
Thursday, September 13, 1973.

Impossibly young Gary Busey, Keith Carradine and Scott Glenn star as former soldiers turned bikers wandering through 1919 America. They're on their way to California when they stop in Bingo, Nebraska. Some pushy loudmouthed kid challenges Carradine to race his brother, played by Dan "Grizzly Adams" Haggerty, who drives an anachronistic souped-up jalopy. Blonde biker China (Doria Cook) tells Haggerty, "I'll bet you've got a tiny pecker and a slow car!" Consarnit! The infuriating bikers flee to a remoter-than-remote farmhouse inhabited by two mysterious women – Oriole (Tina Herazo) and Acacia (Hilarie Thompson). They get high – except for high-strung Busey – and party like only people in 1919 can. The bikers mock the girls' Native American heritage and show everyone what shitty racists they can be. Acacia almost gets raped. Oriole gets vengeance – repeatedly – as she casts the titular hex. One guy gets his face chewed by an owl. Another dies when an old pistol explodes in his hand. In one shocking and effective sequence, Cook gets harassed by various animals, hallucinates that a thorn is thrust into her eye and is swallowed up by the earth for her troubles. *Hex* boasts beautiful forlorn shots of endless rolling grasslands and antique motorcycles courtesy of stuntmen George Goodwin Dockstader (whose gravestone reads simply "Hollywood Stuntman") and Bud Ekins, who performed Steve McQueen's famous motorcycle jump in *The Great Escape*. Herazo and Carradine fell in love on the set of *Hex* and remained an item throughout the '70s. Isn't that nice?

In London, England and France pledge to link England with continental Europe by means of a

EASTGATE Cinema City NO 1
STARTS TONIGHT
Features: 7:35 and 9:23 pm

WHEN WAS THE LAST TIME YOU WERE AFRAID... REALLY AFRAID?

[PG] :::

HEX

20th Century Fox Presents 'HEX' Starring KEITH CARRADINE • SCOTT GLENN with HILARIE THOMPSON as Acacia and TINA HERAZO as Oriole

32-mile tunnel running underneath the English Channel.

$2 billion. That's all it'd cost. A steal, really.

Planned are three tunnels, 32 miles in length – 23 miles of which run underwater – with a service tunnel for good measure.

21 years. That's all it'd cost. A steal. Really.

The violence of time passing.

Earnest Ball takes the stand in Tuscaloosa today.

Ball, from Alabama, is on trial for assassinating Tuscaloosa policeman John Thomas with a 12-gauge shotgun.

"I looked at him in his eyes and he looked in my eyes. His eyes blinked and then I saw he had a gun and the gun fired. All I knew to do was grab my gun and fire back," Ball states.

Earlier in the day of the shooting, he shattered the glass of his ex-wife's front door.

That's why the police were there in the first place.

Community property laws give him the right to do so, Ball says. All he wanted to do was see his five kids before he left town for California, he says. The people of Tuscaloosa were against him, he says.

He saw a bucket of Kentucky Fried Chicken in the kitchen of his ex-wife's home. He says that the Kentucky Fried Chicken company conspired against him because he was running a fried chicken eatery.

There's a man lying on the floor outside the bedroom.

Deader than fried chicken.

Old and poor are the 11 men who die of smoke inhalation at the Washington Hill Nursing Home in Philadelphia this morning.

The alarm system fails. The only thing the retirees can do is sound the alarm the old-fashioned way.

They scream and scream.

A boyfriend of one of the nursing home attendants purportedly said yesterday that he would "burn the place down."

It's one of four nursing home fires that occur between 1972 and 1974 in the city of Philadelphia. These infernos will in turn ignite inspections and tighter enforcement of fire safety regulations. A January 1974 inquest by the United States

Department of Health, Education, and Welfare will find that 59% of America's 7,318 Skilled Nursing Homes have grave fire safety violations.

Grave.

How quickly do you think you could get away from smoke and fire right this instant?

How quickly do you think you could do it 50 years from now?

They think that there may be another man trapped in the rubble. Searching for him becomes agonizingly slow and slowly agonizing as time runs out.

Come on, folks. While he's young.

THE PYX
Thursday, September 13, 1973.

Detective Sergeant Jim Henderson – played with singular passion and intensity through the constantly surprising talents of Christopher Plummer – has to figure out if heroin-addicted hooker Karen Black fell, jumped, or was pushed from the top of a Montréal skyscraper. Could a mysterious cult be to blame? Why, yes. Yes, it could! The cult holds a sinister mass, complete with heavy ambient ambiance and grotesque masks. Imagine a cross between *Christiane F.* and *Rosemary's Baby* and you get the general gist. Troubled Catholic Henderson is incredibly bummed out because his wife died and of course now he has all sorts of regrets to color his actions and the choices he makes. *Of course!* A pyx, so you know, is a container for the consecrated body of Christ to be taken to people who are too sick or invalid to make it to church to do their thing. For once, it's kind of refreshing to have the hero fail to save the girl. He never had a chance, really. The many flashbacks to Black's life that lead up to her fatal fall make the film that much more introspective and contemplative. A metaphor for addiction – to anything, be it a cult or a cut – *The Pyx* also recalls a time when people thought that cults were going to infiltrate everything and make people mindless slaves to shiny things and sparkling drudgery. It was retitled *The Hooker Cult Murders* decades later for the benefit of bored late-night television watchers in Montréal.

If you've got a traffic ticket in Kentucky, now you can pay the fine in blood.

Blowing through stop signs or traffic lights. Speeding. Reckless driving. Come on down to the Central Kentucky Blood Center in

Lexington and donate a pint of blood.

They city already has your sweat and tears, so why not?

They're weeping for joy in Rome, Maine.

A slightly-above-average kid inexplicably hoists

a 3,000-pound tractor when it flips over onto a teen farmhand, pinning him beneath its crushing weight.

18-year-old sudden strongman Arthur Hinkley tells investigators, "I don't know how I did it. I can't remember anything."

Think of a time you witnessed something violent.

How much can you remember? Half of it? All of it?

Think of something else that was violent that happened to you. How much do you want to remember? Half of it?

None of it?

They're crushing Victor Jara's fingers today.

The coup lashes out, reaching into as many aspects of Chilean life as possible. It moves with frightening speed, attacking threats both real and imagined.

Soldiers propping up the new regime of Augusto José Ramón Pinochet Ugarte round up thousands of Chileans. The opposition. Imprison them in Estadio Chile in Santiago. Jara, one Chile's most beloved singers and poets, is caught and tortured by his guards.

They break his hands. Then his fingers. One by one.

Then they try to crush his spirit. They ask him to play guitar.

After they blow his brains out and fill him with bullets, they mount his corpse at the entrance of the stadium for everyone to see as they come and go.

An example.

A sacrifice.

A body.

THE CHAPERONE

Friday, September 14, 1973.

Marsha and her boyfriend Brian meet up with a couple of other teen couples and head off to her dad's cabin in the mountains. Not so fast, Marsha! Dad sends his maid Mildred to chaperone the whole bunch. Mildred is also a secret lesbian who has the hots for Marsha and every other girl on the trip. Marsha gets slashed while swimming. Mildred blames Brian, whom she discovers has a crazy sister who chopped up her husband! That's why you go up to the mountains in the first place – to get *away* from horseshit like that. Soon more people go missing and die horribly. Mildred sure is a crappy chaperone. Press materials promised an "Erie, Hitchcockian" ending, so you can probably guess what happens. Or not!

A fight at midnight.

That's what Samuel Moore, 29, and A.D. Lyons, 53, were involved in last Monday. Moore was in Lyons' apartment when Lyons allegedly pulled out a .22 and shot him in the head.

The moment of death is at issue today.

As usual.

Moore has no brain activity. He's on life support. This is what's keeping his heart and kidneys functioning. His heart goes to a 52-year-old construction worker in an operation at Stanford. His kidneys go to two women, aged 52 and 62, at a hospital in San Francisco.

Lyons' defense is also a philosophical one: at what point is Moore alive, and at what point is he dead?

Did Moore die when Lyons shot him in the head? Or did Moore truly die only when his heart was extracted?

Neurosurgeons pronounce Moore "neurologically dead" before the extractions of his organs were approved.

Moore's sister Rose Green admits, "He would have wanted his organs to help other people. It would have been his decision."

She's all for having the plug pulled.

But not before Samuel Moore can finally do something with his life.

At the 8,000-foot elevation point of Yosemite National Park, Johnny Pages, 6, comes up to a group of hikers and tells them that he's hungry.

He's been trying to find his way out of the Park on his own ever since he got lost in it last night.

He says he saw a coyote and a bear fight. The bear won.

The coyote lives to fight a bear.

HIT!
Friday, September 14, 1973.

FBI agent Billy Dee Williams rallies a team of experts to take down the French heroin cartel who sold the drugs that killed his daughter. Having had personal experience with losing loved ones to drugs themselves, they're more than happy to straight-up assassinate the cartel members, one after another. Richard Pryor plays a rare semi-serious role here as a Naval engineer and reluctant killer – which is nice because the man does have range. It must have been real weird to be a Vietnam veteran and come back from the War and then go to the movies like this in which the only thing that proves your worth as a person is how good you are at continually killing. Conversely, 1973 is also the year that David Carradine makes his film *Americana*, a quiet and redemptive meditation on war and healing, but it won't be out for another decade. Penthouse loved it. It helps to be patient.

A noose loops down around her hands. They're tied behind her back.

In the bedroom. A baby weeps in a crib near her.

That's how Dorothy Lovrencevic, 26, is found by her husband Michael, 27, when he comes home from work in Pine Township, Pennsylvania.

In the bedroom. Fully-clothed.

The car's gone. That's strange. She must be in the house.

In the bedroom. Face up. A scarf in her mouth.

THE NIGHTMARE THRILLER OF THE YEAR!
DOUBLE FEATURE
POOR PRETTY EDDIE 7:20
LESLIE UGGAMS SHELLEY WINTERS
MICHAEL CHRISTIAN as Eddie and SLIM PICKENS
TECHNICOLOR A WESTAMERICA RELEASE R

To pull off a job no one would ever dare,
you need a team no one would ever believe.
Singles 2.00
Couples 3.00
HIT! 9:00
BILLY DEE WILLIAMS · "HIT!"
RICHARD PRYOR PAUL HAMPTON GWEN WELLES
R RESTRICTED
CINEMA

No signs of rape. No forced entry. Nothing stolen. Nothing to indicate a struggle.

"Please take care of them," Michael said as he hands his two children to the neighbors. "My wife's been murdered and I've called the police."

Neighbors don't notice anything suspicious. Not even when the car slides out of the driveway and off into the woods, where it's found later.

On Tuesday, they'll charge James Allen Long, 16, with the murder. He lives only a few miles away. His mother and Dorothy used to play cards together.

No disciplinary issues at school. A purported "loner."

244

To pull off a job no one would ever dare,
you need a team no one would ever believe.

Hit!

BILLY DEE WILLIAMS "Hit!"
RICHARD PRYOR PAUL HAMPTON GWEN WELLES

..ALAN R TRUSTMAN and DAVID M WOLF ... HARRY KORSHAK ... SIDNEY J FURIE

R

Starts TOMORROW

167th ST. TWINS
8 BLOCKS WEST OF I-HAVAII
SHOP CENTER 652-3961

Brandt's
FLAMINGO
Lincoln Rd., Miami Beach

WESTCHESTER
Cinema
223-0016

KENDALL MALL
TWIN CINEMA

SURF
COLLINS at 74th ST

27th AVE.
DRIVE-IN
N.W. 27th Ave
at 85th ST

NO. DADE
DRIVE-IN
N.W. 27th Ave
at 171 at ST

His English teacher, John Seftas, doesn't believe Long did it. "I still am filled with disbelief," he says. "They are going to have to prove it before I believe it," he says.

Seftas took the kid under his wing. "It appeared he needed someone to talk to," he explains. During fishing trips they'd take throughout Pennsylvania, they talked about Long's problems.

"He had friends in school," says Seftas.

"He was not paranoid about things here," says Seftas.

Circumstantial evidence – a type of gravel, a boot mark, hair samples – will convict him. An autopsy reveals that Dorothy had "sexual relations" preceding her death.

He gets 5-to-10 years for voluntary manslaughter next year on July 3.

He gets out in 1977. Circumstantial evidence turns out to be a little too circumstantial. He always maintained he didn't do it.

And then there's this.

On August 23 of 1974, police arrest Long's uncle, Henry J. Heastings.

On New Year's Eve of 1956, Long's mother Mary flees to her parents' house after a particularly vicious beating by his father, Floyd A. Long, 23. She holds infant James, only six weeks old, tightly in her arms during her escape. Floyd follows them there. He's 5'4." "An extremely strong man with a violent temper," they call him.

She told police that she stabbed Floyd to death in self-defense.

The charges were dismissed.

During James' murder investigation, Mary reveals to Police Chief Richard Baer that in fact she had not killed her husband.

Floyd beat her brother Henry violently earlier that day. Henry plunged a butcher knife through Floyd's lungs and into his heart as Floyd lunged at him.

Henry did it. Defending his sister. Defending himself.

He's cleared of all charges on September 5, 1974.

A SCREAM IN THE STREETS
Friday, September 14, 1973.

Two detectives are hot on the trail of a cross-dressing rapist-murderer in the Los Angeles area. This means you get to see lots of beautiful location shots of bygone Southern California, mostly filmed in the San Fernando Valley. When they're not trying to catch that crazy creep, they stop robberies and chase perpetrators. One guy who wastes a shopkeeper goes flying through the door of a Hungarian deli in slo-mo to get away from them. Apparently a cross-dressing rapist-murderer is hard to spot, because he sure does kill a bunch of people. He even hangs out with an undercover policewoman who acts like it's no big deal that she's with this strange man who fits the description of the maniac that's currently being pursued by the police department! *A Scream in the Streets* is the kind of film where people watch "stag movies" while the "fella" and his "old lady" "ball" and then smoke "grass." Also: a guy surrounded by liquor bottles whips his masseuse half-to-death in a massage parlor; a Peeping Tom roams the city; a reasonably riveting car chase at the end; and all manner of perversity dripping from the city's pores as the detectives try to do their job. Also: some people have some sex.

It's late morning when a woman in Rancho Cordova, California, puts her 18-month-old son in bed for his nap.

There's a knock on the door.

She ignores it.

Then there's a funny sound at the back of the house. She sees a man trying to break into the window of one of the bedrooms.

He sees her watching him.

He escapes. This gives her enough time to lock every door and window she can. She calls her husband. Tells him what's going on.

Shortly thereafter, the man comes back. Almost breaks through the door between the kitchen and the garage.

She's got a handgun. Tells him he's dead meat if he keeps coming.

He leaves.

She calls the Sacramento Sheriff's Department.

He then smashes all the way through the broken door. They struggle over the gun. She gets off a shot. Over his shoulder.

247

He flees. She passes out.

The Cat Burglar of 1972-1973. The Cordova Meadows Burglar. The East Sacramento Flasher. The Visalia Ransacker. The Creek Killer. The Diamond Knot Killer. The Original Night Stalker. The East Area Rapist.

This is what people had to deal with, living in and around Sacramento in 1973.

Of course, some of these apparently different madmen are the same person. But people don't know that, in the here and now. They just want to live their lives.

They just want them to go away.

So that they don't have to make other plans.

Watch out for the sealed blue barrels floating in the Gulf of Mexico today.

They're filled with sodium cyanide and potassium cyanide.

Two great tastes that taste great together.

If you add water to these chemicals, then you get cyanide gas.

They fell into the ocean after two ships collided on August 5 off Pensacola, Florida. Tropical Storm Delia, barreling through the Gulf, only muddied the waters by spreading the deadly blue time-bombs far and wide throughout the Gulf. "It's hard to tell what effect the hurricane and current would have," says a Coast Guard spokesman.

"They could be anywhere."

If you could be anywhere – anywhere there aren't serial killers or floating cyanide – you'd be at City Lights Poets Theater in San Francisco to hear Charles Bukowski read his poems. Creation of the Morning Line. Death. Sex Fiends. Best Love Poem I Can Write at the Moment. Eighteen Cars Full of Men Thinking of What Could Have Been. Something for the Touts, The Nuns, The Grocery Clerks and You.

Or you could wait to get the record.

LA CAMPANA DEL INFIERNO
Sunday, September 16, 1973.

Juan gets committed to an insane asylum for three years. When he comes back to the old mansion he calls home, it's a real mess inside. So is he. He also works in a slaughterhouse, which really doesn't help your state of mind if you're already on the edge of sanity. His Aunt Marta (Viveca Lindfors) – who got him committed in the first place – lives nearby with her three daughters. They're living the high life because they're sponging off Juan's inheritance; they also used it to keep him in the asylum. Thanks a lot, assholes. He gets even with them, though – even if he *was* kind of a maniac, and you can totally see why they put him in the asylum in the first place. "Already Fate has dealt the cards," a holy man tells him. "But *I'll* play them!" Juan shoots back. A scene of oxen bearing the titular bell across a pastoral landscape falls beautifully between the Surreal and the picturesque. Director Claudio Guerín fell from the church bell tower on the final day of filming *La campana del infierno* and to this day people argue whether he fell or jumped. Maybe ask Christopher Plummer. Either way, it's pretty sad. An uncredited Juan Antonio Bardem – Javier's uncle – finished the film. Can you imagine hanging out and having a

conversation with Javier Bardem about this film, or *La corrupción de Chris Miller?* That'd be fun!

Meet Buzz Aldrin. Mental depressive.

Speaking from the Space Center in Houston, the second man to walk on the Moon tells all. When he came back down to Earth, his marriage suffered, his career cratered, and he went into a psychiatric hospital.

It happened, he says, because of a "change of life following the flight."

Think of what Buzz Aldrin feels like when someone bumps into him and then turns around and says, "What's *your* problem!" He thinks, "Fuck. I've walked on the Moon and I still have to put up with *this* fucking asshole."

"I think it will make (the public) a bit more aware and hopefully have these things discussed more openly so that a broken arm is looked upon about the same way as a person who has temporary mental depression," Aldrin says.

He's back to his old adventurous self now. Therapeutic drugs. Counseling.

A new memoir called *Return to Earth*.

Geraldine Hughes and Pauline Floyd, both 16, are out dancing at the Top Rank discotheque in Swansea, South Wales.

There's a movie theatre upstairs. It's screening the new film *Live and Let Die*.

Geraldine and Pauline can't afford a taxicab. They hitchhike, only to be intercepted by the person newspapers at the time dub The Saturday Night Strangler. Taken to a wooded area, they're raped. Strangled. Beaten. Found by a retiree near the town of Llandarcy. Abandoned at the entrance of a culvert.

Despite the largest police dragnet in Welsh history, the leads run out in 1974.

Their killer is revealed to be Joseph William Kappen. He dies in 1990. Lung cancer.

The police, working tirelessly to solve the case 30 years after DNA evidence reveals Kappen's identity, exhume his body to be sure. A first in the history of crime. Kappen, an itinerant bouncer, small-time thief and greyhound trainer, once decided that the greyhound he'd taken in as a family pet had become too old. He strangled it to death with a wire on a beach in front of his son.

"You know there are evils out there," says Geraldine's father Jean Hughes in 2003. "But you never believe it will touch on you and yours," he admits.

Before Victor Jara dies today in that stadium in Santiago, amidst inconceivable fear and horror, he writes the poem that becomes known as "Estadio Chile" on a scrap of paper.

† † †

"There are five thousand of us here
in this small part of the city.
We are five thousand.
I wonder how many we are in all
in the cities and in the whole country?

How hard it is to sing
when I must sing of horror.
Horror which I am living,
horror which I am dying.
To see myself among so much
and so many moments of infinity
in which silence and screams
are the end of my song."

† † †

The poem – reproduced here with the kind permission of writer Nain Nómez – is smuggled out in a friend's shoe. In the time following the Chilean coup d'état, Nómez had the poem distributed by hand as a statement of hope and solidarity – person to person, individual by individual – that continued to ring true long after this year is dead and buried.

A bell.

But not from Hell.

LEGACY OF SATAN
Monday, September 17, 1973.

Gerard Damiano follows up *The Devil in Miss Jones* with this vision of occult fricker-frackin' in New York. Bored boosh-wah housewife Maya (Linda Christian) is elected by prophecy to become cult queen and consort to the sinister minister Dr. Muldavo. The cast sits around and engages in bush-league theological debates that are so tedious that you want a Bible salesman to come in and start a long conversation with you about Jesus. The cult performs rituals to give Maya wacky dreams. Of course those dreams spill over into her waking life and drive her around the bend as she enthusiastically murders people left and right. She falls for the Doctor – by way of devotion, he cuts her throat open with the razor-sharp metal crescent seen in the newspaper ads for the film – but another acolyte, Aurielia, gets jealous. Aurielia lets Maya's weak husband George out of his basement prison and gives him a magic sword by which he vanquishes the cult. With Electronic Rhythms Created by Arlon Ober and Mel Zelniker That Do Absolutely Nothing For Your Boner. It was doubled with either *Blood* or *The Texas Chain Saw Massacre* throughout its theatrical run, courtesy of Bryanston Distributing. They worked so hard to sell it! Maybe they should've hired a cult to get the group discount on movie tickets. With other new groups of thinkers emerging throughout 1973 – African Theological Archministry; Ásatrú; Church of the Creator; Heaven's Gate; Jews for Jesus; Raëlism; and Vajradhatu – Damiano was nothing if not perceptive of the tenor of the times. Christa Helm – who played the tastefully-named The Blond Blood-Farm in *Legacy of Satan* – was a widow by the time the film was made. She's knifed and bludgeoned to death at age 27 in West Hollywood on February 12, 1977. It happens in the same neighborhood where actor Sal Mineo dies in 1976 after a knife gets stuck in his heart. Speculation rages that she has a "frank and intimate" diary of her celebrity sexual adventures and recordings to back it all up. Her murder remains unsolved.

I wonder what music they played at Hugo Winterhalter's funeral.

He dies today. Cancer.

"There was a time there when everything he touched turned to gold," a spokesperson at RCA Records recalls about the easy-listening maestro. In the '50s, Winterhalter had a #1 hit alongside Eddie Heywood with their song "Canadian Sunset."

Given the backlash against easy-listening music that's been growing steadily since the '50s, it's somewhat amusing to see that the quote from his *New York Times* obituary online translates through OCR software as "There was a time there when everything he touched turned to acid."

His funeral on Wednesday will be private. It may be that there's no one left now who remembers what music they played there. Little details of big events have a habit of falling away into oblivion first.

The violence of progress.

Jane Jarvis, director of music and programming in 1973 for Muzak – the easy-listening background music played in businesses to optimize worker productivity with a technique known as "Stimulus Progression" – reveals in a *New York Times* interview, "Ten o'clock is peak fatigue period, and 2:30 in the afternoon is even more so. You have to combat boredom and fatigue. So the music gets more abrasive, punchier, brassier."

It's all highly orchestrated.

Gene Leroy Hart is on the run.

He's been at large since escaping from the Mayes County Jail in Pryor, Oklahoma with two other prisoners.

He stays on the run for years until he's arrested April 6, 1978 after an extensive manhunt

throughout the backwoods of Oklahoma. He's a suspect in the June 13, 1977 murders of three Girl Scouts, aged eight, nine and 10, in a tent at Camp Scott in Mayes County. Brutal murders. Nauseating and unthinkable.

The things you don't know until it's too late.

Today, Deputy Premier Péter Válya, 54, experiences hideous agony at a Budapest hospital from burns suffered Saturday evening while he visited the Lenin Metallurgical Works factory in Miskolc, Hungary.

An ordinary workplace accident. Slip and fall.

Directly into a pit of molten iron ingots.

Caught between iron molds, the heat fuses his nylon safety suit to his body.

He only has today to live.

So do you.

DYING ROOM ONLY
Tuesday, September 18, 1973.

Jean (Cloris Leachman!) and Bob (Dabney Coleman!) are vacationing marrieds driving back home to Los Angeles through the Arizona desert. They wind up at a roadside greasy spoon/motel and decide to stay there for the night. The lead heavies are Jim the cook (Ross Martin!) and customer Tom (Ned Beatty!), who Jean thinks have kidnapped Bob because she can't find him anywhere. Jean thinks that Vi (Louise Latham?), the motel's front-desk lady, is also in on it but she can't figure out how. Apparently there have been a string of disappearances and the sheriff (Dana Elcar!) knows something's up. More people die but Dabney escapes in time to star in *The President's Plane Is Missing* in October, while Cloris survives so she can be on *The Migrants* in February with Ron Howard. Only on ABC!

In Roselle, New Jersey, the body of 19-year-old sociology major Ann Logan lies in the woods near Seton Hall University. Strangled.

She fought. She fought hard.

Using every ounce of her strength. Using everything she knew about karate and self-defense. The police think that her killer has all sorts of scars on him now from fucking with the wrong person.

Ultimately, serial killer Robert Zarinsky becomes the prime suspect in her murder. The woods are in walking distance of his house.

In 2008, a DNA test reveals that his isn't the DNA found on Logan's body.

Investigators remain adamant that, all things considered, he's still guilty.

In 2008, he dies in prison. Pulmonary fibrosis. A disease that scars the lungs.

Makes it impossible to breathe.

In Santa Cruz, Herbert William Mullin, 26, gets life in prison for the murders of 10 people committed from October 13, 1972 through February 13 of this year.

The kids in high school voted him "Most Likely to Succeed."

He succeeds today in keeping silent and ignoring his family seated behind him in the courtroom as they wait for his sentencing.

Mullin killed all those people, he swears, so that he might offer up sacrifices in order to stop earthquakes from tearing California apart.

On February 21, 1973, a magnitude 5.2 earthquake off Point Mugu causes $1,000,000 worth of damage in Ventura County, California. It's the strongest earthquake in the county's his-

Tale Of Danger

*Emmy-winner Cloris Leachman is left alone and terrified by two sinister men —
Ned Beatty and Ross Martin (left to right) when her husband disappears in a dingy
roadside diner in "Dying Room Only," at 8:30 p.m. on ABC.*

tory — that anyone knows of, anyway. "It felt like the end of the world," says Richard Rodriquez, manager of the Mayfair Market in Oxnard, where 10 years later I myself would play Galaga to near-total distraction, totally unaware of anything shakin' beyond trying to tape Dr. Demento off the radio that week and the fact that the film *Curtains* had one of the scariest ad campaigns I'd ever seen.

Elsewhere in California, singer and "Cosmic American Music" composer Gram Parsons dies.

At the Joshua Tree Inn, the sometime member of The Byrds — and architect of their country rock opus *Sweetheart of the Rodeo* — is shot up with liquid morphine.

Provided by an unknown woman.

He'd said he wanted to be cremated and have his ashes spread over Cap Rock in Joshua Tree National Park, where he and Keith Richards from The Rolling Stones used to get high and look for UFOs.

On the other side of the country, in Durham, New Hampshire, at about 9:45 p.m., a married couple hears a loud *thud* outside their home.

The husband goes outside to see what's landed. He hears "garbled voices" and noises like electricity issuing from the top of a tree in his yard.

Back in the desert, Gram Parsons breathes his last.

Anywhere but here.

TERROR ON THE BEACH
Tuesday, September 18, 1973.

Hippies in dune buggies terrorize parents Dennis Weaver and Estelle Parsons as they try to protect their kids – Susan Dey and Kristofer Tabori – amid the beautiful seaside backdrop of Pismo Beach, California. Their leader is as Mansonesque as you can expect from a television network with a motto like "CBS is Easy on the Eyes!" Weaver plays his character as a put-upon pipe-smoking pacifist. His son wants to fight. He'd probably be one of those guys who die in Vietnam the minute he steps off the troop transport. Good thing the war's over. Isn't it? The freaks freak out the family by trying to drive them off the road and making a mannequin part of their gang. Conversely, there's a lot of hugging going on in this film. If you ever get a chance to visit Pismo, it really is very deeply pretty. The mass butterfly migration that ends at Monarch Butterfly Grove happens from October to February, and there's a big wide beach where you can drive your RV right beside the water. Just like in the movies.

Mary Cairns is 8 years old.

When she's sentenced in a Glasgow, Scotland court to 18 months' detention for stabbing an 11-year-old twice in the lung with a bread knife during a fight, she screams.

"I want my mummy," she screams. Continually.

In the courtroom, her mother weeps. Her daughter screams as she's carried away.

Screams all the way out the door. Screams when she's carried down to the cells beneath the court.

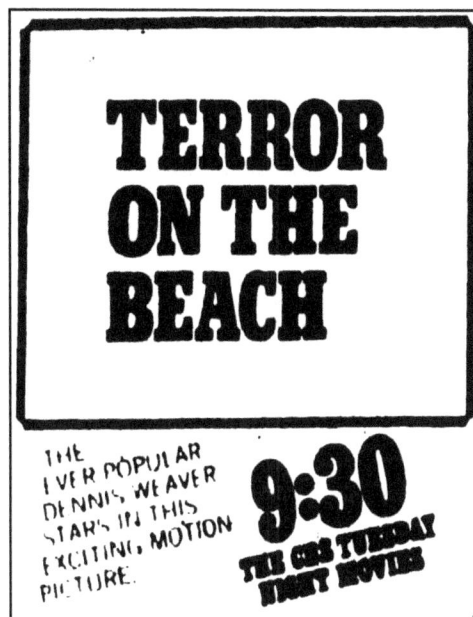

TERROR ON THE BEACH

THE EVER POPULAR DENNIS WEAVER STARS IN THIS EXCITING MOTION PICTURE.

9:30 THE CBS TUESDAY NIGHT MOVIES

Other recent Scottish criminal court cases involving children include a 10-year-old boy sentenced to five years for raping a seven-year-old, and another 10-year-old on trial for murder. Mary is, however, the youngest child to ever be tried in Scotland.

By December, Mary will be freed. Public uproar. Outcry.

Hues.

The laws that put her there in the first place are now due for review. She gets three years' probation and placement under psychiatric care.

She skips along, playful and childlike on her way home. Leaving the court behind.

Presumably.

Hurricane Ellen, the strongest storm of this year's season, gathers strength in the Atlantic.

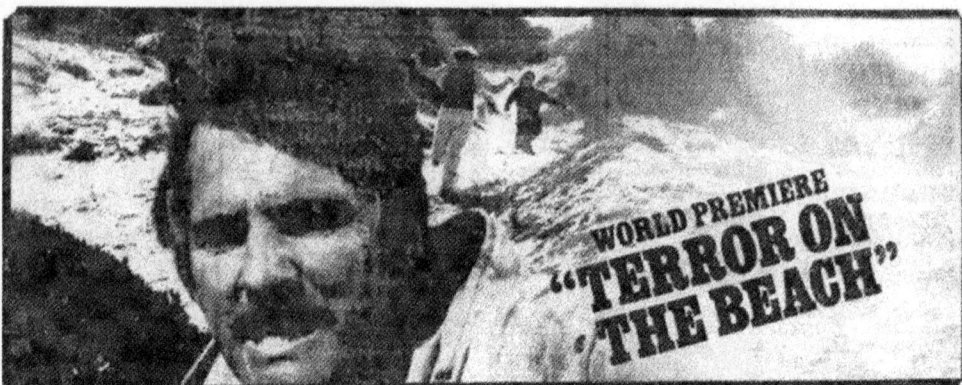

WORLD PREMIERE
"TERROR ON THE BEACH"

Well on its way to becoming a Category 3 hurricane, its winds reach 115 miles per hour, arriving at the totality of its strength further north than any storm yet known.

How much of a storm is defined by its eye?

How much of a storm is defined by what passes beneath its gaze?

Holly Springs, Mississippi. The Holly Theatre burns down. Possibly because of a gas leak.

Gutted.

It's still burning. Refusing to die.

This isn't the first time that it has.

On December 15, 1949, 20 minutes after the end of the last show, gas fills the auditorium of The Holly. Explosion. Demolition. Conflagration. It sets fire to the store next door. Kills a family of three – Dr. and Mrs. H.R. Davidson and their four-year-old son. While searching for the source of the gas leak with the store owner, Dr. Davidson is outside the building and downstairs when it explodes. He runs to their apartment above the store to save his wife and child.

They've recently moved to Holly Springs from New York City. Their bodies are found in the ruins of the shop. Where they fell. Together.

That was then, this is now.

A fireman is taken to Marshall County Hospital today. Smoke inhalation.

Before he goes to the hospital, black funeral home director C.F. Brittenum, 24, rushes to help him. Brittenum's funeral parlor sits next door to The Holly.

Another fireman pushes him away from the injured man. Brittenum pushes back.

White policeman Rex Bell, son of the pushed fireman, sees this and punches Brittenum out. Bell and his partner arrest him a few minutes later in the funeral parlor. Beaten by both of them, he says.

Assault on a police officer, they say.

Does no good deed truly go unpunished?

Ask the hurricane.

SATAN'S SCHOOL FOR GIRLS
Wednesday, September 19, 1973.

Martha Sayers, a student at the swanky and haughty Salem Academy for Women, hangs herself in the living room of her sister Elizabeth's house in Los Angeles. Sleuthing Elizabeth enrolls at Salem under a fake name, because of course on TV you just go get a fake driver's license over from the guys in MacArthur Park and then you get to go to college. She meets some of Martha's classmates – future Charlie's Angels Kate Jackson and Cheryl Ladd among them – and weird things happen around the school. Headmistress Jessica Williams frowns and schemes and soon there's another suicide. Elizabeth finds a cellar with a spooky portrait and another dead girl in it. Professor Delacroix (Lloyd Bochner) gets so distressed that he runs away and gets caught in a swamp. Students show up and turn him into a piñata. If you ever wanted to see Cheryl Ladd beat a guy with a stick, this is your movie! Suave Dr. Clampett (Roy Thinnes) tells the Headmistress what's really happening and she loses her mind. Elizabeth discovers Clampett leading a cult meeting. Her so-called "friends" turn on her because they believe he really is Satan and they want to get on his good side! Klutzy Satan sets the school on fire and all those dummies burn up while Elizabeth saves the Headmistress. Then he vanishes! He doesn't even offer to help clean up! What a surprise!

Apopka, Florida. A cocker spaniel named Mayor. 11 years old. Arthritic.

He's going to die today.

Today was the day his death sentence was set to be executed. So to speak. This is because there have been 18 complaints about Mayor biting kids. Seminole County Commissioners had no choice but to put the dog down for the safety of the public and for the good of the community.

Not so, says Cora Lee Marden.

The 66-year-old lives in alone a modest home in the middle of a remote orange grove. Her husband Ralph died on July 23. Her two daughters died very young.

She knows something about the value of life.

"It's all so ridiculous the way this case developed and how this dog came so close to death," she says, stepping forward to adopt Mayor.

And so she saves his life.

In Milwaukee, an alderman suggests psychological screening for all police department applicants. In order to "eliminate the psychopaths and odd-

7:30

ABC Wednesday Movie of the Week

"Satan's School for Girls" deals with a young woman's investigation into the unmotivated suicide of her sister at an exclusive girls' academy. Starring in tonight's motion picture are Roy Thinnes, Pamela Franklin, and Kate Jackson.

balls from the police force," says he.

On a panel at Marquette University's Multi-culturral Center, he also suggests hiring more minorities at top levels of the department, as well as including a more involved level of community oversight into the actions of the police.

Pat Curley is a new member on the staff of the D.A.'s office. She maintains that cops often "derive vicarious thrills by asking a rape victim to recount all the intimate details."

The evil that other men do.

In outer space, Laërtes unveils itself.

A minor planet, it's discovered today near Jupiter's orbit by Dutch astronomer couple Ingrid and Cornelis van Houten. They find it, together, by looking at photographs taken at California's Palomar Observatory by Dutch-American astronomer Tom Gehrels.

Laërtes the planet was named for Laërtes the Argonaut. He's the father of the famous Greek adventurer Odysseus.

Laërtes' father was Arcisius, a son of Zeus.

The god of lightning. Justice. Order.

Better up there than down here, sometimes.

TOM
Wednesday, September 19, 1973.

"You think things are going to be better for you after the War?" "You mean because I'm black?" "Yeah." "I don't think things are going to be a hell of a lot different." Jim – a former GI, played by director Greydon Clark – goes to Watts to deliver a letter to the family of his black friend who died in Vietnam. Pretty soon he gets hassled by anyone and everyone in the inner city. His friend's brother runs a gang and they don't like him. Aldo Ray and Jock "Tarzan" Mahoney play a pair of deeply abusive racist cops and *they* don't like him. Soon everyone is at each other's throats. The gang crashes a hippie pool party and promptly scandalizes all the pearl-clutchers and monocle-droppers there. It's pretty weird to see Tarzan be such a raging asshole. The real moral here is that the desperation, distrust and despair in both Vietnam and Watts are like living things. *Tom* composer Ed Cobb produced and wrote "Tainted Love" for singer Gloria Jones in 1965 – as a B-side! – which enjoyed a prosperous second life when Soft Cell covered it in 1981.

In Sacramento, California Highway Patrolman Earl L. Doyle offers hitchhiker Glen Johnson, 29, a ride.

To a safer spot.

When he approaches Johnson and his friend near the South Sacramento Freeway, he asks if they have any weapons.

Johnson does.

He pulls a .38 from his pocket to show him.

Ask a question, get an answer.

California Medal of Valor recipient Doyle answers back by firing three shots into the hitch-hiker.

"Husband and father," it says on Johnson's grave.

Later, Doyle was said to have whirled around. Fired twice from behind the squad car as the other man cocked his pistol and aimed at him.

Under the body lies the pistol with the hammer cocked and the live round in the chamber.

In Paso Robles, California, three people are blown to smithereens and four more are injured when the wares of Duke's Smoke Shop mix with an unexpected gas leak.

The roof caves in. Walls fall down. The windows of nearby homes shatter.

Those that could be saved from the smoking ruin are pulled out of their would-be graves by citizens who rush in from the surrounding streets to help.

"I wanted to make somebody else feel as bad as I did," says a nameless Vietnam veteran in a Georgia prison. He's serving a life term for murder.

He speaks behind a screen. Concealed. Tells a panel of sociologists, priests and policemen his sorry story.

They're trying to figure out why Atlanta has become so violent.

In 1970, the veteran killed a kid in a passing car.

"I was very violently mad and had a feeling of not caring about myself or anyone else," he admits.

What would have defused this particular ticking time-bomb? Not having a gun, he says. Also, having "Somebody to talk to … a person who was sincerely concerned."

A headline screams, "Veteran tortured by heroin addiction recalls slaying."

The killer says, "I see the problem not in drugs but in myself."

Who do you believe?

Why do you believe that person?

What do you do then?

★ ★ 872-1331 ★ ★
NAVARRO
TWIN DRIVE-IN SCREEN 1
OPEN 7:00 STARTS 7:30

HORROR HIGH

R

He made an 'A' in
TERROR!
Ask His Teachers If You Can Find One
STARRING
PAT CARDI — ROSIE HOLOTIK
JOHN NILAND
**PLUS THE DALLAS
COWBOYS**

HORROR HIGH
Thursday, September 20, 1973.

Pat Cardi plays Vernon Potts, a hectored, harried and hassled high-schooler who perfects a potion to punish the parochial pricks who perpetually punch him at school. Even the janitor is a grade-A bastard to him. Austin Stoker plays Lieutenant Bozeman, a cop who only wants to understand what in the hell is going on after a bunch of kids and teachers wind up wretchedly slaughtered. People get dismembered by paper-cutters, dumped into acid vats and stomped on with baseball cleats. The girl who loves Vernon for his mind weeps piteously. A favorite of mind-warped late-night-TV during the '70s and '80s, it was usually experienced under the title *Twisted Brain*. Jekyll & Hyde stories are not generally germane to this volume because they're so dependent on an outside stimulus (a transformative serum) to unlock the violence inside. This one, however, remains unusually sleazy and angry and so we include it here for general overall perspective. Its world premiere took place in Irving, Texas. That's where Lee Harvey Oswald was living in 1963 before John F. Kennedy's assassination. Frank Beard, the drummer from ZZ Top, was getting ready to be a freshman at Irving High School in 1963. Today, in 1973, he's got a hit with ZZ Top's *Tres Hombres* LP. They're playing University of Southern Mississippi's Reed Green Coliseum in Hattiesburg tonight. He's probably at the premiere in spirit.

It's the only tree around.

A pecan tree.

Death is set in motion by small, almost inconsequential things. You'd never even think to look for them.

isle of view drive-in
EVERITT AVENUE / 785 4110

TONIGHT
HORROR HIGH 7:30
DRACULA'S CASTLE 9:15

There is something evil out there...
Possessed by a force that
doesn't belong to this world
—and it's going to kill me!

CROWN
INTERNATIONAL
PICTURES presents

HORROR
HIGH   COLOR

PAT CARDI · ROSIE HOLOTIK · JOHN NILAND · AUSTIN STOCKER
JOYE HASH · JEFF ALEXANDER · JAMES P. GRAHAM · LARRY STOUFFER
JAMISON FILM COMPANY · A CROWN INTERNATIONAL PICTURE

2ND FEATURE   -G
"BLOOD OF DRACULA'S CASTLE"

A pilot with a heart condition runs three miles from a motel to an airport.

The guitarist. The comedian. The agent. The manager.

The voice.

Almost past that tree. Almost in the air. Almost got it.

Almost.

Death sets in motion the smallest things.

You'd never even think to wait for them.

Until you finally do see.

By the time you do – in an instant – small things become incredibly consequential.

Prather Coliseum. Northwestern State University. Natchitoches. Louisiana.

One hour later, he was dead.

When your life flashes in front of your eyes, do you think it happens in chronological order?

Revenge began it
...terror ended it!
TONITE 7:30 & 9:30

an eye for an eye

PG

OUT-'PYSCHO'S
'HITCHCOCK!

NO ONE ADMITTED AFTER THE FIRST MURDER!

FRI. "HONG KONG CAT"

CINEMA CITY
ROCKER RECLINER CHAIRS · TEL. 549-0030
BRAINARD RD AT I 91 HARTFORD

NEXT TO VALLE'S

AN EYE FOR AN EYE
Friday, September 21, 1973.

Man-child-with-a-bowl-cut Mr. Rabbey hosts a public-access television kids' show. Some of the kids are being abused by their parents. So, he kills the parents. Scenes of offscreen verbal abuse heaped upon various children are somehow even more unsettling when you can't see the adults speaking the words. The extended dissociative abuse makes time slow to an absolute crawl. One little girl gets slapped hard in the face and thrown to the ground by her snarling mom. You'd think that once Mr. Rabbey found out about all that abuse, he'd cool it with his Punch-and-Judy puppet show thing because it'd traumatize the kids all over again! He even brings his puppets along when he commits his murders. What a trouper. So you know how bonkers he is, you get to see constant close-up shots of Mr. Rabbey's sweaty freaked-out eyes. Re-released in 1975 under the title *The Psychopath*, in case you forgot how subtle the film was.

"An epidemic of violent thought."

That, says renowned Los Angeles coroner Dr. Thomas Noguchi, is what we're experiencing in our lives as they are lived today.

Thinks. Alleges. Suspects.

The medical examiner casts a dire forecast.

"We are boiling in a sort of pressure cooker. People are becoming more susceptible to suggestions of violence. Motion pictures are hounding us. People are fantasizing acts of violence. There is a chain reaction of hysteria."

A chain reaction. The hallmark of hysteria.

Reading that litany as it is written, you'd think that these are situations that are inescapably linked.

One follows.

Another.

Speaking today at the culmination of a three-day crime investigators' seminar at the County Police Academy at North Park in Pennsylvania, Noguchi maintains that in the past 18 months in California, cults practicing human sacrifice have been ramping up their nefarious activities. That the hours between 11 p.m. and midnight and from 2 a.m. through 3 a.m. are prime times for murders. That – of the 1,000 murders in Los Angeles in 1972 – 150 were linked with sex, and many of those victims were young women.

Don't forget the suicides, either.

Violent thoughts are what you have when you think of the Piper Twin Comanche B that crashes today in the woods near Florence, Wisconsin, killing all 6 aboard.

It isn't found until September 30.

Violent thoughts are what come to mind when

you've read Tuesday's obituary of Noreen Kumeta. She died in a car wreck in Barrington Hills, Illinois last week.

Her husband Donnie Rudd isn't convicted until July 2, 2018 of savagely beating Noreen – a librarian for the Quaker Oats Company – sticking her lifeless body in the family car and staging the accident to collect on a $100,000 insurance policy.

Violent thoughts are what cross your mind when you hear that British-American Tobacco Corporation accountant David Heywood has been kidnapped by Argentine gunmen.

He's freed on October 20. Unharmed. Well-fed. Sympathetic toward his captors.

Remember: it can *always* be worse.

EL RETORNO DE WALPURGIS
Saturday, September 22, 1973.

Back in olden times, witch-hunter Ireneus Daninsky (Paul Naschy) persecutes the Countess Elizabeth Báthory de Ecsed, burning her alive and hanging her acolytes. You know – the things that plants crave. Thirsty for revenge as well as blood, she puts the zap on his bloodline. Wouldn't you? Her descendants turn great-great-great-granddummy Waldemar Daninsky into a werewolf after he accidentally kills one of their own – because apparently after all those generations, he's still kind of a putz. Bring on the bloody murders! Most people think it's an axe-wielding escapee from the insane asylum who's doing all the killing. And it is! Once again, the English-language dubbing is some of the most consistently entertaining around. "The blood of a virgin! The jaws of a wolf!! The night of a full moon!!!" Daninsky falls in love and of course it's doomed from the start. He can only be freed from his lycanthropic curse if his new love kills him. How do you start a conversation over dinner about *that*?

They finally figured out what happened with Donald Bonin's wife.

Investigators initially thought she was a passenger in the car that swerved over the double-yellow line on Highway 1 near Point Mugu yesterday and collided head-on into Bonin's car.

Then burst into flames.

Right before it ejected its hood and sent it directly through the windshield of a sportscar passing by the rolling disaster.

They find her in the other car, suffering from massive head trauma.

Donald Bonin, 45, and Betty Bonin, 51, have been married for only one week.

Had.

20 years working on New York's Central Railroad is a long time.

It only takes a split-second for retired conductor William Edstrom, 67, to make the decision to end his life with the pistol in his hand.

It takes a slightly longer time for his sister to find what's left of him.

Edstrom's wife Marie died on August 13.

Who knows when he finally decided which way to turn?

In Sydney, Australia, two brilliantly-colored mountain lory parrots – normally seen in the distant bush country of the continent – make their nest in the ruins of the Savoy Theatre on Bligh Street.

Poet and Nobel laureate Pablo Neruda dies tomorrow in Santiago, Chile.

Unexpectedly.

Speaking of hunting witches.

Neruda, famous for his *Cien sonetos de amor* (100 Love Sonnets), leaves behind a body of work that now transcends him. A record of our better nature.

Something you can count on.

SHE CRIED MURDER
Tuesday, September 25, 1973.

Fashion model Lynda Day George accidentally sees Telly Savalas push some lady onto the train tracks down in the Toronto subway. She calls the cops to tell them what happened. Guess who one of the cops is. It's an interesting role for Telly because it falls perfectly between his acting jobs this year as both psycho (*Senza ragione*) and policeman (*The Marcus-Nelson Murders*). Mike Farrell – two years before joining the cast of M*A*S*H – plays Telly's partner. I wonder how many cops feel bad for not seeing the warning signs when their partners commit horrible crimes. Telly chases her through the subways while she keeps asking people for help – of course, in true '70s fashion, no one gives a rat's ass.

15 minutes into prison guard Earl F. DeMarse's shift, he's dead.

Stabbed. Multiple times. 26 years a cop.

Marquette Branch Prison. Understaffed. Overworked.

The guards see DeMarse's demise and agitate to strike. They vote 121-17 in favor of a strike.

The Governor has to come in and beg them to stay on the job.

At what point do you realize you've got nothing left to lose?

When the knife rips a hole in the skin?

In Farmington, West Virginia, four bodies are pulled from the wreckage of the Number 9 mine.

An explosion in that mine killed 78 workers.

In 1968.

There are still 38 miners missing down there.

Sara Kaznoski, a miner's widow, rejects an offer of $10,000 in compensation from the coal company.

"It's not a matter of money," she says, asking, "Don't you think we deserve a grave to go to?"

Kenneth James Dartt, 40, a police sergeant in Oregon, Ohio, is found in his car. Parked in his garage.

Carbon monoxide poisoning.

A president of the Oregon Fraternal Order of Police. A 10-year veteran of the force. A Marine Sergeant in Korea.

A wife. Two daughters. Two brothers.

End of watch.

SAVAGE ABDUCTION
Wednesday, September 26, 1973.

Attorney Richard Ridelander hires wealthy warped weirdo Harvey to kill his cheating wife. Energetically sweaty maniac Harvey (Joseph Turkel) likes killing – and mannequins, and panties, and necrophilia – so much so that he blackmails Ridelander into getting him more girls to violate and defile. Ridelander then pays a biker gang $10,000 – $62,200.88 in 2022 money – to kidnap and deliver two girls to Harvey. The gang picks up hitchhikers Jenny (Tanis Galik) and Faye (Kitty Vallacher) and makes them strip and smoke doobies. Romeo, one of the bikers, saves the girls when he realizes how boring and clichéd their deaths are going to be. Stafford Repp – Chief O'Hara from the '60s *Batman* TV series – appears as Abe, one of Ridelander's law

partners. He only had about a year left to live at this point. Turkel showed up about a decade later as Dr. Eldon Tyrell in *Blade Runner*. Galik is really into crocheting these days! There should've been way more crocheting in *Blade Runner* than there was.

Anna Magnani. 65. The actress. Pancreatic cancer.

Ed Kemper. The killer. Six female hitchhikers. Pleads insanity.

Glenn Miller. Bandleader. Vanishes on a flight over the English Channel in 1944. They say they've finally found his airplane.

Perry McKinney. A blind man. Arrested for murder. Sightless for eight years, his guide dog

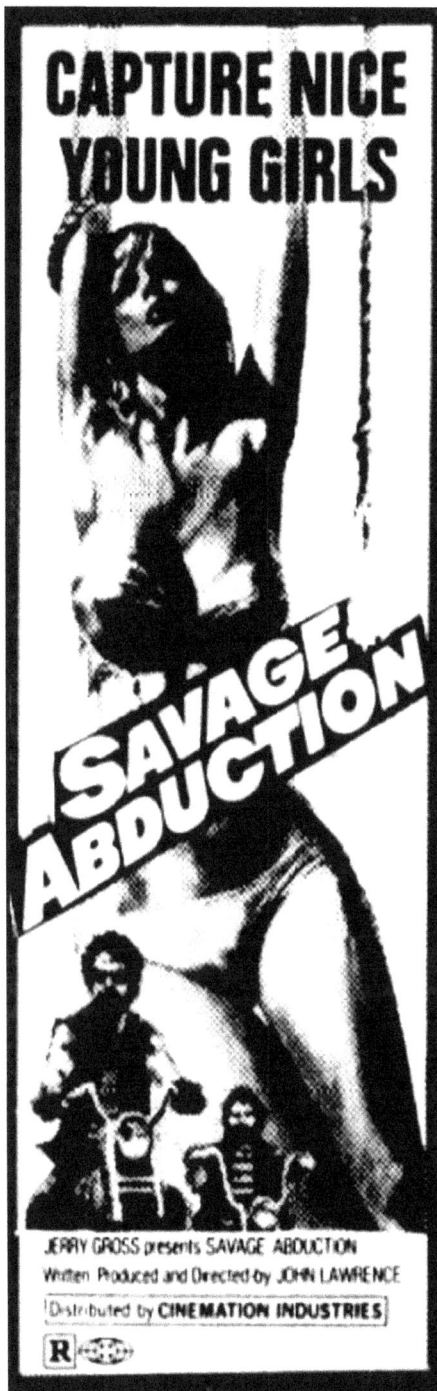

CAPTURE NICE YOUNG GIRLS

SAVAGE ABDUCTION

JERRY GROSS presents SAVAGE ABDUCTION
Written Produced and Directed by JOHN LAWRENCE
Distributed by CINEMATION INDUSTRIES

R

helps him run away. Neighbors hear gunfire, and then find a body.

Philip C. Kaufman. The record producer. Arrested today at his home in Van Nuys, California. Charged with grand theft for helping steal Gram Parsons' body and cremate it in Joshua Tree National Park, per Parsons' request.

Margaret Shortal. 83. Standing on the porch on the second floor of her home in Milwaukee. Hanging out the washing. The porch gives way. She does not survive.

People.

When you know so little about them, it's easy to fill in the blanks in their lives.

What do you imagine?

What do you suppose?

IOANNIS O VIAIOS
Saturday, September 29, 1973.

Vastly underrated Greek director Tonia Marketaki was only 31 when she made this insightful, riveting character study of Ioannis Zachos, a young psychopath who stabs a girl to death in Athens. He becomes something of an antiheroic celebrity when he goes to trial and snookers everyone with his sensitive patter. All the press attention stokes not only his narcissistic ego and the vanity of his insanity, but also his need for attention by the family of his victim. Talk about barking up the wrong tree! He gets a life sentence in a psychiatric hospital but he never really changes or feels remorse. That's not what he's all about. If you think you're going to find any kind of redemption or growth here,

keep dreaming. A rare and crucial film in that it asks larger questions about responsibility both individual and communal, the nature of masculinity, and what it means to be an individual adult human being operating a particular way within a civilized society.

Viggo Hinrichsen.

Not a man. A ship.

A ship filled with barrels of highly toxic hydrogen chloride.

A ship with a crew of two where there should have been five.

That's how you're supposed to do it.

It's not supposed to be uninsured. It's not supposed to be so flimsy. So slipshod.

It's not supposed to sink to the bottom of the Baltic Sea.

In southern Sweden, off the island of Öland, circling salvage ships deploy their cranes to pull the noxious cargo out of the ocean.

Captain Kurt Mester, 48, and his stepson, Leichtmatrose Heinrich Backers, 25. Rescued before being eaten up by sickly yellow clouds of chloric acid hydride transformed by water to become volatile hydrochloric acid. The chemicals blossom skyward, flowers of death sprouting from the sunken ship's putrefying corpse, killing everything in their path.

What also bubbles up from the bottom to the top of public knowledge today is the discovery of the secretive movements of the broken-down ships that transport dangerous shiploads through Swedish waters.

To save money.

Mester will be fined thousands. Kept in custody, away from his home. He can't even captain a boat anymore after today.

Well, he's not supposed to.

"All my fortune is in the sunken ship, I do not have a single penny left," he says.

All gone now.

Last night in Vienna, the poet Wystan Hugh Auden gives a reading to the Austrian Poetry Society at the Austrian Society of Literature.

W.H. Auden, author of the poems "The Age of Anxiety," "The Unknown Citizen," "Funeral Blues," and the upcoming collection *Thank You, Fog*.

W.H. Auden, whose lifelong consumption of alcohol was so legendary that he could drink a concrete statue of Oliver Reed under the table.

W.H. Auden, self-described "comic poet" whose penchant for the trenchant was his defining quality.

W.H. Auden, this morning, is dead.

His chosen last words were "This has never happened to me before."

The violence – slowly, slowly – of poison.

'GATOR BAIT
Monday, October 1, 1973.

Alligator hunter Desiree (Claudia Jennings) wants revenge on the family who killed her little sister. The murderous brood thinks she killed one of their own when in fact it was the son of the local sheriff who really did it. She doesn't care and kills as many of the odious dipshits as she possibly can. The plucky, resourceful and barefoot bayou siren throws everything from snakes to shotgun blasts at them on her way to vengeance, and the seamy, sweltering atmosphere of the swamps practically pulsates through the screen. From today, Claudia Jennings has almost exactly six years left to live.

In Ohio and Virginia, police investigate claims by Vietnam veteran Jack Paul Reale, 24, that he's killed six people since last year.

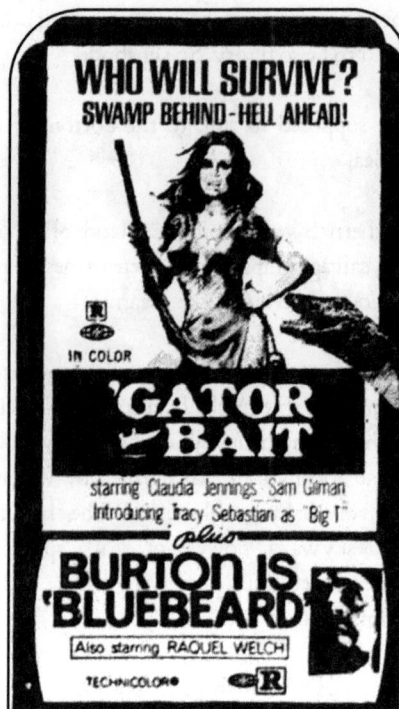

WHO WILL SURVIVE?
SWAMP BEHIND - HELL AHEAD!

IN COLOR

'GATOR BAIT

starring Claudia Jennings Sam Gilman
Introducing Tracy Sebastian as "Big T"
plus
BURTON IS 'BLUEBEARD'
Also starring RAQUEL WELCH
TECHNICOLOR®   R

Old men. Sexually mutilated with a blunt jack-knife.

They've found the body of George Nicholson, 70, in Reale's apartment in Hampton, Virginia.

He tells the police that he won't harm women, though. Investigators are under the impression that he "seems to revere them."

This sentiment is at odds with the discovery of the bodies of the mother and daughter of an old man who owned an antique store. The general consensus is that Reale had to kill them when they accidentally caught him killing the old man.

Worship and sacrifice, intertwined.

They've found the last body from the crash on September 27 of Texas International Airlines Flight 655.

Tomorrow, L.D. Davis, 50, of Pine Bluff, Arkansas, reveals that he knew he should leave Flight 655 before takeoff. It had been delayed to board three Army colonels who had missed the flight. Davis saw his chance. Took it.

L.D. Davis. The survivor.

Like Cary Grant missing the flight in 1943 that killed 24 in Lisbon.

Like Elizabeth Taylor missing the 1958 flight that killed her husband Mike Todd.

Like Waylon Jennings missing that 1959 flight that killed Buddy Holly.

Davis departs the airliner because he had a "strange feeling, vague feelings, something just wasn't right." He'd seen one of the doomed stewardesses on an earlier flight a few days before the crash.

"She had the saddest eyes," he says.

L.D. Davis dies peacefully at the age of 87 on July 27, 2011 in Little Rock, Arkansas. Married to his loving wife Eva Jean Davis from 1974 until the day he died. 13 grandchildren. 10 great-grandchildren.

Sometimes it's the violence that *doesn't* happen to you that changes your life forever.

ISN'T IT SHOCKING?
Tuesday, October 2, 1973.

Police Chief Daniel Barnes (Alan Alda) notices that a lot of old-timers in his small New England town are dying unexpectedly. Is it from natural causes – or is it murder? You, the audience, find out the killer's identity right off the bat but they, the characters on the TV screen, take more than one hour and thirteen minutes to figure it out. Not including commercials. Starring Will Geer as a chain-smoking coroner, Louise Lasser as Barnes' sassy receptionist, and Ruth Gordon as the whimsical old lady that Barnes thinks will probably take the ol' dirt nap next.

In Fort Thomas, Kentucky, an 80-mile chase across the state ends with the capture of two fugitives.

Wilmer Scott, 35, and William Sloan, 24, tell the cops that they've killed six.

At a motel in Falmouth, Kentucky, they kill the night manager and two brothers.

In Lexington, Kentucky, police find the body of Episcopal minister John K. Barnes, the nude body of his daughter and the body of his son.

They even beat up the family's German Shepherd.

The minister's wife, who was not home when her loved ones were murdered, was attending an Episcopal Church convention in Louisville.

Mixed blessings.

On Friday, at St. Hubert's Church, nestled amidst the bluegrass of Locust Grove, Kentucky,

the reverend and his children are buried.

St. Hubert's is a young church, only four years old. Minister Barnes and his children are the first to be buried in its cemetery.

Barnes, who was murdered the day before his 47th birthday, once said that he'd wanted to make the little church "a beauty spot."

"Thank you for conducting the service," his widow Mary Agnes tells presiding Bishop William Moody.

Edmond O'Brien stars in "Isn't It Shocking?"

"I loved your family," the Bishop tells her. "We all did."

Mary Agnes Barnes, later Mary Agnes Melton, will be buried beside them in 2012. In the years that follow their deaths, she becomes a philanthropist. A drama critic at the *Lexington Herald*. A generous benefactor of the Lexington Opera Society. Bringing as much beauty and music to the world as she possibly could in the 40 years since the murder of her family.

It's all she knows how to do.

In Englewood, Tennessee, a 12-year-old boy opens his eyes in bed at night and sees a colossal disc hovering above the trees outside. It makes no sound. A voice, as though standing right beside him, says, "You are not supposed to see this."

Not supposed to. Did anyway.

NIGHTMARE HONEYMOON
Tuesday, October 2, 1973.

David comes back from a tour of duty in Vietnam to marry his Mississippi bride Jill. Jill and David skip out on the wedding reception. Aggrieved, her father sends her brothers to bring them back. Hiding out in a grubby little backwoods motel, they accidentally witness hired assassins bumping off the motel manager. Why doesn't The Mafia like Jehovah's Witnesses? They don't like *any* witnesses! The killers beat David and rape Jill. The couple tries to go about their married lives after that like everything's normal – but of course the only thing that will bring everything back to normal is revenge. Bloody, bloody revenge. David takes advantage of his finely-honed killer instincts, hunts them all the way to New Orleans and makes their last night alive a living hell. Does he do it for Jill? For the both of them? For himself? "Please ... do not see it with someone you love," screamed the considerate ads. Behind all this exploitation rests a portrait of the emotional lives of two people who have suffered through a horrifically violent event together – and what that experience does to them as people individually, and together as a couple. You'd think they'd really be able to understand one another because of what they went through together, right? It's not always that easy. People process their violent experiences differently. Even when you think your experience intersects with that of someone who was there with you in the shit, sometimes you've actually got two disconnected lines laid on top of one another, never meeting as they move in opposite directions.

They've arrested two men in Jacksonville, Florida for the mass murder on January 18 of the seven Hanafi Muslims living out of the house that Kareem Abdul-Jabbar donated to them.

Five of the murdered were children.

Four of those children were drowned.

All this in retaliation for Hanafi leader Hamaas Abdul Khaalis' letters to 50 ministers of the Nation of Islam, condemning their leaders.

Khaalis was not at home the time of the murders.

In New Norway, Alberta, a gas well explodes. A pillar of toxic fumes erupts from it like a cobra, sending hundreds from their otherwise-peaceful Canadian homes.

It's "sour gas," otherwise known as hydrogen sulphide – a gas that is colorless, stinking of rotten eggs and highly flammable – that spurs them to flee.

The oil company spokesman says that the well "got away from them."

In Topeka, a hitchhiker pulls out a pistol and assassinates a state trooper when he bends down to check out the hitchhiker's belongings.

Edward E. Mitchell. 22. Already wanted for the shooting death of his father in Cayuga Heights, New York.

Do **NOT** See It With Someone You Love!
THANK HEAVENS, IT'S ONLY A MOVIE!
THANK HEAVENS, IT'S ONLY A MOVIE!
THANK HEAVENS, IT'S ONLY A MOVIE!
THANK HEAV...   ...NLY A MOVIE!
THANK HEA...   ...LY A MOVIE!
THANK HEA...   ...LY A MOVIE!
THANK HEA...   ...Y A MOVIE!
THANK HE...   ...Y A MOVIE!
IT'S ONLY A MOVIE!

NIGHTMARE H♥NEYMOON

Jim Thornton. 52. On the force for 24 years.

Some see responsibility as a calling. Others hear that calling and it's only voices in their heads.

Mitchell steals Thornton's police cruiser. Trades shots with the policemen who respond.

Is surrounded. Is killed.

He's been on the run for his father's murder since Sunday morning.

It used to be that the only times a person had their name published in a newspaper were when they were born, when they got married, and when they died.

No clue about what he was doing on the drive between New York to Kansas.

No idea why he did it.

No reason that ever got published in a newspaper, anyway.

THE LAUGHING POLICEMAN
Saturday, October 6, 1973.

Walter Matthau and Bruce Dern play cynical cop/misunderstood cop as they try to find the killer behind a machine gun massacre that happened on a bus in San Francisco. Matthau's partner was one of the victims, shot while following some leads of his own that obviously went nowhere. With a crazed hostage-taking amputee, obligatory-but-enjoyable car chases through the storied streets of 1973 San Francisco, and all the casual police brutality you've come to expect from a police story like this.

In East Berlin, an unnamed man, 34, dons a scuba diver outfit and slips into the River Spree.

Completely unnoticed by the guards at the Berlin Wall. Their orders are to shoot citizens on sight if they're caught trying to escape to the West.

The barbed wire. The machine gun emplacements. Patrol boats.

He outwits them all.

Removing his flippers, he walks into a nearby West Berlin police station and tells them what's what.

How did he escape? It's very simple.

He hitches a ride on the bottom of a freighter making its way down the Spree.

The escape is a brief bit of good news in a year when five others meet their deaths near the Wall.

Trying to get out any way they can.

AT 1:30-3:20-5:10-7:10-9:25

Colonial
153 N. Main St. Midtown Plaza

THIS MOVIE IS SO REAL IT MAKES EVERY OTHER MOVIE ON THIS PAGE LOOK LIKE A MOVIE.

The Laughing Policeman

R · COLOR BY DE LUXE · 20 FOX

WALTER MATTHAU
BRUCE DERN

A 15-month-old, accidentally suffocated after his parents try to silence his cries, moments before their successful exodus.

A worker who falls from a speeding train near the border.

Horst Einsiedel, the engineer machine-gunned while climbing a ladder, millimeters from freedom.

Another engineer, who fashions a bulletproof suit for his escape. Gunned down as a crowd watches, despite his best-laid plans.

A boy who falls into the Spree and drowns as guards stand by and do nothing.

A boy who dies five years to the day after the murder of his sister, a 21-year-old in East Berlin. Thrown into the same river as her brother.

The violence of coincidence.

UNA VELA PARA EL DIABLO
Monday, October 8, 1973.

Marta and Verónica. Sisters. A Spanish inn. Pretty young girls check in. They never check out. Laura Barkley. Her sister: murdered. Trying to find the truth. Flashback: Marta. Left at the altar. Lashes out. Sadistically. Kills lively young ladies who only want to have a little fun. Kills one in front of her own baby. God said to do it. Somewhere. Probably. Wish you were here.

Think of how much violence occurs when things don't go the way they're "supposed to."

Roger Caryl. 18. Once an Eagle Scout. Now a cowboy in Avon, Montana. Killer of four yesterday.

Hunted today.

Angered because he claims that he's owed money by the owners of the ranch.

Previously ensconced in a mental institution in Illinois. Calls himself Tex McCord when his victims first meet him.

He walks into the ranch house. Purportedly tells the people inside, "This is hello from Tex."

And then starts shooting.

He completes his assigned responsibilities in 2004 during a pre-release program in Butte, Montana.

Paroled in 2005.

Victims' families oppose it. Caryl tells some of them that he doesn't remember killing all those people. Says he was under the influence of drugs and alcohol.

Aren't you supposed to remember something like killing a bunch of people?

He quietly lives out his monitored life in Muskogee, Oklahoma.

Wondering if this is how life was supposed to be.

In San Francisco, the Lavender Panthers patrol the city, facing off against passersby who might harbor detrimental intentions behind their greetings.

So renowned are the Panthers for bashing gay-bashers that *Time* itself profiles them today. Led by Pentecostal Evangelist and Gay Pride Parade co-founder Rev. Ray Broshears, 38, the Lavender Panthers walk the streets of the city each night, armed with pool cues, chains, whistles and red spray paint. Broshears vows to claw fear into the hearts of "all those young punks who have been beating up my faggots."

You'd think that the police are supposed to handle things like this.

Sometimes it seems like they've vanished.

In Newport, Vermont, the police chief of the nearby village of Barton rests in stable condition after being admitted to a hospital.

In hysterics.

"Did you hit me?" he says to nurses at the hospital.

Over and over.

It's been 24 hours since he was the subject of a substantial police manhunt. His cruiser is found, abandoned, with a window smashed in.

The only other thing investigators find strange about his car is a "dark stain."

Something that isn't supposed to be there.

But still is.

MANCHESTER CINEMAS

ABC 1 & 2 DEANSGATE. Tel 832 2112
(1) THE TOWERING INFERNO (A).
70mm Big Screen Stereo Sound.
Sep. perfs Sun 3 0: 7.30. Weekdays
12.45, 4.0, 7.30.
(2) Andy Warhol's BLOOD FOR
DRACULA (X).
Cont. 1.20. Main film 1.30, 5.05,
8.45 Prog. 3.15, 7.0.

ABC ARDWICK   273 1141
MURDER INFERNO (X)
1.30, 5.5, 8.45
A CANDLE FOR THE DEVIL (X)
3.20, 6.55

BADLANDS
Tuesday, October 9, 1973.

Kit and Holly fall in love and live inside a dream. They kill to maintain their place within that dream. Holly gets tired of it all. She turns herself in. Kit is captured. He jokes with a crowd. He fascinates them. Is executed sometime later. Based on real events. You can look those up later. This is more about the dream.

"I am not trying to be cruel. Do you understand?"

That's what Judge Leander J. Foley tells Doris Scalici, 39, when he sentences her. Three years. Manslaughter.

She helped her new boyfriend Terrance Robinson, 27, kill her ex-boyfriend Glen Leith, 54, in April. Beaten. Dragged off. Dumped in a creek near her home.

Also, she's blind.

She says she couldn't help it. Says that it happened after "an incident" between her 10-year-old daughter and Leith.

Robinson said he'd dump her in the river if she didn't hit Leith.

Jesus and Evelyn Trevino head to their home in Jerry City, Ohio after finishing their shifts as night janitors at Bowling Green State University.

Their mobile home, in which they live with their eight children, is on fire.

The flames rise through the twilight to meet the

IN 1959 SHE WATCHED WHILE HE KILLED A LOT OF PEOPLE

BADLANDS
STARRING MARTIN SHEEN, SISSY SPACER AND WARREN OATES
WB   PG

first rays of dawn.

The back door is sealed shut. The children can't get out.

And Jerry City doesn't have any fire hydrants.

The children, ranging in age from one to nine, suffocate to death. Jose, the eldest, is the child they put in charge while they were at work.

The loss is total.

Elvis and Priscilla Presley got divorced today.

The 500th person to jump off the Golden Gate Bridge will die tomorrow.

The violence of ruined expectations.

MARKLAND MALL
CINEMA I
457-8101

LAST NIGHT:
"American Graffiti"
(PG) 7:00-9:00

He was 25 years old.
He combed his hair like James Dean.
He was very fastidious.
People who littered bothered him.
She was 15.
She took music lessons
and could twirl a baton.
She wasn't very popular at school.
For awhile they lived together
in a tree house.

In 1959, she watched
while he killed a lot of people.

Badlands

Starring MARTIN SHEEN · SISSY SPACEK
and WARREN OATES   PG

FRI.-SAT.-SUN.
5:30-7:30-9:30
MON.-THURS.
1:30-3:30-5:30-7:30-9:30

ARNOLD

Friday, October 12, 1973.

Stella Stevens plays a blonde bombshell ex-flight attendant who has to marry millionaire Arnold in order to get his millions – but only after he's dead. They get married at his funeral. She also has to stay faithful to him, and presumably not run off with other corpses. The marital funeral is presided over by none other than Minister Victor Buono. Jamie Farr, Roddy McDowall, Elsa Lanchester, Farley Granger and others are viciously avaricious as they try to find more riches in Arnold's house, only to be dispatched forthwith in numerous ways – with Arnold rubbing their faces in it up until the very end. He's such a control freak that each day the tape player in his coffin regales the survivors with all the gory details of the previous day's murders. Death by cold cream. Death by immurement. Death by overly-tight suit. You know. The usual.

Edmund Emil Kemper III is judged to have been sane and aware when he killed eight women earlier this year.

He narrates books on tape during his future days in prison.

Jack Paul Reale is extradited to Virginia to answer for the murders of six men.

Reale is rarely if ever mentioned in the history of American mass murder after 1973.

In Albury, New South Wales, Australia, Bronwynne Richardson, 17, goes missing.

They'll find her body, strangled at the edge of a lagoon, two days later.

Arnold is a scream!

They'll find a suspect, Colin Michael Newey, 61, in South Australia in 2014.

It'd be nice to tell you that Newey finally goes to trial for Richardson's murder.

It just wouldn't be true.

In Rhode Island, Craig Chandler Price – known in the '80s as The Warwick Slasher – is one day old. Isn't he cute?

He has no idea, does he.

In Sacramento, the California Highway Patrol announces the addition of blue lights to its crime-fighting dyad of red and amber lights on all of its patrol cars. The three lights now make a "light bar." Studies have found that blue is more visible at night, while red is more visible in daylight. By the spring of 1974, these light bars will become standard equipment on police cars across America.

Something to look forward to.

DOCTOR DEATH: SEEKER OF SOULS
Friday, October 12, 1973.

A grieving widower visits the titular Doctor, an ancient charming carnival conjurer who apparently has the power to bring people back from the dead by transferring withered souls into fresh corpses. He's done it countless times himself over the millennia, moving his essence from person to person as soon as his body becomes too decrepit and grody. He has a tough time finding a soul that'll fit the man's dearly departed wife, so he bumps off a lot of ladies in the process of finding a suitable donor. He also makes out with dead women, which is still a better way to stay young than prune juice and an enema.

It's the last night on Earth for Cynthia Zimniewicz.

She goes missing tomorrow. Skindiving. A field trip with two dozen ecology students from the State University of New York at Binghamton.

Ships search off the north shore of Long Island, near Port Jefferson. The Coast Guard takes part. Helicopters, too.

They're looking. They're realistic.

They're notifying her next of kin.

Floating elsewhere in the Long Island Sound, a fisherman finds a trunk made by the Non-Break-able Trunk Co. Inc., New York.

It's a heavy trunk. 42 pounds of wood and metal, with a black paper skin that makes it seem like another passing wave as it floats by. It could have been in the water anywhere from two days to a week. Could have floated in from somewhere else. Nearby. Somewhere. Maybe.

For decades, the woman in that trunk remains unidentified.

5'1". Shoeless. Long dark hair and nails painted silver.

Strangled.

Maybe both women floated past each other at some point, there in those dark blank waters of the Long Island Sound.

Ships in the night.

DON'T LOOK NOW
Friday, October 12, 1973.

John (Donald Sutherland) and Laura (Julie Christie) grieve for their daughter Christine, who accidentally drowned at their home in the English countryside. Decamping to Venice so John can work, they run into two psychic crones. One of them tells Laura that she can see Christine. Laura and John make love. He starts seeing a little girl running around Venice in a red coat that reminds him of Christine. Laura meets with the psychics; a séance convinces her that John is in danger. Meanwhile, there's a killer at large. Their son gets into an accident back home at school so Laura returns to England to deal with it. Later, he sees her with the two crones on a funeral boat – in Venice! He calls to see what's up with their son. She's been in England all along! Audiences were rather in a lather about the (simulated) sex scene between Sutherland and Christie – but that a husband and wife could have sex under those circumstances – let alone *make love* – in the face of all that crippling, shattering, Holy-God-Almighty-I-triple-fucking-dog-dare-you-to-come-up-with-something-worse level of grief is nothing short of miraculous and people should really just mind their business when it comes to fictitious characters who don't even have a three-dimensional physical form.

Off the coast of France at Sangatte, rescuers trying to save the six sailors trapped inside a capsized ship say that they can't hear anyone tapping on the hull anymore.

Even after they withstood surging waves.

Even after the ship kept sinking.

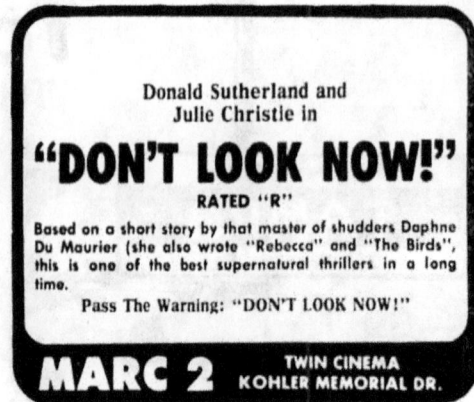

Even after they cut a hole in the hull.

There are no more signs of life.

In Annaghmore, near Belfast, a young man tries to help an old lady escape her grocery store after he'd seen someone from the Irish Republican Army toss a bomb inside it.

Raymond McAdam, 24, saves Lily Nichol, 68, before the bomb explodes and tears him to pieces.

He's the 891st person killed in four years of Troubles in Northern Ireland. But who's counting?

I'll let you figure out which one was Protestant and which one was Catholic.

In Australia, the 320-ton freighter Blythe Star leaves Hobart, Tasmania. Tomorrow, it will capsize in a calm sea on a beautiful day.

10 men make it to the life raft. The vanished ship – the sinking of which remains unexplained – ignites the most intensive search at sea in the history of Australia to date.

And yet.

That raft drifted by lighthouses and near fishing vessels, past tourist spots and within sight of casual coastal watchers. They saw the airplanes searching for them and yet could not make themselves known to their would-be rescuers.

Still they went unseen. Unseen, and given up as lost.

One of the crew dies at sea. Two die when they finally make landfall nine days later.

The search is called off on October 25.

October 25. The day before three of them were found by a local forester after fighting their way through rugged scrub brush, walking for two days to get help.

In Santiago, an autopsy finds that an American citizen killed in Chile during the September 11 coup d'état had been tortured and shot 17 times.

Frank R. Teruggi, 23. Peace activist. Journalist. Ham radio operator.

If you read the news today, you'd think he was the only American citizen to have to have died there.

If you saw Costa-Gavras' 1982 film *Missing*, you'd know that journalist Charles Horman died there, too.

Sometimes it takes time to catch up to what really happened.

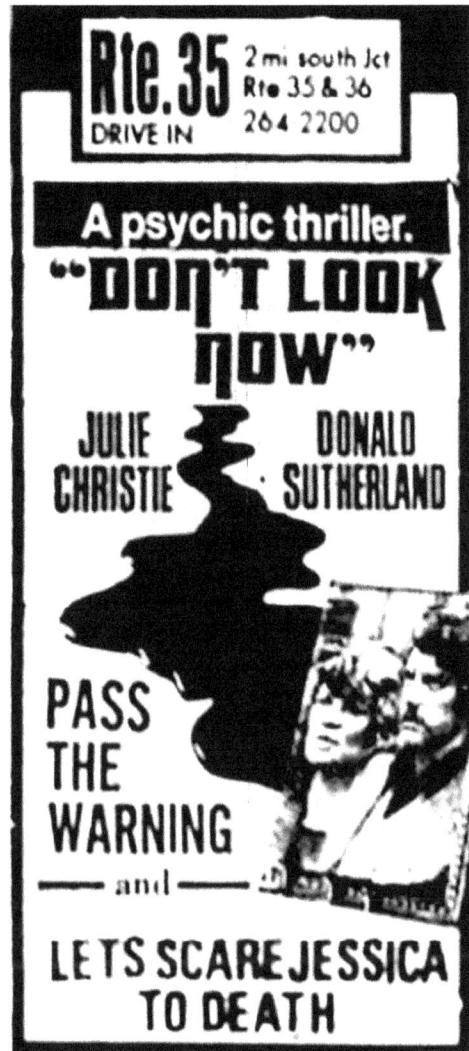

An orgy of the damned!

"It happens beyond madness — where your mind won't believe what your eyes see."

Starts Today

Tales that Witness Madness

Kim Novak Joan Collins Jack Hawkins Donald Houston Michael Jayston
Suzy Kendall Peter McEnery Michael Petrovitch Donald Pleasence

THIS THRILLING CO-FEATURE
AND "Let's Scare Jessica To Death"

R

| 362 4862 THEATRE
abc ST. FRANCIS
MARKET near 6TH | 647 1261 THEATRE
NEW MISSION
MISSION at 22nd | 587 1000 THEATRE
EL REY
1970 OCEAN AVE. | 585 1234 DRIVE IN
MISSION
500 GUTTENBERG |

Barg. Mats. Daily til 1:00
"Tales" 12:30,3:45,7:05 &
10:25 "Jessica" at 2:05
5:25 and 8:45pm.

"Tales" 6:40 & 9:50p.m.
"Jessica" at 8:20p.m.

"Tales" at 8:35p.m.
"Jessica" 7:00 & 10:10

Open Weekdays at 6:45
Open Weekends at 6:30

— ALSO AT THESE THEATRES & DRIVE INS THROUGHOUT THE BAY AREA —

EAST BAY	OAKLAND	AUTO MOVIES	FREMONT	SAN JOSE	SAN JOSE
LUX THEATRE	OAKLAND	ISLAND AUTOMOVIES	ALAMEDA	CENTURY ALMADEN 1	SAN JOSE
TOWER THEATRE	OAKLAND	SHOWCASE THEATRE	CONCORD	JOSE THEATRE	SAN JOSE
EASTMONT 4 THEATRES	OAKLAND	PENINSULA		MERIDAN QUAD 2	SAN JOSE
PLAZA 1	SAN LEANDRO	CARLOS THEATRE	SAN CARLOS	MOONLITE AUTOMOVIE	SANTA CLARA
SOLANO DRIVE IN 2	CONCORD	SAN MATEO THEATRE	SAN MATEO	WINCHESTER DRIVE IN 1	CAMPBELL
SHOWCASE CINEMA 1	ALAMEDA	PENINSULA DRIVE IN	BURLINGAME	MONTE VISTA DRIVE IN	MTN VIEW

TALES THAT WITNESS MADNESS
Monday, October 15, 1973.

Jack Hawkins visits his pal Donald Pleasance in the insane asylum he runs. He tells Hawkins four stories that revolve around the asylum's patients. A boy with crummy back-biting parents has an invisible tiger for an imaginary friend; a photograph commands the weak-willed to do its bidding; Joan Collins gets dumped by a man who falls in love with a killer tree log; and Kim Novak has to deal with cannibals at a luau. These EC Comics adaptations are always great at putting movie stars in deeply weird dramatic situations they'd never be in otherwise, but no matter how bizarre they are, at their essence they exist to moralize and to scold. It was the final film for Jack Hawkins – in May, he'd gone to the hospital to get fitted for an artificial voice box and wound up hemorrhaging out his throat. His voice here is dubbed, likely by the actor Charles Gray, who played Blofeld in *Diamonds Are Forever*. Novak's role was supposed to be played by Rita Hayworth but she walked out suddenly during filming, possibly due to the onset of the Alzheimer's disease from which she dies in 1987.

The cops are in pursuit of the UFOs that visit Pine, Louisiana today.

Late last night and early this morning. Five of them. Red-orange and hurtling through the woods. Almost attacked a cop car.

On October 11, on the Pascagoula River in Mississippi, Charles Hickson and Calvin Parker are fishing when they're taken by three eyeless creatures to a strange craft, after which they're examined and released.

CAPITOL STARTS TOMORROW! 7-BIG DAYS!
DOUBLE THE TERROR DOUBLE THE SHOCK
AN ORGY OF THE DAMNED!
It happened beyond madness where your mind won't believe what you eyes see!!
"TALES THAT WITNESS MADNESS"
Starring Kim Novak Joan Collins Jack Hawkins
CREATURE BLUE HAND
KLAUS KINSKI · DIANA KERNER

The creatures' skin wrinkles like an elephant's. Their long arms taper into claws.

Hickson and Parker stick to their story for years. Years of ridicule, scorn and disbelief.

With a reception like that, it's no wonder those aliens haven't come back.

It wasn't unidentified flying objects that took Carolyn Yvonne Kingston away.

It was the bullets pumped into her head by the as-yet-unidentified robber who shot her in front of her two young sons at her family's store in Salt Lake City in 1971, leaving her for dead.

The thief also murdered a deliveryman there and would have killed another if his gun hadn't jammed while he's escaping.

Carolyn suffers ever since. Wasting away. Liver failed. Brain massively damaged.

She dies today, shortly after being admitted to a Salt Lake City hospital.

If anyone deserves to get a planet after all that, it's Carolyn Yvonne Kingston.

At the Huron Cement Company building in Milwaukee, painter's helper Richard E. Fikes, 22, steps backward to take a look at things.

This would be completely unremarkable except for the fact that he's on scaffolding. Several stories up.

The guide ropes slip from his hands. He plummets into the frigid waters of the Menomonee River.

"Someday we'll meet again!
Never to sever.
Soon Peace will wreathe her chain
Round us forever.
There may we all unite
Safe from the dark of night
In the Eternal Light
Happy forever."

Two steps forward.

DER FLUCH DER SCHWARZEN
SCHWESTERN
Tuesday, October 16, 1973.

Insatiable blood-drinking females express their
sexuality in all sorts of fun ways in this, director
Joseph W. Sarno's take on the Countess Elizabeth
Báthory de Ecsed story that's big on boobs and
bongos and basement bacchanalia. A doctor and
her brother are driving near Castle Varga. Their
car breaks down. Soon they're swallowed up in a
ritual of transference and resurrection with head
villain Wanda Krock (Nadja Henkowa). Baron-
ess Varga was burned at the stake 400 years ago
but she still has a few big fans like Wanda that
would really like to hang out with her again.
Wanda's enthralled girls have lots of sex by the
light of dong-shaped candles. Wanda is assisted
in all her mad schemes by Samana, played by
Claudia Fielers, who will kill herself in Munich
on February 20, 1975 by drinking poison during
the filming of Robert Furch's *Lysistrata*.

A butcher knife with a broken blade.

A stick, stained with blood.

That's how Dorothy Sanchez's life ended.

It's also how the lives of her daughter Toni,
15, her son David, 14, and family friend John
McGrail, 19, all ended.

Near an area in California's San Bernardino

Mountains known as Lost Lake, their bodies are
found by hikers.

Kidnapped Monday. $7,000 demanded of
Sanchez's mother.

Money demanded, more than likely, while the

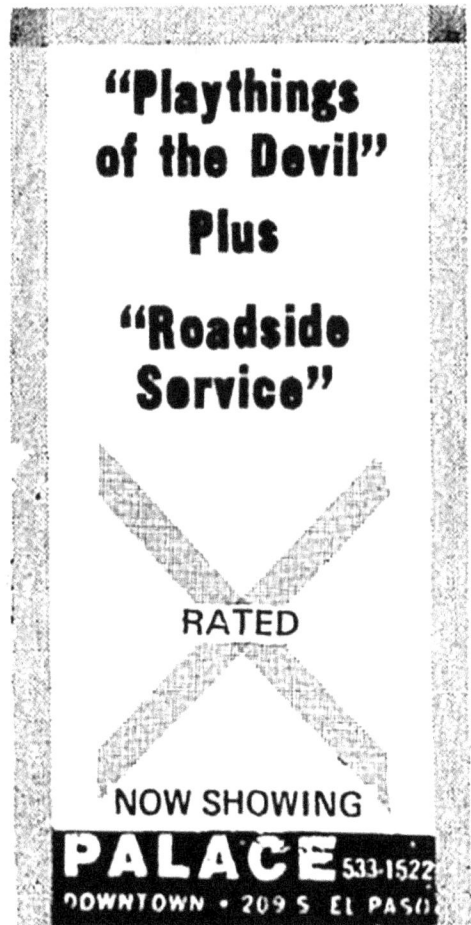

MERCED
THEATRE 722-6000
17th and J Street

X ADULT X
LATE SHOW
TONITE
Doors Open 11:15
Starts 11:30
No One Under 18
Admitted
ID Required

"PLAYTHING
Of The DEVIL"

AND

"SEX & The
OFFICE GIRL"

On February 22, 1986, three people will be killed at Lost Lake after an overnight campout. Two are found dead in their sleeping bags.

When police divers plumb the lake to look for clues, they find Richard Thomas Glass, 33, dead in a sunken Ford Courier pickup truck.

In time, it will be revealed to have been a murder-suicide: shotgun blasts to the heads of the sleeping campers.

Then, a self-inflicted shotgun blast to his chest, the moment Thomas' car slid into the depths of the lake.

No motive. No connection.

No amount of blood that can bring back any of them.

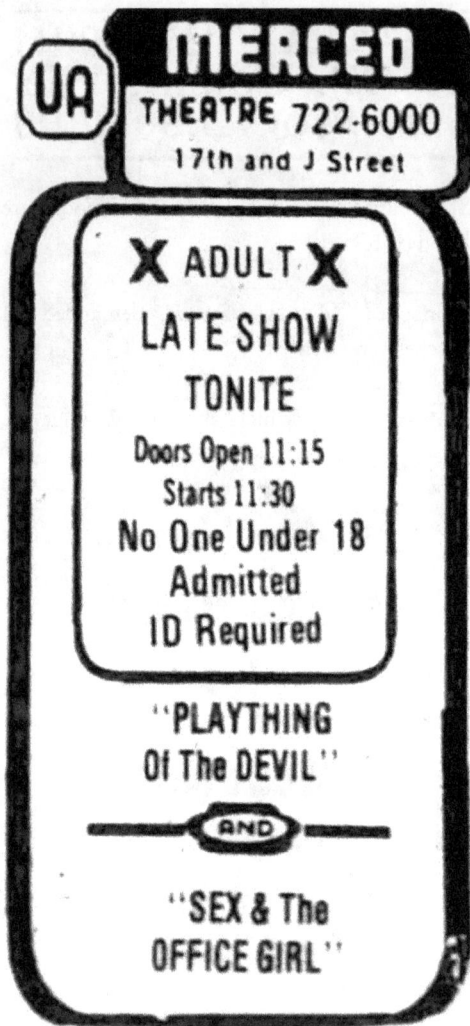

bodies were still warm.

Multiple stab wounds. Bound hand-and-foot. Sanchez, disemboweled.

After they catch the man who takes the ransom money, police arrest Sanchez's ex-husband, Norbert "Tony" Meier, 31, and two accomplices.

Two of them get life in prison next year.

LES ANGES PERVERS
Thursday, October 18, 1973.

Wealthy tycoon Sir Thomas Hilton lies on his deathbed while all his greedy heirs hover like stylish vultures. The family attorney reads the will that says that they get money if they live up until a particular age. Just like Bing Crosby's will! Of course this means that most if not all of them will die horrible premature deaths – brained by a mace; groped by poisonous metal fingers; slashed by a straight-razor – suited to their respective levels of greed and spite. A semi-nude freakout party is a real highlight, and the copious amount of sex in the film – punctuated with weirdly chaste kisses – kicks off with the morbid butler and the maid having sex on the old man's brand-new coffin! People deal with grief in different ways, I guess. Camille Keaton is by far the least dopey of the entire bunch. Go, Camille! Boo, everyone else!

On the outskirts of Meridian, Mississippi, two boys, aged one and three, burn to death in their family's Toyota station wagon.

Their mother shops at a store in the mall. They've been left alone in the locked car.

No idea how it could have happened.

It just is, right now.

In Marseille, police board a jet and liquidate a 35-year-old society matron who had hijacked it.

She says she wants to go to Cairo and end the Yom Kippur War. It's raging in the Middle East currently, with the forces of Egypt and Syria arrayed against Israel.

It's also over in a week.

Patience, virtue, et cetera.

The French press condemns the police action. They say she was simply a momentarily deranged person and would've mellowed out accordingly.

"Such brutality is surprising," observes Paris newspaper L'Aurore, appropriately aghast.

It is still 1973, after all.

Walt Kelly, the brilliant cartoonist who for 26 years illustrated the newspaper comic strip Pogo, dies in Woodland Hills, California. Diabetes. Complications. 60.

Pogo, the optimistic everypossum who embodies the goodness of the human condition, remains famous for one quote in particular.

"We have met the enemy and he is us."

SEXCAPADE IN MEXICO
Friday, October 19, 1973.

Three dudes go to Mexico to score with some hookers. They have a lot of weird simulated overacted sex, like a bunch of young guys that have seen a pantomime of sex without ever really having experienced it. Elsewhere, virginal blonde Tracy and her boyfriend Michael talk about finally having sex. Her parents bicker about how to dole out discipline to their daughter. "Why don't you just put her in a glass cage!" her liberated father blusters. Her mother, who's having a secret affair, gets huffy. Beneath all the sex is a simple melodrama about flawed middle-class dummies and their usual problems and hang-ups. Tracy and Michael retreat to Mexico, where they finally consummate their relationship. Later, they encounter the still-horny dudes, who proceed to rape Tracy. "Nobody knows who they are, or where they are," one of the rapists gloats about their new captives, employing some reasonably chilling logic. She and Michael ultimately get revenge on the dudes, but no one really wins in scenarios like these. Filmed on location in Mexico, with stock footage of real live Baja 500 races, because apparently Michael is really into that kind of thing. Rowles (Shannon Cooper), Leonard (Louis Ojena) and Abner (Stewar Andrews) are violently grimy, and a more vicious bunch of opportunistic scumbags you won't see all year.

Spewing carcasses of meat.

That's the sight that greets the survivors of the Greyhound bus that's been destroyed by a tractor-semi-trailer truck on the New Jersey Turnpike.

CINEMA 35

SEXCAPADE IN MEXICO

(X) COLOR

At 7 & 10

Filmed on location in Mexico with actual "BAJA 500" race scenes

(X) IN EASTMANCOLOR

OAK DRIVE IN THEATRE

BOX OFFICE OPEN 7:30 TO 10:00 P.M.
SHOWTIME 8:00
TWO SHOW NIGHTLY
Abilene Hiway 84
Ph. 625-4226 · Coleman

"SEXCAPADE IN MEXICO"

WED.-THURS.-FRI.-SAT.

(X) Must be 18 years old and show proof.

Near Bordentown. 15 to 20 people killed. Possibly more. The truck blew a tire. Lost control.

Swerved into the lane.

As the truck hurtles through a guard rail after colliding with the bus, its forward momentum carries it down down down the embankment.

Leaving a rain of meat and horror in its wake.

A car hits the bus wreckage as the truck hurtles down. It folds like an accordion.

All dead.

Tomorrow, in San Francisco, Richard Hague, 30, and his wife, Quita, 29, will take a stroll near their Telegraph Hill home.

They'll be kidnapped by a group of men. Hustled into a van. They'll fondle Quita, a reporter for the Industrial City Press.

Then someone will slit her throat with a machete. It nearly decapitates her.

They'll do the same to Richard. They'll leave him for dead.

He lives.

Police secretly consider these murders and others like them to be the beginning of the killing spree of a group of Black Muslims in the San Francisco Bay area that ultimately becomes known as the Zebra Murders. "Zebra" is the name of the police radio band dedicated to investigating and communicating about the murders committed by the group. A group known as The Death Angels.

Nude in an icy ditch.

That's how they find Gale Weys, 19, who vanishes today while hitchhiking to see her parents in Kamloops, British Columbia, Canada. She's discovered on April 6, 1974.

Police believe her death may be connected to that of another woman killed in a park near here. That her death may be connected to scores of other murders over the years of women, mostly young, mostly Indigenous.

Mostly unsolved.

The Highway of Tears Murders stretch onward into the present-day, a road the end of which has not yet been reached.

Death at every turn.

"Turn over, I'm going to shoot you."

That's what Nancy Lee Hall, 36, tells her daughter, Patti Marshall, 14.

It's Nancy's birthday. She's trying to kill as many people in her family as she can.

Her husband. Her eldest son.

She keeps shooting until there's no one left to kill.

In Wheaton, Maryland, a suburb of Washington, D.C., police find Walter Marshall, 16, and his brother George, 12, steeped in a pool of blood that's soaking through the bottom bunk of their bedroom. George has been shot in the head by Nancy. He's still alive, though.

Her daughter Toni Hall, aged 2, is also still alive.

She regains consciousness in the hospital in the afternoon.

Another son, Joseph, 10, survives because Nancy sent him to mail some letters shortly before 6:30 a.m., when the slaughter began.

You'd be surprised how much damage a .22 revolver can do.

But it does.

And it did.

WRVQ'S MIDNIGHT ADULTS ONLY MOVIE

"case of the smiling stiffs"

FOR THAT LITTLE BIT OF ANIMAL IN EACH OF US!

(X)

GUARANTEED AS FUNNY (AND AS WILD) AS "TARZ & JANE"! Cheetah & Boy

CASE OF THE FULL MOON MURDERS
Wednesday, October 24, 1973.

Emma, a lady "vampire," is on the loose in Miami. She gives such great oral sex during the full moon that her victims have heart attacks and die smiling. In her waking life, she's nagged at by her roommate Caroline for being stingy with oral. Ironically enough! She stalks the night in a pretty gossamer blue two-piece that's really billowy and striking, watching all sorts of people enjoying sexual congress. A couple of detectives act like they're on *Dragnet* and try to figure out what the hell is going on. Harry Reems plays a reporter who's always on the make, even while he's investigating The Full Moon Murders for The Evening Star. Poor Harry. Directed and produced by Sean S. Cunningham, this was the first film he produced after *The Last House on The Left*. It's a far cry from working with David Hess, that's for sure. Edited by Steve Miner, the future director of *Friday the 13th Part 2* and *Friday the 13th Part III*. And *Warlock*. And *Soul Man*. What a weird career.

There's a sniper near the Ingleside Police Station in San Francisco.

No injuries. A late-night spree. Six shots. Sounds like a .22, police say.

They search near San Francisco City College, under a waning crescent moon, to get a better fix on the menace.

On August 29, 1971, some men walk into Ingleside. They murder police sergeant John V. Young with a shotgun. Injure a clerk.

No suspect in today's sniper assault is ever found.

Does that sniper ever think about the night they got away with it?

Is it something about which they can tell their grandchildren?

Or was it simply an itchy trigger finger that needed scratching?

On that day in 1971, the Black Liberation Army became a suspect in the shooting.

The police station was scoped out – as it were – in the hours before that shooting by a brunette in a blonde wig.

Right before a bomb blew up a nearby Bank of America.

On this day in 1973, Marilyn Buck sits in a prison cell.

No wigs or bombs in sight.

The onetime University of California at Berkeley student is charged with running guns for the BLA. The only white member of the group, purportedly.

Judge Samuel Conti disregarded all the letters of support and testimony for Buck.

Says he wants to "save others from being killed." She's also under indictment in Arizona, Oregon and Texas for even more gun-related troubles.

Ten years. In a federal penitentiary.

How penitent she truly would be is anyone's guess.

In 1985, she and six others will be convicted as part of the "Resistance Conspiracy" responsible for a series of symbolic bombings along the East Coast.

Symbolic in that the actions are statements.

The softest of all possible targets.

This is, ostensibly, their protest against American foreign policy in Central America and

YOU'LL RIP A ZIPPER LAUGHING
OUTRAGEOUS!! HILLARIOUS!!
ZANY!!

SEX ON THE GROOVE TUBE [R]

1:15, 2:50, 4:30, 6:15
7:50, 9:30
11:00

abroad. In July of 1985, group member Elizabeth Ann Duke will be released on bail. She escapes and goes underground.

She's still out there, somewhere.

Buck will publish poetry up until the very end, when she's released on July 15, 2010 from the Carswell Federal Medical Center in Fort Worth, Texas. Dies from cancer of the uterus, three weeks later, at home in Brooklyn.

A lifer.

Now.

In Washington, D.C., Congress passes a bill to halt the use of lead-based paint in toys, cookware and federally financed housing.

You know – to help the poor people.

Lead paint can cause blindness and death in children who nibble on paint chips the deliciousness of which is legendary.

Lead in the bloodstream can also lead to a violent loss of impulse control.

You can't always blame it on the moon.

ORDEAL

Tuesday, October 30, 1973.

A pushy insufferable tycoon (Arthur Hill) seeks revenge on his faithless wife (Diana Muldaur) and the young prospector (James Stacy) who left him to rot in the desert when he breaks his leg while checking out a hot mining tip. Vengeance turns to redemption as he finds his way out of the hellish wasteland and he realizes he was just on an incredible power trip all along. Meanwhile, his wife wonders if he's really dead. The local sheriff starts getting suspicious. "Ordeal" would be a slight understatement when describing the life of James Stacy in 1973. On September 27, while riding his motorcycle with his galpal Claire Cox, 26, along Benedict Canyon in the Hollywood Hills, a drunk driver sideswipes them, severing their left legs. "Lying there," Stacy later recalls, "I thought, gee, I'm okay, there's nothing wrong – and tried to stand up. Then I realized I didn't have a left leg." The accident also severs his left arm. Cox dies nine hours later. In 1976, a civil jury awards Stacy $1.9 million in a settlement, also granting $400,000 to Cox's husband John and her young daughter Leah.

Nebraska. 1958.

Caril Ann Fugate accompanies her lover Charles Starkweather on a cross-country murder spree that kills 11.

He said he was going to kill her family if she didn't come along. She's only 14.

She watches *Badlands* alongside Martin Sheen and Terrence Malick next spring at the Women's Prison in York, Nebraska. Has nothing to say.

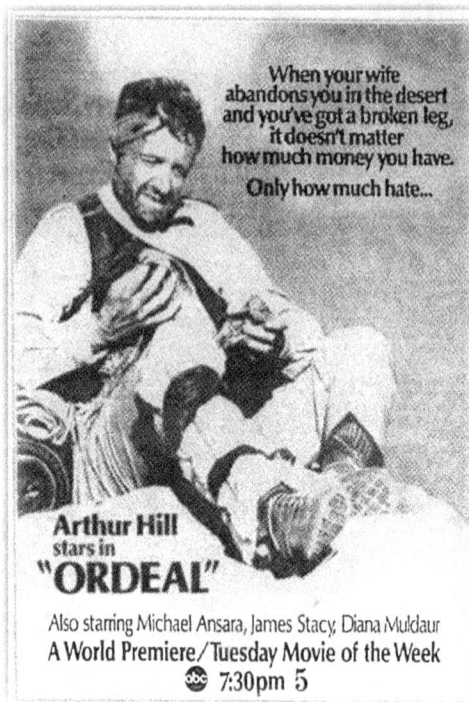

When your wife abandons you in the desert and you've got a broken leg, it doesn't matter how much money you have. Only how much hate...

Arthur Hill stars in "ORDEAL"

Also starring Michael Ansara, James Stacy, Diana Muldaur
A World Premiere/Tuesday Movie of the Week
7:30pm 5

What does she know?

Today, Fugate sees her life sentence for her role in those murders commuted. She's up for parole in 1976.

She said she was his "willing accomplice." Victims' families take issue with the ruling.

Beyond belief.

What do you do with your life once someone hands it back to you?

Battery. Rape. Deviate sexual assault.

That's what Ronald Rennert, 30, is charged with today in Chicago.

Valedictorian. Football player. Scion of the U.S. Adhesive Corporation family.

Septuagenarians. Widows. Raped and robbed while visiting the graves of their husbands.

He's been embroiled in one level of deviance or another since 1960. That's his life.

In Atlanta, freed prisoner Cecil "Sheephead" Kelly thinks about the past.

In 1947, on the outside, he kills a man with a butcher knife in a fight during a card game.

Jailed longer than anyone else in Georgia prison history, Kelly once killed a prison guard during an escape attempt.

He thinks about how he'll adjust to life on the outside.

He's 48 now.

"I never felt so good in my life. It thrills me, from my soul all the way up, to feel God's cool, free air on me on the outside of prison walls after 33 years," he says.

He wants to make speeches to the youth of the free world. To tell them to avoid doing the things that led him to his sorry fate. "I regret every crime I have did," Kelly says. "I regret spilling people's blood. In younger life, people don't think too much, but once you get up in age a little and you go back over your life, you feel sorry for the wrongdoing that you have done."

"Because it don't take life long to run out, this day and time."

J'IRAI COMME UN CHEVAL FOU
Wednesday, October 31, 1973.

Young Aden Rey kills his maniacal mother and hides in the desert. He meets a dwarf named Marvel, who can fly, turn night into day and communicate with animals. Aden takes Marvel to experience the wonders and the miseries of the city. Instead of the fish-out-of-water adventures that usually lead to slapstick and wacky misunderstandings in most movies, here you get fetishism, cannibalism and murder. An army of Christians guns down a nude boy. White-robed lunatics in the desert surround a dragged skeleton. A man gives birth to a skull. In one scene, a "civilized" audience puts Marvel in a cage with a lion but this lion really knows that Marvel loves him so much, so he won't eat him! Directed by Fernando Arrabal – who, with Alejandro Jodorowsky and Roland Topor, created the shock doctrine of the Panic Movement, a fount from which their collective Surrealist creativity springs, evocatively evident throughout this puzzling, maddening work of art. In 1983, the Supreme Court of Canada decrees that the Canadian Broadcasting Corporation must go on trial for obscenity charges stemming from a 1976 television screening of the film. In 1984, Judge Jean-Pierre Beaulne judges the film not obscene. Shocking, yes. Repulsive – oui. But not obscene. Also, he says, the acting in the film is excellent. As if you needed another reason to see it!

It's Halloween.

Teamsters Union leader Jimmy Hoffa is on Dick Cavett tonight. He's gone in a year-and-a-half.

Vanished. Perpetually enigmatic.

Lisa Ann French is nine. She's trick-or-treating in Fond du Lac, Wisconsin. She knocks on the door of the nearby house of the man who will be forever known as The Halloween Killer.

They search for her for days.

They find her. A black plastic bag flutters in the wind.

On the banks of the Iowa River, in Tama County, Iowa, the body of Helen Mae Bown, 61, is finally discovered.

They've been searching for her for weeks.

Even now, as you read this, they still don't know if it was an accident or murder.

Possibly drinking. Possibly with brutal friends. Possibly in possession of the kind of information that would lead a grand jury to be convened to investigate certain matters.

Too few know what really happened now. Too few knew remember really what happened then.

This is the last Halloween before the poison.

The poison that taints the public imagination.

One year from now, Ronald Clark O'Bryan, 39, laces a batch of the sugary-sweet powdered treat known as Pixy Stix with potassium cyanide. He gives one Pixy Stix package to his son Timothy, and one to his daughter Elizabeth.

Timothy will eat some and die. Painfully.

Un film D'ARRABAL

ANDRO' COME UN
CAVALLO PAZZO

EMMANUELE RIVA · GEORGE SHANNON · HACHEMI MARZOUK
TECHNICOLOR

Neither Elizabeth nor her friends ever taste any of the tainted candy.

Because you have to think of the future.

O'Bryan is in debt to the tune of $100,000.

He does it for the life insurance.

A KNIFE FOR THE LADIES
Wednesday, October 31, 1973.

Sheriff Jarrod (Jack Elam) thinks that maybe this Jack the Ripper feller they've been reading about in the newspapers might be the one who's killing pretty young thangs in the town of Mescal. Enter a suave, scintillating private eye by the name of Burns – but Jarrod is gonna be horn-swoggled if he lets that dadblasted city boy solve this rag-fraggin' case. The concept of a Western serial killer isn't so ridiculous when you consider the out-west outrages of murderers Felipe Nerio Espinosa (Colorado, 1863), The Bloody Benders (Kansas, 1871-1873), Alferd Packer (Colorado, 1874), the Servant Girl Annihilator (Austin, 1884-1885), and William Henry Theodore Durrant (San Francisco, 1895). There is some conjecture that Jack the Ripper was in fact an American surgeon. As early as 1913, a St. Louis doctor by the name of Dr. Francis J. Tumblety was a suspect; Dr. Thomas Neill Cream was suggested as a suspect in John Cashman's newly-published book *The Gentleman from Chicago*; and so was American mass murderer H.H. Holmes, although the culpability of these individuals is always subject to dispute, consarnit.

In Dublin, Seamus Twomey, Kevin Mallon and Joe O'Hagan get ready to go home.

People watch as they board an Army helicopter that touches down in the Mountjoy Prison exercise yard.

A helicopter that later will be discovered to have been hijacked.

Twomey, leader of the Belfast Brigade of the Provisional Irish Republican Army, won't be

caught again until 1977.

On Mt. Everest, mountain climbers scale a different kind of height entirely.

Trouble is, they're now completely blind.

While scaling the then-unconquered southwest face of Mt. Everest too quickly, the eyes swelled up in the skulls of Hisahi Ishiguro, 28, and Yasuo Kato, 24. Bulging out of their skulls. Atmospheric pressure. A temporary effect. It happens. They're abandoning their attempt.

With an eye toward continuing later.

Above Venezuela, José Gabriel Lorenzo Ruiz is flying high.

WARNING!
When the Ripper
Slashes—
Grab Your
Throats and Pray!

Hang him. Shoot him. Bury him.
Nothing can stop the maniac
and his blood lust for ladies
naked and dead!

BRYANSTON PICTURES present:
A SPANGLER-JOLLY PRODUCTION

KNIFE
FOR THE
LADIES

COLOR [R] From Warner Bros A Warner Communications Company

Until the pilot of the Avensa DC-9 that he's hijacked tells him that they don't have enough fuel to make it to Cuba.

He hijacked the plane to save his ailing father in Havana.

The jet approaches Maiquetía International Airport near Caracas.

José puts his revolver to his head.

He's never felt so low.

LA MANO SPIETATA DELLA LEGGE
Saturday, November 3, 1973.

A bunch of double-crossing crooks find out that the capo of a rival gang is in the hospital. One of them dresses like a cop, infiltrates the hospital and wastes the capo and a nearby nurse besides. Then they find out that people saw them do their crimes so now they have to bump *them* off, too! Philippe Leroy stars as the increasingly demoralized police inspector who tells people they'll be safe in witness protection but they get killed anyway. He raves, "I turn violent – but I haven't lost touch with reality when it comes to the result of violence!" Klaus Kinski shines as an impeccably-dressed, mostly silent hitman. In one scene, he watches himself in the bathroom mirror as he strangles a witness, emotionless as she dies in his arms. In another, he jams a blowtorch into a slap-happy rapist's crotch and burns his nuts off – right after he sticks a revolver into the side

of the raped girl and pulls the trigger! The crooks dressed like cops get more done than the actual cops themselves.

G.F. Gardner. Ejected out the window of an airplane at 25,000 feet.

The fan on engine #3 of the Douglas DC-10 disintegrates.

Fragments of the fan erupt through the fuselage. Through part of the right wing. Two of the other engines.

Decompression of the cabin is swift and catastrophic.

A stewardess. In tears. Says she served him a drink moments before he went out the window.

Mr. and Mrs. Mark Smith were playing cards when the cabin of the National Airlines flight descended into chaos. "I turned to Mark," she says, "and I said, 'I think we've had it'."

The airplane makes an emergency landing at Albuquerque International. Some injuries. Some scars.

Computer simulations attempt for months to determine where the body of Gardner, 47, fell.

Still. Nothing. He's still out there. Somewhere. There's some talk that his remains were found in 1975 in central New Mexico during the construction of the Very Large Array of radio telescopes on the Plains of San Agustin.

Beyond that, it is unclear.

In Sacramento, 13 people die on a Greyhound bus when it hurtles head-on into the pillar of a highway overpass.

They call it the "Gambler's Special."

They're on their way back from a weekend at the casinos in Reno. "The guy practically ran us off the road," says driver and witness Bernard Norton of Sacramento. "He had to be doing 90 or 100, because my wife was going 70."

The bus driver, Douglas Moore, 26, of Hayward, dies instantly. Hurled 60 feet up the freeway, along the shoulder.

With his seat. And his steering wheel.

The bus splits open lengthwise, spewing its contents across the approximate length of a football field.

A missile full of people. Straight into a concrete pillar.

Dead center.

By Monday, the County Coroner will say that Moore was neither hopped up on drugs nor blotto on booze.

Further, George Nielson says, Moore had "an amazingly healthy heart."

Years later, they still won't know why it all happened.

At Cape Canaveral in Florida, the satellite known as Mariner 10 launches today.

On its way to Mercury and Venus.

Magnetic fields. Radio noise. Gravitational slingshots.

The usual attractions.

Because Mercury is so close to the sun, scientists in 1973 are "fairly certain" it cannot support earthly life.

Fairly.

The plucky little satellite continues sending images, measurements and transmissions until March 24, 1975. Commands will be sent. Programs will run.

Transmissions will end.

Conceivably, it's still up there. Orbiting the Sun.

Only as dead as you want it to be.

THE GIRL MOST LIKELY TO...
Tuesday, November 6, 1973.

Stockard Channing plays smart-but-scorned college girl Miriam Knight. Changing colleges often, shut out of love or even real friendship, she still keeps putting herself out there – until her roommate gives her some roses during the play in which she's acting. Roses to which she's allergic. Totally humiliated by her uncontrollable sneezing, she hops in her car, drives too fast and gets in a massive car wreck. After reconstructive surgery, the bandages come off and she's beautiful. Since no one who's mistreated her can recognize her anymore, she murders them one after another. Detective Ralph Varone (Ed Asner) tries to put it all together and in the process falls in love with her – just the way she is! Ed and Stockard make a weirdly cute couple. Co-written by Joan Rivers, who probably put way more of her own frustrations into Channing's character than anyone was ready to discuss.

In the borough of Liberty, Pennsylvania, Shane Klein, 25, is arrested.

He's been knocking on the doors of women on the north and south sides of town. Posing as a paramedic.

He comes in. Sits them down. Breaks the news that he's got to give them a "spot check" to see if they've got VD.

"Held on morals," say police.

He has the attitude down. He's plausible enough.

TUESDAY MOVIE OF THE WEEK
THE GIRL MOST LIKELY TO ...
ED ASNER
JOE FLYNN
STOCKARD CHANNING
Meet the ugly duckling who turned into a gorgeous swan with murder in her eye.
A WORLD PREMIERE
8:30

Knows precisely how much shame he can use to compel women in 1973.

In Ventura, California, a train conductor and engineer are flash-frozen by a flood of liquid propane. As a prank, five kids released the brakes on the railcar tankers. When they reach the end of the track, they collide and rupture.

Conductor Joe Mason, 60, will die of his injuries after midnight. Engineer Tony Emanuel, 54, will hold on until Friday.

Not much longer.

Three tanker cars. Rocketing down the tracks at 50 miles per. The first comes out of nowhere, hits the locomotive engine and showers the men with chemicals so cold that they burn away flesh on contact.

They probably didn't know what hit them.

Neither did the kids, who are now in custody for their deaths. Manslaughter.

It doesn't seem real.

Also like a bad dream: three black men armed with shotguns and cyanide bullets ambush and assassinate Oakland School Superintendent Dr. Marcus Foster. Deputy Superintendent Robert Blackburn collapses after being wounded in the same attack. Foster writhes in agony on the ground as one of his killers steps over Blackburn to deliver the gunshot that ends Foster's life.

Is it not a coup de grâce. There is no mercy here.

In a few days, the "Symbionese Liberation Army" – so new a prospect that newspapers present it in quotation marks, some of which are possibly sarcastic – claims responsbility. You can read all about it in the *San Francisco Examiner*, owned by William Randolph Hearst.

In Los Angeles, Gilbert Perez tells police that his brother William says he's dismembered one of his girlfriend's children.

At first, Gilbert doesn't believe him. Doesn't know if it's real or not.

William Vela Perez, 30, tells police that he found Mary Ann Vitali's three-year-old daughter Lisa dead in her bedroom last Sunday. Doesn't know anything about how she died.

The brothers wrap Lisa's body parts in plastic and bury them in makeshift graves strewn pell-mell across five miles of streets and canyons and gravel pits throughout the suburbs of Sun Valley and Tujunga.

William Perez was arrested last year for beating another child of Vitali.

In May, they'll both be convicted of second-degree murder. Perez beat Lisa to death.

Would they last long in prison?

Not likely.

BLADE
Wednesday, November 7, 1973.

In New York City, serial killer Peterson – played by Jon Cypher, the eternally-annoyed Chief of Police Fletcher Daniels on *Hill Street Blues* – is on the loose. Detective Blade – played by John Marley, the horse's ass who gets the horse's head in his bed in *The Godfather* – is on his trail. One of the victims is a senator's daughter, so now Blade has to deal with cover-ups and political fallout on top of everything else as he pursues his quarry through the mean streets and beautifully gritty exteriors of 1973 New York City. The angry, sadistic murderer – who isn't concealed in the slightest – assaults his victims using martial arts techniques and really, really hates women. Like Robin once said to Batman, "He's a paranoiac who's a menace to our society!" Marley's face here is almost heroically lined with decades of hard life and laughter. Just like a cop. With Morgan Freeman in a brief role as a militant who would in real life probably be irritated that more people don't ask Morgan Freeman what it was like to play him in *Blade*.

The Great Red Spot on the planet Jupiter is a storm.

Two shots. Dead instantly.

A storm that has raged with uncontrollable violence and inconceivable fury for untold hundreds of years.

Four more shots. Dead instantly.

No one knows why it's red. No one knows why it's formed the way it is.

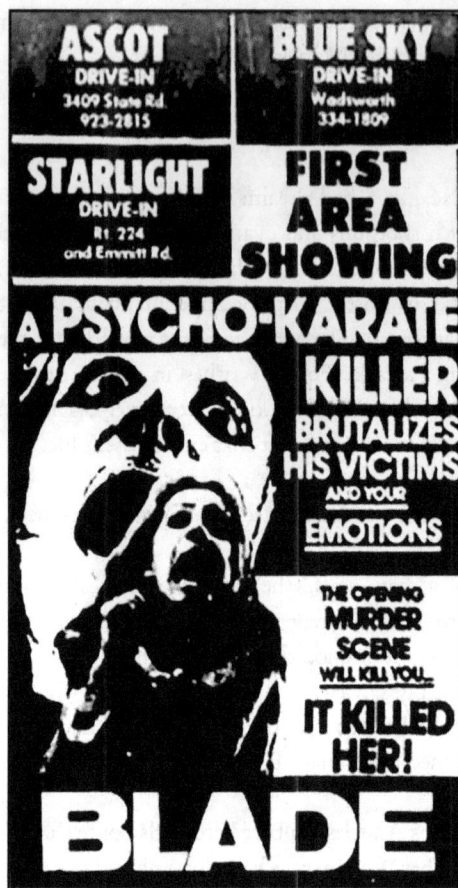

An unknown man enters a bar in Modesto, California and assassinates brothers Michael and John Varner.

A storm larger than the Earth itself.

Hells Angels. Dead in the New Era Club.

Pioneer 10, the spacecraft launched on March 2, 1972, is 15 million miles away today from Jupiter and yet the photographs of The Great Red Spot that it takes and transmits to Earth are stunning and sobering in their magnificence.

"What do you think of this?" the man says before opening fire.

The first spacecraft to Jupiter. The first man-made object to exit the Solar System.

Their friend Raymond Piltz is in the car outside. Sleeping. Misses the whole thing.

The first one to make it out.

The three men were on their way back from a funeral for a Hells Angel who died in a shootout the week before.

Its ultimate destination is a vantage point slightly more than 80,000 miles away from Jupiter. It's getting closer now. Closer and closer.

Trying to understand a disturbance.

They're burning books in Drake, North Dakota today.

"The burning of the books is not significant," Superintendent Dale Fuhrman says. "It's just one way of getting rid of them."

They get rid of English teacher Bruce Severy, too. Happily, not by fire.

Students and parents protest the "obscene language" of Kurt Vonnegut's novel *Slaughterhouse-Five*. Also up in flames is *Deliverance* by James Dickey, and assorted short stories by Ernest Hemingway and John Steinbeck.

None of the members of the Drake School Board has ever read any of the books.

The violence of sacrifice.

ENOUGH TO BLOW THE TOP OF ANY ORDINARY COP...
BUT NOT BLADE!

THE STREET WISE COP WHO MAKES THE LAW WORK...
EVEN IF HE HAS TO BEND IT A LITTLE!

CROOKED COP CORRUPTION
BLACK MILITANT THREATS
POLITICAL COVER UPS
WHITE LAW & ORDER PHONIES
RABBIT KILLER MURDERS

BLADE

JOSEPH GREEN PICTURES PRESENTS

BLADE . JOHN MARLEY COLOR [R]

PLUS: TOM TRYON in The NARCO MEN [PG]

MANHATTAN	BROOKLYN	QUEENS	SUFFOLK	CONNETICUT
HARRIS 42nd STREET	BANCO	CITY LINE STRAND FAR ROCKAWAY CAMBRIA HEIGHTS	REGENT BABYLON	PARIS WETHERFIELD
WEST END 125th STREET				

THE CASE OF THE HOODED MAN
Monday, November 12, 1973.

Unseen for decades until it screened in September 2018 in Los Angeles as part of the 24-hour *Sesión Continua* marathon of erotic cinema produced by Bradford Nordeen's "Dirty Looks" initiative, this is a crime film in which young men are raped and robbed by a stocking-masked man. As soon as the crime is solved and the rapist gets dealt with, the action switches to a leisurely half-hour orgy accompanied by the sound of elephants. *You* try having sex while elephants stomp and trumpet around you and see what that does to *your* libido. Or your mind! Another quick and easy film full of amateurs, it enjoyed a long weird life in adult theatres across America throughout the '70s.

In Laos, someone throws a grenade into a cinema in the capital city of Luang Prabang. Nine people die; six injured. Police don't know who would throw fire into a crowded theatre, or why.

War is over if you want it.

Just not all at once.

In Sikeston, Missouri, the Old Morehouse Theatre continues its process of disintegration. It's been a razed and ruined wreck ever since it was ravaged by fire on Saturday morning. The theatre, vacant and devoid of film for almost 25 years, was set on fire because the owners requested that it be destroyed that way.

The things you used to be able to get just by asking for them.

In Marysville, California, some boys go down to

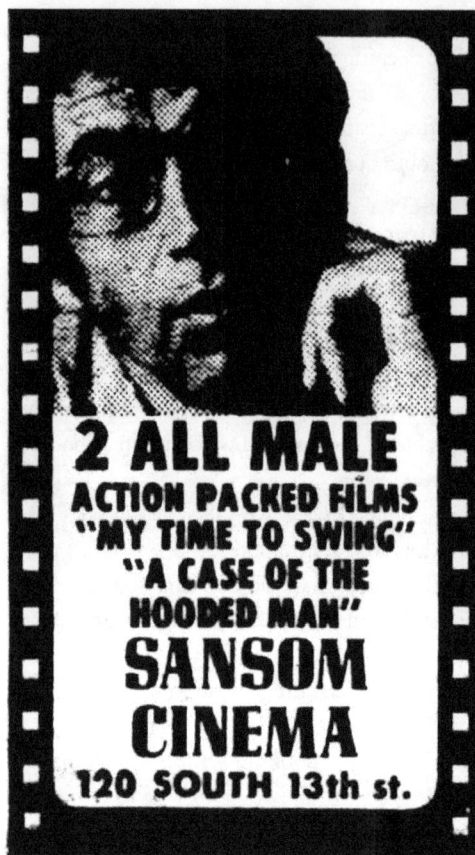

a dam on the Bear River to shoot targets.

For fun.

What they find are the bodies of two girls, missing since Sunday after they went out shopping and never came back. Murdered by shotgun. Valerie J. Lane, 12, and Doris K. Derryberry, 13.

Best friends until the end.

No motive for their murders that anyone knows of right now. Detectives work around the clock for weeks. Months. Years. It never ends.

Except for the two cousins ultimately found guilty of the crime in 2014.

DNA testing makes the dead rise again to talk and point an unwavering spectral finger that reveals their killers.

In another week, four boys will be executed at Gitchie Manitou State Park in Iowa. Murdered by shotgun. No leads. No connections. There is a survivor, though.

There's always a survivor.

IL FIORE DAI PETALI D'ACCIAIO
Tuesday, November 13, 1973.

Il fiore dai petali d'acciaio means "The Flower with Petals of Steel." It's also a sculpture with which rich surgeon Dr. Andrea Valenti kills his lover Daniela. Accidentally. He gets rid of the body – but someone's watching him. Taking photographs. Daniela's obstreperous half-sister Evelyne suspects his involvement. She calls Inspector Garrano to help her nail the guy. As it so happens, red-hot *lovah* Valenti once had a wife who apparently went bananas after he deflowered her. He shoved her into an insane asylum so he could go about his business, performing delicate surgery and buying unnecessarily deadly artworks. Evelyne gets murdered with the same sharp flower petals and Garrano swears he'll figure out who killed whom. Also, two girls make love underwater. Oh, get over it. It's a film that's as much about the death of a relationship – and all the lives subsequently touched by that death – as it is about a clumsy, horny bonehead.

In Stockton, California, mass murderers Willie Luther Steelman and Douglas Edward Gretzler are questioned in prison by the police.

Authorities think the two men may have killed 17 people from California to Arizona throughout October.

The two killers say they've killed others. These may simply be convenient lies.

Steelman, 28, from California, and Gretzler, 22, from New York, came together to rob and kill during their time as shiftless drifters.

A couple in a mobile home near Mesa, Arizona.

A man in the desert outside Tucson. A man in a sleeping bag in the Superstition Desert. Two men in Phoenix.

Grocer Walter Parkin, 33, and eight others die in a home in the tiny hamlet of Victor, California on November 6. University of Arizona students Patricia and Michael Sandberg are shot in the head while bound and gagged.

Together.

This is the sixth mass-murder case in California in four years.

That you know of.

Carol Jenkins, 18, who also lives at the Parkin home, returns from a date, late on the evening of the murders.

She goes to bed, not knowing that elsewhere in the house there are nine corpses.

Steelman will die on death row in 1987. Liver disease.

Gretzler gets executed by lethal injection in 1998.

To the victims' families witnessing his execution, Gretzler says, "From the bottom of my soul, I am so deeply sorry and have been for years for murdering Patricia and Michael Sandberg. Though I am being executed for that crime, I apologize to all 17 victims and their families."

He also gets a last meal of six fried eggs, four chewy strips of bacon, two slices of buttered white toast, a cup of coffee, and two Classic Cokes with ice.

Did something good grow out of all that?

In Paris, off the Champs-Èlysées, Italian fashion designer Elsa Schiaparelli dies from complications of a stroke that befell her seven weeks ago. Her designs – which found kinship with Surrealists Salvador Dalí, Alberto Giacometti and Jean Cocteau – remain a groundbreaking vision of couture backlit with the brilliance of genius and the color Shocking Pink.

Finding beauty amidst death, blood and violence. It's a survival strategy.

At least, it should be.

SYMPHONY HUNT. AT MASS. 262-3888
CARROLL BAKER
R
"THE FLOWER WITH THE DEADLY STING"
AND "ACROSS 110TH STREET"

THE RUNAWAY SISTERS
Friday, November 16, 1973.

Suzy and Wendy stay with their mournful damaged widower uncle Max while their mother is in the hospital. He rapes Wendy. They run away. They hitchhike and are picked up by an overacting truck driver who threatens them with a hammer if they don't surrender to his demented demands. They wrest the hammer away, bash his brains out and run away. They finally make it to the big city – possibly Copenhagen – and meet a sleazy conniving lady and her dopey sex-crazed son running a boardinghouse. They simply cannot get away from people taking advantage of them! What happens next will shock you. It may nauseate you. You may wonder where your cat is right this minute. Originally double-billed with *Deap Throat*, then *Dear Throat*. "You girls should have stayed at home." Quite!

"I can't find my sister and I can't find the kids."

In downtown Los Angeles, the Stratford Apartments building is on fire.

Midnight brings the horrors of an inferno to its residents. Mostly poor people who couldn't find anywhere else to live.

"A furnace with a chimney" is what people call The Stratford. A furnace that burns 24 people to death. Injures 52 others. At least.

In terms of sheer numbers, it's the worst fire in the history of Los Angeles.

In terms of every life affected by the fire, it's the worst fire. Period.

In the blazing wooden three-story building at 821 West Sunset Boulevard, some choose to leap from the upper floors.

Onto mattresses. Onto bushes.

Onto the sidewalk.

Elias Gonzalez-Sanchez and Gustavo Gomez, both 19, wake up sleeping residents by frantically knocking on doors. They save four babies thrown down to them from upper floors by parents.

Jorge Orantes, 15, saves another boy when the fire chases his mother out of an upper-story window. She throws the child. Orantes catches him.

She catches the pavement and dies.

The bodies of five children are found gathered around a woman's body in the smoking ruin, stars in a constellation of misery and heartache.

In the aftermath of the disaster, no one knows exactly who's died. Even though the walls were thin and the living conditions cramped, few at The Stratford knew each other.

They were too busy trying to make it through another day.

There is a suspect in the fire. Michael Altenburg, 18. Held on suspicion of murder. 24 charges.

Soon to be 25.

Arrested while he slept on a bus bench.

He's released in February. False confessions. He

describes places in Los Angeles despite never having been to any of them before.

Six months later, investigators remain mystified as to the cause of the fire.

Arson? A television, heater, lamp and refrigerator, all plugged into one sorry little extension cord? Teenage girls sniffing glue down in the lobby?

Investigators are also mystified as to how Stratford tenant Wayne Tedrick got stabbed in the back moments before the flames consumed him.

Wait, what?

THE SEVERED ARM
Friday, November 16, 1973.

One day, a dude gets a package. Opening it, he finds some dude's severed arm inside. Oh, you shouldn't have! He calls up one of his dudes and they reminisce about that one time five years ago when they went spelunking with a bunch of other dudes and they got trapped in a cave and they all thought they were going to die of starvation so they chopped off the arm of one dude so they could have a snack but then they got rescued moments later. *Molded.* The other dudes from the group are stalked and disarmed, apparently in revenge for being so antsy. The original one-armed dude is catatonic, and then disappears – so it can't be him. Or can it? Can you handle the pulse-pounding conclusion? Even if you can't handle it, would you ever admit it, you big chicken?

The philosopher Alan Watts dies today.

Someone dies and what comes next is are the autopsies of both a body and a life.

Alan Watts put many minds at peace throughout his life and beyond it.

He dies because he drinks too much.

The previous two sentences could have been connected by the word "but."

Unnecessarily so.

One thing leads to another.

One thing does not cast aspersions on another.

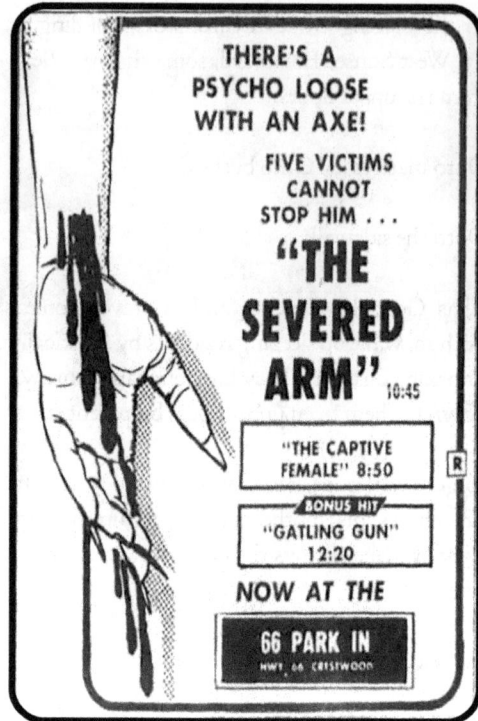

THERE'S A
PSYCHO LOOSE
WITH AN AXE!

FIVE VICTIMS
CANNOT
STOP HIM . . .

"THE
SEVERED
ARM" 10:45

"THE CAPTIVE
FEMALE" 8:50

BONUS HIT
"GATLING GUN"
12:20

NOW AT THE

66 PARK IN
HWY. 66 CRESTWOOD

One thing does not cast disappointment into the light reflected by another thing.

One thing follows another.

Imagine a flower – one that you want very much to blossom – that fulfills its truest self, somewhere in the world. Only you don't know where it has.

And yet you have all the time in the world to find it.

It won't die. It's out there, waiting for you. Just for you.

You, in your own time.

That's Alan Watts.

ARMED SERVICERS
Saturday, November 17, 1973.

Three former Vietnam POWs sit around, peel potatoes and bullshit about what great sex they've had in their lives. While two of them come back to an instant sexy reception from their lovers, the third finds out that his girlfriend turned into a hooker hooked on heroin by her dealer while he was gone. Did I mention that this is an erotic film? Soundtrack selections include "Reveille Rock" by Johnny & The Hurricanes; The Ventures' "War of the Satellites," "Exploration in Terror" and their version of the *Twilight Zone* theme; and "Fools Rush In" by James Burton. The surprisingly inspired easy-listening background soundtrack acts as a secondary narrative: the two guys who come back to pleasure and the swinging life get smooth music, while the third guy gets Floyd Cramer's sorrowful renditions of "Making Believe" and "You Don't Know Me" playing behind him as he makes love to his girl – until he finds out that she's really fallen on hard times, is duly repulsed, and runs off to crawl into a bottle. The end!

"I'm not a crook."

That's what President Richard Milhous Nixon tells the 400 reporters that have gathered in Orlando, Florida to get his hot take on the Watergate scandal.

"I've earned everything I've got."

That's what he says in his very next breath.

That second part tends to get lost in the shuffle of history. Sort of like how, right after Dr. Frankenstein screams "It's alive!" in the 1931

version of *Frankenstein*, what he says next is, "In the name of God – now I know what it feels like to *be* God!"

It isn't about innocence.

It isn't about right or wrong.

It's about entitlement.

It's about doing everything he thinks he should do because he is who he is.

But not because he's the President of These Here United States.

Because he's Richard Milhous Nixon, goddammit.

For him, it isn't about the ideals that built the nation.

It's about his legacy. The posterity that is owed to him. He worked hard and you get what you want after you've worked so hard.

Don't you?

Obstruction of justice? Sure. Payoffs to people who broke in to the Democratic Party headquarters to spy on the opposition and gather intelligence to use against them? Has to be done. Covering it all up?

Of course. It is, literally, a matter of course.

What good is it being the most powerful man in the free world if you can't do any of that?

The violence of impotence.

IS IT TOO SOON TO TALK ABOUT '72...
THAT TIME PAUL AND VALERIE FELL IN LOVE AT FIRST SIGHT AND BEGAN SEARCHING FOR A PLACE TO HAVE AN AFFAIR

FROM THAT COMPANY!!!
IT'S ONLY A MOVIE!
IT'S ONLY A MOVIE!
IT'S ONLY A MOVIE!
IT'S ONLY A MOVIE!
IT'S ONLY A MOVIE!
IT'S ONLY A MOVIE!
IT'S ONLY A MOVIE!

WARNING!
NOT RECOMMENDED FOR PERSONS OVER 30!

—AND They kept searching until they found... COLOR R
"THE HOUSE THAT VANISHED"

SCREAM...AND DIE!
Tuesday, November 20, 1973.

Director José Ramón Larraz brings you yet another one of his erotic, insular portrayals of passions that go way too far in this, a film popularly known as *The House That Vanished* and one that you should know is only a movie, only a movie, only a movie. Nudities. Creakiness. Slaughter. Valerie and her lover Terry sneak into a mansion in the forest. He wants to burgle the place but then they happen to see a shadowy man with a switchblade murdering a girl sitting on his lap. Terry vanishes. Valerie is stalked. The sadistic killer wears black gloves. She tries to take people to the house where it all happened. Too bad! It vanished, dummy! She later gets mixed-up with young psycho Paul, who makes grotesque masks and loves his aunt a little too much.

In West Berlin.

Four missing. Four hospitalized.

The top three floors of a five-story apartment, demolished.

A father and son try to kill themselves. They turn on the gas.

It's one thing to kill yourself. What about the people you take with you, accidentally, on the way out to Kingdom Come?

This just in.

It was two kids — one of whom was busted last weekend for stealing a car — that blew up the place.

Suspicion.

ARE YOU PLANNING AN AFFAIR?
Starts TOMORROW!
A TRUE HITCHCOCK-TYPE THRILLER!
WE CAN GIVE YOU 7 GOOD REASONS NOT TO HAVE YOUR NEXT AFFAIR AT "THE HOUSE THAT VANISHED" AND THEY'RE ALL DEAD!!
① George
② Marsha
③ Ted
④ Linda
⑤ Ronnie
⑥ Alice
⑦ Larry
"THE HOUSE THAT VANISHED" R
CO-HIT DRIVE-IN ONLY! SHOWN AT 7:15 & 9:00 at the ESQUIRE
ESQUIRE CINEMAS AIR CONDITIONED
ALFRED HITCHCOCK'S PG FRENZY NEWPORT DRIVE-IN

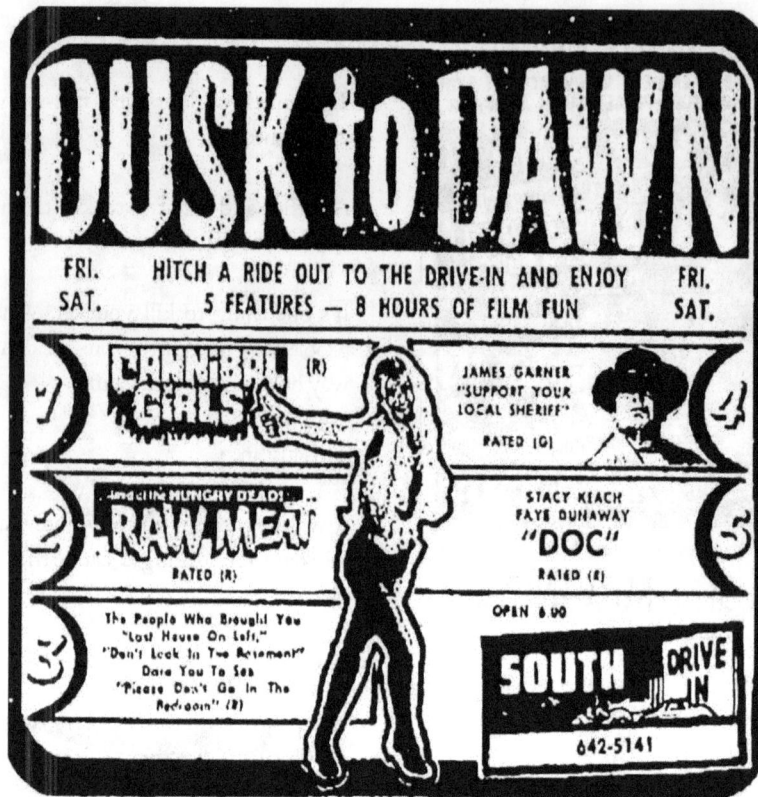

Seven injured in the gas-explosion demolition of a four-story building, the top three floors of which collapsed.

Newsflash.

The father of the boy who was busted for theft found his suicidal son and his young friend passed out in the building. He went for help.

No word if he'd turned off the gas first.

Then: explosion-osion-osion-osion-osion.

Five dead. Seven hurt.

And we're back.

Just in time for A Charlie Brown Thanksgiving. Sponsored by Dolly Madison.

Bakers of all kinds of neat-to-eat treats.

This is the one where Lucy holds the football for Charlie Brown to kick, and even though she always pulls it away right before he kicks it and falls flat on his ass, he thinks that she'd never trick him like that on a national holiday like Thanksgiving.

She wouldn't do that again, would she?

SCREAM, PRETTY PEGGY
Saturday, November 24, 1973.

Artist and college student Peggy Johns (Sian Barbara Allen) starts work as a housemaid in a creaky old mansion in the Hollywood Hills owned by caustic Bette Davis, who lives with her strange sculptor son Ted Bessell. Bette's daughter is apparently on holiday in Europe but actually she's certifiably insane and lives above the garage. You know, like The Fonz. George Thornton, whose daughter Agnes used to be the housemaid, comes by looking for her. He vanishes. Peggy tries to make friends with the girl above the garage. She fails to heed the warnings – much to her great and lasting dismay. Directed by Gordon Hessler and co-written by Jimmy Sangster – no stranger to compelling '70s horror, they. When people reminisce about life in the '70s, one thing they mention is the amount of weird, distressing films like this that they used to

see on TV all the time. A formative period.

In Mexico City, there's a manhunt going on.

50 agents since Thursday. 19 rape-murders over a series of months. They call the killer The Naucalpan Strangler.

It's interesting how often old news reports describe female victims as "pretty."

The murders may have been committed by one person, or several.

There's some speculation that the news reports of the putative strangler inspired other cats to copy the crimes.

No witnesses. A lot of speculation.

Including how someone dressed as a woman

might have been able to get close enough to the victims to rape and murder them.

"Women here have started to panic," the police admit.

The exploits of the sex-killer will be published in American newspapers for three days in late November 1973.

Then, no more.

Not everything that bleeds leads.

They're tearing down the Regent Theatre in Rochester, New York.

It's a long and involved process that drags the theatre to a decidedly gory and ignominious end. The neighborhood, which has filled the 1,400 seats of The Regent over the years since it opened in 1914, is treated to a long, languorous look at the forlorn guts of the cinema, spilling out of the holes in its walls gashed open by the wrecking ball. The balcony seats sit empty, gazing out through a haze of demolition, into a city that fills those seats with nothing now but entropy and amnesia.

All to make one more parking lot for an increasingly flat world.

Tomorrow night, Albert DeSalvo, 42, the rapist, burglar and serial killer alleged to be The Boston Strangler, will himself be murdered in the hospital at Walpole State Prison in Massachusetts. Stabbed in the heart. Many times.

In prison, he started a thriving business by

assembling wire and jewels into fashionable necklaces and selling them through the mail.

You know. Chokers.

CRY RAPE!
Tuesday, November 27, 1973.

A lady (Andrea Marcovicci) gets raped and then goes through yet another ordeal when the police hassle her with their cynical bullshit that really isn't necessary or welcome at a time like this. A suspect is identified, tried and ultimately convicted, but who knows if they got the right guy! Features one of the all-time greatest plot twists in the history of television. I don't know where I should place the sarcastic air-quotes in that last sentence, so you'll have to do it yourself.

So you win $3.7 million in a malpractice suit.

The problem? You've only got seven years left to live.

A judge awards Albert Gonzales that $3.7 million today in a malpractice suit against both Mercy Hospital in Sacramento and Dr. John G. Nork, 45, an orthopedic surgeon in Martinez, California. All because of Nork's unnecessary back surgery on Gonzales in 1967.

Incompetence. Paralysis. Cancer.

Nork has a couple of other malpractice suits pending against him. He's also under investigation by the California State Board of Medical Examiners.

Most of the needless back surgeries he performed were on poor people.

Scores of those poor people show up to testify against the doctor who had made their lives misery incarnate.

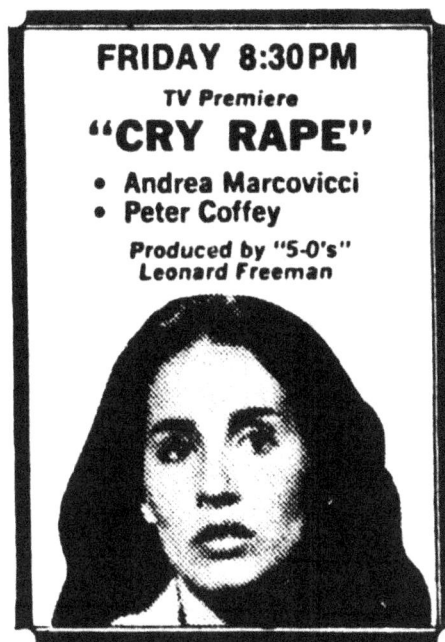

FRIDAY 8:30 PM
TV Premiere
"CRY RAPE"
• Andrea Marcovicci
• Peter Coffey
Produced by "5-0's"
Leonard Freeman

Judge Abbott Goldberg, breathing righteous fire in his summation, proclaims, "Here have come the poor and the maimed and the halt to testify against their once-beloved physician for the wrongs he committed against them with evil purpose."

A 1982 news brief calls Nork the one doctor who has been "sued for malpractice more often than most any doctor in the country."

John G. Nork remains in trouble with the Board as late as July of 2000.

Albert Gonzales dies in 1981, aged 39.

His epitaph reads, "Absent from the body, present with The Lord."

Thank God for that.

Cry Rape Offers Mature Viewing For Best Show

In a hospital room in Miami, Mary Axelson Cropper, 41, beats her mother, playwright Mary McDougal Atkinson, 82, to death.

Atkinson once wrote a Broadway play called *Life Begins*, about waiting in a bed in a maternity ward.

Waiting for her daughter to be born.

Miami Metro detective Charles Mussoline sums it up. "The mother was afraid of the daughter – but she still loved the daughter and figured that love would conquer the problem between them."

Brain haemorrhage. The nurse comes into the room and finds the elder Mary in her bed, weeping and drooling blood.

The younger Mary promises her mother for years that she would kill her. That she'll burn her house down.

Then she turns around and asks for money.

Cropper's aunt, who requests that her name be withheld from newspaper reports, doesn't know or understand why her sister was so endlessly hated by her daughter.

"Even now, she would want to protect her daughter," she says.

Yesterday, Genie – the child discovered in Los Angeles in 1970 to have been so abused and neglected that she reverted to a notorious near-silent feral state of non-development – was interrupted during her learning exercises with physical therapist Sue Knox.

Two people dressed as Woodsy Owl and Smokey Bear stand before her.

The violence of good intentions.

OUTRAGE
Wednesday, November 28, 1973.

Finally! An ABC Movie of the Week that understands the true meaning of the word "outrage"! A bunch of young reprobates terrorize everyone around the suburb of Oak Meadows (in reality, the beautiful bucolic town of Rolling Hills Estates, due south of Los Angeles). They do silly shit like dump garbage into an old lady's swimming pool, or stick garden hoses through windows and turn them on. When they get bored of doing all that, they zero in on Dr. Jim Kiler (Robert Culp) and his family. One of the lead scummers is played by Nicholas Hammond, formerly known for his angelic voice in *The Sound of Music* and soon to be known for the heroism of his television role as Spider-Man. They try to corrupt his daughter, so Jim tries to reason with them, and then their parents. Nothing. Worse than nothing, actually – he gets outright hostility and a satanically stupid level of self-deception in those parents about what their children are really like. On top of that, the cops won't do anything. After one particularly loathsome attack on his family, Kiler explodes and smashes the kids' coveted material possessions, getting revenge not so much because he savors it but because he only wants them to stop bothering him and his family forever. Culp's clenched teeth should've won an Emmy for this film. Not all of Robert Culp, I mean. Just his teeth.

Is a community still a community if there's only one person living there?

John Riffey is the only person inhabiting the small town of Tuweep, Arizona.

Throughout the 20th century, there are villages,

OUTRAGE
WEDNESDAY
MOVIE OF THE WEEK

A WORLD PREMIERE!
How far can you push a man before he takes the law into his own hands? The true story of an angry man, starring Robert Culp and Marlyn Mason

abc 7:30

hamlets and gores – mostly in the Dakotas – that remain alive even with fewer than 10 residents.

The demise of these heartland places could be blamed on the death of industry, the death of The Rust Belt, or the death of The American Dream.

The death of a small town usually happens when

no one's looking.

When there's no one left to see.

Tuweep sits on the inside edge of the Grand Canyon National Monument.

If you wanted to visit John Riffey, the Highway Department's map makes you overshoot Tuweep by 10 miles.

Riffey, who started as Superintendent of the Grand Canyon National Monument in 1940, lost his wife in 1962.

Now it's only him, there in Tuweep. It's been that way since 1969.

Will be that way until 1980.

His second wife, Meribeth, visits him from Washington each spring and summer. She dies in 1993. Buried beside him. Graves covered by vast endless desert skies.

It's been two days since Michelle Maenza, 11, vanished from Rochester, New York.

They find her today, dead in a ditch in Macedon, New York. Very near where Wanda Walkowicz was found in Webster. Not far from where Carmen Colon was found near the towns of Churchville and Chili.

Not far. Still miles from home.

Cormac McCarthy's new novel *Child of God*, ready to be delivered unto bookstores across America tomorrow, tells the tale of Lester Ballard. Ballard, an increasingly isolated man, descends into cannibalism and cave-dwelling even as he becomes a mythos unto himself in the mountains and hollers of Tennessee.

A child of God.

Which God, exactly, remains unclear.

PENA DE MUERTE
Thursday, November 29, 1973.

It's a bit of a leap to go from a title like *Pena de muerte* (Death Penalty) to a title like *Violent Blood Bath* – but anything that gets people to see another performance by Fernando Rey is *un sueño hecho realidad*. Rey plays Oscar Bataille, an aging judge riddled with anxiety. While on vacation in Pontevedra in Spain with his devoted, increasingly-destroyed wife Patricia (Marisa Mell), he starts reflecting on his life and the things that he's done. A money order sent to an executed man makes headlines. Is one of the criminals to whom he gave the death penalty alive and living it up and killing people like in the old days? Other crimes for which Rey had condemned various men to the guillotine start happening again, copycat-style. It doesn't help that he's obsessive-compulsive and increasingly paranoid – or that there's a judgmental guy (Espartaco Santoni) who seemingly knows much more than he should and is writing a book about his career. *Pena de muerte* is a much more sympathetic portrayal of mental collapse, old age and regret than you'd expect. "To condemn a man to death is not a means of murder?" the judge is asked. "I recognize the difference is subtle," he replies.

A boxer. In New York. In 1938.

Fred Apostoli. World middleweight boxing champion. Lifelong friends with Joe DiMaggio.

Now in San Francisco. Now at age 59. Now in 1973.

He works as an executive in novelty promotional advertising these days.

And then – like *that* – he doesn't.

A heart attack. On the job.

Fred Apostoli has pulled off what might be one of the most sensible job transitions in the history of professional boxing.

When you're in sales, however, there *is* a fair amount of beating your head against a wall.

Once, he was a bellhop.

They called him "The Hard Luck Champion." Emphasis on the "The."

Courageous. Blessed with stamina. Beloved. He was beloved.

He hit hard.

He hit real hard.

An American dream.

KARATECI KIZ
Saturday, December 1, 1973.

A mute girl (Filiz Akin) lives off in the hinterlands with her kindly old florist father. A gang of escaped convicts shatters their serene idyll by invading their home, robbing them, raping her and killing her dad. The shock of all that violence is so intense that she gets her voice back. She immediately vows to learn karate and get revenge – some of it in extreme slow-motion. I wonder how many martial arts dojos there were in Turkey in 1973. A handsome placid enigma (played by Ediz Hun, who later became an MP for the center-right Turkish Motherland Party) guides her tactically and philosophically. It helps that she's pretty handy with a gun – and she sure does cut a great figure in her red turtleneck, platform heels and black leather ensemble. She hears his echoing, goading voice in her head every time she achieves maximum vengeance. Makes a great double-bill (as *Karate Girl*) with *They Call Her One Eye*.

Burt Levin always enjoyed sailing out on the open ocean.

They'll find his body washed up tomorrow on Rincon Point Beach, slightly north of Ventura, California.

He was on his way to Anacapa Island, 11 miles off the coast.

The ends of the earth.

Levin, 45, takes off early today in his 27-ft. catamaran.

They'll find it capsized, three miles out to sea.

Alone. Without him.

Adrift.

The coroner doesn't know what did him in.

Could have been a sudden storm. Could have hit something while sailing.

What that something might be, however, is unclear.

Men Go And Come
But Earth Abides

That's what's inscribed on his tombstone. His wife Ann never remarries. She dies in 2011 at age 83.

Almost twice as old as he was when he died.

I Give My Life Essence Willing To
Allow New Life To Thrive

Sometimes the best perspective you'll get into the life of a person is at the side of their grave.

da una disperata storia d'amore   nacque il seme della violenza !

diretto da
OCLAOMA ASHIM

INSEGNAMI AD UCCIDERE

con: EDITH HUMMER · JHON ELMESSER · OTTO REGAN · FRITZ FALCUVER

EASTMANCOLOR

SHURAYUKIHIME
Saturday, December 1, 1973.

In 19th-century Meiji-era Japan, four muggers assault a family. The husband and son are murdered. The wife gets gang-raped. She kills one of the muggers and winds up in jail. Dying in childbirth, she whispers to her newborn daughter that her only purpose in life is to avenge the family by killing all their tormentors in the most horrible, painful ways imaginable. 20 years later, she becomes Lady Snowblood. The problem with that 20-year preamble is that once you get to the point that you finally get your revenge, when you've finished – well, then what? It's not like you can go run out and get a job washing dishes. Sure enough, she tracks them down and kills them – but what happens if one of *their* kids wants revenge because of *her* revenge?

Meanwhile, near Jupiter.

The Pioneer 10 probe sends back a beautiful bounty of images of the giant planet.

The image we see of an impenetrable world emerges more clearly than ever.

Arthur C. Clarke thinks there might be jellyfish-like beings swimming in the atmosphere.

Gerard P. Kuiper – for whom the Kuiper belt of dwarf planets and comets is named – does not concur. "Life is a chemical impossibility on Jupiter," scoffs he.

Carl Sagan thinks Jupiter is a star that failed to reach its full potential.

After Jupiter – and a fly-by of the Jovian moons

Callisto, Europa, Ganymede and Io – Pioneer 10 will encounter Neptune and Pluto.

In 1983, it leaves the solar system.

Out there, receding into the infinite darkness of space, its presence reminds us that the human species is meant for greater things than vengeance and murder. That we can in fact surpass the era in which we seem more likely to destroy the planet than we were to transcend it.

It represents humanity at its finest.

At its bare brutal essence, Pioneer 10 shows us that acts of human violence are so small in the face of the endless cosmos that they may as well not even exist.

Half-a-billion miles away from Earth, more violence happens on Jupiter in a fraction of a second than will ever happen on this planet.

It shows us that there's more to life than all this.

THE WICKER MAN
Monday, December 3, 1973.

Some asshole cop shows up on an island to save some asshole kid. He finds a whole island full of pagan assholes, and, because he's a Christian asshole, he thinks that they're all total assholes. The island assholes say that the asshole kid never existed. Then he meets the asshole that runs the place. A hundred years ago, some asshole said that they should sacrifice another asshole because some asshole gods wanted them to be exactly the kind of assholes that would do an asshole thing like that. He saves the asshole kid from being sacrificed – but it turns out the little asshole was luring him into a trap set by all the other assholes. What an asshole! He finds out that those asshole gods think that he's the perfect asshole to sacrifice because he fits their four asshole requirements perfectly: he's a nosy asshole, he's an asshole cop, he's never had sex (what kind of asshole his age has never had sex?), and he's a foolish asshole. He tells the asshole that runs the place that actually it's Nature that's being an asshole – and when the asshole sacrifice fails and the asshole crops die, they're going to come looking for another asshole to sacrifice. He thinks the cop is just being an asshole so he and the rest of the other assholes push him into a giant wicker effigy that they light on fire, the assholes. The assholes on the outside sing some asshole folk song while the asshole on the inside prays and curses the asshole islanders. Then the whole asshole thing falls down, the poor asshole dies and the asshole sun sets. Assholes.

A guy in Valparaíso, Chile will sell you his eye for $35,000.

He wants to buy a house for his family. To give his little girl a good education.

Doesn't say which eye you'll get, though.

MAGNUM FORCE
Tuesday, December 4, 1973.

San Francisco. Gangsters, pimps and drug dealers are systematically liquidated. Inspector Harry Callahan puts the pieces together and finds out there's a squad of vigilante killers on the police force, hell-bent on taking out the city's human garbage. "Man's got to know his limitations" is Callahan's credo in this film – as much a personal philosophy as it was a challenge to the audience to really think about how much they understood the character of "Dirty" Harry Callahan. Even the rotten cops don't get what he's all about. "I'm afraid you've misjudged me," he tells them after finding out that they want him to hang out and kill. Screenwriter John Milius explains his understanding of the Callahan character in a 1976 interview in *Film Comment*: "My Dirty Harry scripts never had Harry knowing any girls too well other than hookers, because he was a lonely guy who lived alone and didn't like to associate with people. He could never be close enough to a woman to have any sort of affair. A bitter, lonely man who liked his work." A scene of a pimp feeding a prostitute drain cleaner would be cited as an inspiration for the April 22, 1974 Hi-Fi murders in Ogden, Utah, during which three enlisted Air Force airmen robbed a home audio shop. Hostages, Drano, et cetera. You get the gist.

At 8:56 this morning, President Richard Milhous Nixon goes to the Oval Office.

At 10:33, the President and The First Lady honor the arrival of President of the Council of State of the Socialist Republic of Romania and his wife, Mrs. Nicolae Ceaușescu.

Secretary of State Henry Kissinger is there, too.

At 3:07, he holds a press conference and announces a new Federal Energy Administration, with Deputy Secretary of the Treasury William E. Simon designated as the future Administrator of said Administration.

There's an oil crisis this year.

An embargo. Since October.

The Organization of Arab Petroleum Exporting Countries cuts back oil production to those countries they feel were sympathetic to Israel during the Arab-Israeli War.

Truck drivers across America strike to protest the limited gasoline supplies the Administration doles out.

They strike with bombs. Sometimes.

Long, long lines of cars and trucks twist through gas stations throughout America.

In some states, "odd-even rationing" of gasoline takes place. This means that if the last digit of a license plate is odd, gasoline is only available to the vehicle on odd-numbered days of the month. Even-numbered license plates, same deal.

At 10:15 this evening, the President's dinner party watches a performance of Gioachino Rossini's opera *The Barber of Seville*.

Or, The Useless Precaution.

Inspector Harry Calahan...
#1 on the list of the nation's endangered species!

Clint Eastwood
is Dirty Harry in
Magnum Force

STARTS TUESDAY

SEX PSYCHIATRIST
Wednesday, December 5, 1973.

Dalana Bissonnette plays a housewife who gets molested by her psychiatrist. He takes advantage of his patients under the guise of therapy and closure. He also has two oversized statues of Laurel & Hardy overlooking everything on the couch – Laurel & Hardy, clearly, two of the most explosively erotic men ever to walk the planet. Through hypnotic regression, he gets into her mind and makes her increasingly pliable and willing as she thinks back to what made her sexual encounters so intense. Lots of flashbacks. Lots of incest. Lots of tasteless misconceptions about the nature of psychiatry and therapy. The Sex Psychiatrist and the Hungry Hypnotist probably knew each other. The shabby, furtive, one-room sexual escapades of '70s pornography are often ridiculed and scorned – but, in their way, those rooms represent the small, insular spaces which sexual people transform until they're worlds that exist unto themselves. They are three dimensions transformed into another little-known dimension: that of private life.

In Milwaukee, two 14-year-old friends get in an argument.

Words are exchanged. Words turn into fists. Fists turn into a .22, fired by one boy into the other boy's chest.

Because what are friends for?

Raymond Donaldson, 14, remains in serious condition at County General Hospital.

The reason for their fight? A pizza.

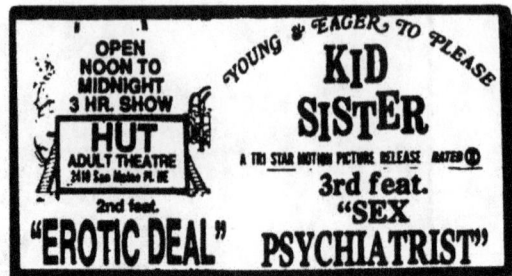

OPEN NOON TO MIDNIGHT 3 HR. SHOW
HUT ADULT THEATRE
2nd feat. "EROTIC DEAL"
YOUNG & EAGER TO PLEASE
KID SISTER
A TRI STAR MOTION PICTURE RELEASE RATED X
3rd feat. "SEX PSYCHIATRIST"

Who knows why people do the things they do sometimes?

Dr. Lester L. Luntz. One of the most influential figures in the field of 20th-century criminology.

Influential, and relatively unknown.

Today, he's giving a talk to 6th graders in West Hartford, Connecticut. Explaining all about what it's like to be a dentist.

Last month, Lippincott published his magnum opus, *Handbook for Dental Identification*.

He shows the kids all kinds of skulls. Dog. Calf. Human. Baby monkey.

He doesn't go too far into the fact that he's used his inestimable skills at dentistry to identify hundreds of unidentified bodies in Connecticut simply by what he can tell by looking at their teeth.

"I don't know if I got any converts to come over to be dentists," he explains modestly, adding, "But I was able to explain what's involved in the career, and show some interesting side aspects of it."

Near Carnegie, Oklahoma, three high school sports coaches driving down Highway 9 see lights flashing in the road ahead of them.

Instead of an accident or an ambulance, it turns out to be a man in "blood-red pants, with green flashing lights on his shoulders and what resembled a welder's mask with a red flashing light on top."

It comes toward them. They leave as fast as they possibly can.

Too much to comprehend all at once.

MANEATER

Saturday, December 8, 1973.

In this TV take on *The Most Dangerous Game*, animal trainer Carl Brenner (Richard Basehart) has two big Bengal tigers that he calls his "babies." After a run-in with RV-driving city folk Nick and Gloria Baron (Ben Gazzara and Sheree North) and their youthful pals Shep and Polly (Kip Niven and Laurette Spang), he decides to use his tigers to hunt them down as they bumble through the mountain wilderness without the slightest idea what's coming for them. Brenner cuts their gas line and tells Shep that the tigers are coming for them – but it'll be a really great chance for them to work on their survival skills! The night-time scenes are a drag if only because they make it hard to see those beautiful tough tigers. In one especially tense scene, Ben and Sheree make breathing tubes out of reeds and submerge while the tigers swim toward them. Most tigers I know wouldn't be able to sit through the last 15 minutes.

In Rochester, New York, police release a sketch of a suspect in the murder of Michelle Maenza.

She's a victim of the enigmatic '70s serial killer ultimately known as The Alphabet Killer.

The names of all the victims have double initials. Their bodies are found in places the names of which matched those initials.

Coincidence, or compulsion?

Carmen Colon, 10, in 1971. In Churchville, New York.

Wanda Walkowicz, 11, on April 2 of this year. In Webster, New York.

Michelle Maenza, 11. Vanished November 26. Found in Macedon, New York.

All strangled. All gone.

They're poring over Maenza's coat to see if there's any evidence that can lead them to a suspect.

The police telephone tipline keeps ringing.

Ringing and ringing.

Years later, in California, more women will go missing. When they're found murdered, it turns out that their names also have double initials.

The killer even murdered another girl named Carmen Colon.

As of 2022, the tipline remains open.

Quieter, but open.

344

EL PROFETA MIMI
Thursday, December 27, 1973.

Ignacio López Tarso plays Ángel "Mimí" Peñafiel, a childlike simpleton and self-styled prophet in Mexico City. He lives with his mother, a geriatric religious fanatic who spent years in prison for the murder that Mimí committed when he saw his drunken father stepping out with a prostitute. By strangling other random prostitutes, he thinks he's saving them from their sad and sorry lot in life. He falls in love with Rosita, a poor girl...who turns out to be a prostitute! What's a damaged fuckup to do?

They're still finding bodies of girls buried in an orange grove in Titusville, Florida.

They've already found four. Brevard County Sheriff Leigh Wilson indicates a link between the four girls.

11 other women have been reported missing in the area in recent days.

Two teens find the body of the latest girl in the grove. Nude, like the others.

A suspect. Arrested at his trailer park home nearby.

At last report, no charges filed.

They are murders that will occupy precisely one day of national newspaper coverage. It's as though the orchard pulls each victim back down with long implacable fingers of dust into the blankness of oblivion.

Some news reports mention the death of Carolyn Jean Bennett, whose body was found in the grove on December 25.

Carolyn Jean Bennett dies in Brevard County nine days after her 17th birthday.

On November 11, 1973.

On the other side of the world, Lucy Partington, 21, vanishes in Cheltenham, England.

An English Literature student at Exeter University, her fate remains unclear until her skeletal remains are discovered on March 6, 1994.

In the cellar of serial killers Fred and Rosemary West.

269 miles up, aboard the American space station Skylab, astronauts watch the Comet Kohoutek reach its closest approach to the Sun this year before it leaves the solar system.

Kohoutek's path through the Universe is vast and elliptical. It won't be back here for another 75,000 years.

Leaving a distinct lack of death and catastrophe in its wake.

No sign of anything greater than itself.

No impulse toward anything apart from forward momentum.

No direction other than away.

Away from 1973.

INDEX TO FILM TITLES

So you think you saw a movie in this book but you can't remember the title because you remember things differently? Well, you're in luck.

The titles and dates for films in A *History of Violence* (1973) are the titles under which those films first appeared in press materials, and the earliest-known dates that each of those films was screened or made available publicly.

In some cases, this information comes from a review of a screening that happened before a film's wider release.

In others, the release date is anything from a world premiere to a sneak preview.

For working titles, the years cited are the years in which those titles first appeared.

If you see the word "Variety" in parentheses, that means that *Variety Magazine* was the first place an alternate title appeared.

If you see the word "TV" in parentheses, that was the title it had when it got shown on TV – often how most people discovered it in the first place.

If an alternate title purportedly exists but isn't included here, that doesn't mean that it doesn't exist. It simply means that I couldn't find it in the arcana of the archives. I realize that I may have missed a few. A comprehensive index with every single foreign or alternate title is for another book. Just not right now and not right here and not right this instant. You have to draw the line somewhere.

With your thumb. Across your throat.

Cannibal Girls (April 5, 1973), 93

Carnal Violence (1981):
see Corpi presentano tracce di violenza carnale, I (January 4, 1973)

Case of the Full Moon Murders (October 24, 1973), 303
a.k.a. Case of the Smiling Stiff (1974) (U.S.)
a.k.a. Case of the Smiling Stiff, The (1974) (U.S.)
a.k.a. Case of the Smiling Stiffs, The (1974) (U.S.)
a.k.a. Sex on the Groove Tube (1976) (U.S.)
a.k.a. XXX on the Groove Tube (1977) (U.S.)

Case of the Hooded Man, The (November 12, 1973), 318
a.k.a. Case of the Hooded Man, A (1974) (U.S.)
a.k.a. Hooded Man (1974) (U.S.)
a.k.a. Hooded Man, The (1973) (U.S.)

Case of the Smiling Stiffs, The (1974):
see Case of the Full Moon Murders (October 24, 1973)

Cauldron of Death, The (1979):
see Tipo con una faccia strana ti cerca per ucciderti, Un (August 27, 1973)

Ceremonia sangrienta (September 10, 1973), 231
a.k.a. Blood Ceremony (1973) (Australia)
a.k.a. Bloody Ceremony (1997) (U.S.) (VHS)
a.k.a. Bloody Countess, The (1972) (U.S.) (Variety)
a.k.a. Female Butcher, The (1975) (U.S.)
a.k.a. Female Butchers (1976) (U.S.)
a.k.a. Legend of Blood Castle, The (1974) (U.S.)
a.k.a. Vergini cavalcano la morte, Le (1973) (Italy)

Chaperone, The (September 14, 1973), 242

Chassés-croisés sur une lame de rasoir (1974):
see Passi di danza su una lama di rasoio (January 5, 1973)

Chica de Via Condotti, La (1974):
see Ragazza di via Condotti, La (August 11, 1973)

Clan der Killer, Der (1974):
see Tipo con una faccia strana ti cerca per ucciderti, Un (August 27, 1973)

Cloche de l'enfer, La (1974):
see Campana del infierno, La (September 16, 1973)

Clockwork Terror (1986):
see Gota de sangre para morir amando, Una (August 22, 1973)

Colour of Blood, The (May 10, 1973), 115

Come Deadly (August 10, 1973), 199
a.k.a. Harder They Fall, The (1975) (U.S.)

Corpi presentano tracce di violenza carnale, I (January 4, 1973), 20
a.k.a. Bodies Bear Traces of Carnal Violence, The (1973) (literal)
a.k.a. Carnal Violence (1981) (U.S.) (copyright)

a.k.a. Torso (1974) (U.S.)

Corringa (1972):
see Morte negli occhi del gatto, La (April 12, 1973)

Corrupción de Chris Miller, La (May 17, 1973), 125
a.k.a. Behind the Shutters (1976) (U.S.)
a.k.a. Corruption of Chris Miller, The (1973) (literal)
a.k.a. Sisters of Corruption (1975) (U.K.)

Corruption of Chris Miller, The:
see Corrupción de Chris Miller, La (May 17, 1973)

Cousin Pauline (March 7, 1973), 60

Crazy House (1978):
see House in Nightmare Park, The (March 29, 1973)

Crie...et Meurs (1974):
see Scream...and Die! (November 20, 1973)

Crooked Arrangement (September 12, 1973), 235
a.k.a. Crooked Arrangement, A (1973) (U.S.)
a.k.a. Crooked Arrangements (1974) (U.S.)

Cry Rape! (November 27, 1973), 331

Curse of the Devil (1976):
see Retorno de Walpurgis, El (September 22, 1973)

Cycle Psycho (1970):
see Savage Abduction (September 26, 1973)

Daddy's Deadly Darling (1984):
see Pigs (May 23, 1973)

Daddy's Girl (1984):
see Pigs (May 23, 1973)

Day Well Spent, A (1972):
see Journée bien remplie ou Neuf meurtres insolites dans une même journée par un seul homme dont ce n'est pas le métier, Une (February 28, 1973)

Deadly Honeymoon, The (1972):
see Nightmare Honeymoon (October 2, 1973)

Death Carries a Cane (1987):
see Passi di danza su una lama di rasoio (January 5, 1973)

Death Hires a Hooker (1983):
see Pyx, The (September 13, 1973)

Death Sentence: Pena de muerte (November 29, 1973)

Death Smiled at the Killer:
see Morte ha sorriso all'assassino, La (July 11, 1973)

Death Smiles on a Murderer (1975):
see Morte ha sorriso all'assassino, La (July 11, 1973)

Death Ward #13:
see Forgotten, The (May 16, 1973)

Devil's Crypt, The (1974):
see Plenilunio delle vergini, Il (April 10, 1973)

Devil's Due (March 29, 1973), 88

Devil's Feast (1979):
see Warlock Moon (August 17, 1973)

Caveat Lector.

www.NineBandedBooks.com

www.ingramcontent.com/pod-product-compliance
Lightning Source LLC
Chambersburg PA
CBHW080811280326
41926CB00091B/4163